THE ONION BOOK

Written and Illustrated by

Jan Roberts-Dominguez

THE ONION BOOK

DOUBLEDAY

New York   London   Toronto   Sydney   Auckland

PUBLISHED BY DOUBLEDAY

a division of Bantam Doubleday Dell Publishing Group, Inc.

1540 Broadway, New York, New York 10036

DOUBLEDAY and the portrayal of an anchor with a
dolphin are trademarks of Doubleday, a division of Bantam
Doubleday Dell Publishing Group, Inc.

Book design by Maria Carella

Library of Congress Cataloging-in-Publication Data

Roberts-Dominguez, Jan.

The onion book / Jan Roberts-Dominguez. — 1st ed.

p.   cm.

Includes index.

1. Cookery (Onions)   2. Onions.   3. Cookery (Garlic)   4. Garlic.

I. Title.

TX803.05R617   1996

641.6′525—dc20   95–46574

CIP

ISBN 0-385-47735-X

Printed in the United States of America

August 1996

First Edition

1   3   5   7   9   10   8   6   4   2

To Jessie, an unfailing fountain of collie/shepherd charm and good humor for the past fourteen years. Despite a refreshingly independent nature, she always finds ways to maintain our status as a happy pack. It might be her crowding onto a chair behind me to rest her chin on my shoulder, or riding shotgun in the car with her elbow propped on the armrest or her paw resting on my hand. Or the priceless miles she walks me to get my creative juices flowing. Thanks to her, this writer's days have been far from solitary, never boring, and always overflowing with love.

But even more pertinently, to Steve. For teaching me the significance of low-key humor in a fast-paced world. And for the spirit he brings to our life. As the song goes, we have flown to the moon and played among the stars.

Many people had a hand in this book. To all of them I give a hearty thank-you:

Sondra Brough for her support and research, of course, but most of all for asking, "Why *not* an onion book?"

Jane Dystel, my wonderful agent, who made it happen with her canny vision and unflagging energy.

Judy Kern for being the kind of editor most authors only get to wish they had; and her editorial assistant, Brandon Saltz, for his enthusiasm and excellent taste in cookbooks.

Maria Carella for an elegant book design, and for so enthusiastically merging my art into it.

Michiru Kobayashi, my Oregon State University student intern the spring of '94, for the valuable hours spent researching cooking times and temperatures for roasting garlic.

ZoeAnn Holmes, Oregon State University professor in nutrition and food management, and all of the students in the spring of '94 Experimental Foods course, for helping Michiru with her roasted garlic study. And also, to all the staff and faculty within the college, for tolerating morning after morning of garlic in the air.

Sharon Van Loan, co-owner of southern Oregon's premier fly-fishing lodge and retreat, the Steamboat Inn, and coauthor of *Thyme And The River*, for her gracious loan of two recipes.

Michel Richard, owner and chef of Citrus restaurant in Los Angeles, for his wonderful salmon recipe.

Jim and Jane Robison of Robison Ranch in Walla Walla, Washington, for sharing their fabulous shallots and garlic, and delectable ways to use them.

Ginger Johnston, "FOODday" editor at *The Oregonian*, for great ideas and leads, as well as general support.

Chris Rossi for piquing my interest in green garlic all those years ago.

John Battle of Battle Produce in Traverse City, Michigan, for introducing me to the OSO Sweet Onion; and Rodger Helwig, OSO Sweet Onion director of communications, for his help and information, as well as creative support. Karen and Frank Morton of Shoulder to Shoulder Farms in Philomath, Oregon, for providing me with glorious supplies of green garlic when I needed it the most.

Bob Hogensen for the inspired recipe title "Walla Walla Salsa Salsa," and the entire Crawdad Weekend taste panel. Thanks! Thanks!

My parents, Margaret and Will Roberts, for their support and vigilant attention to trends in onion cookery.

My sons, Ryan and Brandon, for caring enough to ask.

My husband, Steve, for always making sure the music fits the mood, and for being the Chairman of the Board of Stress Management and Great Ideas.

CONTENTS

1

ALLIUMS ABOUND

It was at the ripe old age of twelve that I tackled my first onion quiche recipe. This one was a spin-off from the traditional quiche Lorraine in Julia Child's *Mastering The Art of French Cooking,* and the part that piqued my interest had to do with the onions. In my limited experience, onions were typically relegated to supporting-cast status, worthy of little fuss. But in Julia's recipe, there was a full paragraph devoted to exactly how long and at what temperature the huge mountain of thinly sliced yellow onions sitting on my cutting board should be cooked. The directions were specific: "Cook the onions in a very heavy skillet with the oil and butter over very low heat, stirring occasionally until they are extremely tender and a golden yellow. This will take about an hour."

Imagine that! Devoting so much burner time to plain old onions. What effect could time and temperature possibly have on such a pungent vegetable? In spite of my skepticism, I managed to stick with the directions long enough to be rewarded with the answer. How amazing that this stalwart companion of beer batter and my mother's Texas chili mellowed under the right conditions to smooth sweetness, with a sublime depth of flavor I had never before experienced. It was magical.

Well, a discovery of such magnitude just *had* to be shared with an unsuspecting world. My first opportunity came in a quaint little bistro and deli in the heart of California's Napa Valley wine country. The house specialty being quiche, it was a good bet the management would be thrilled to see their product go from good to "fabulous"—with my help.

I seized an early opportunity to sidle up to the cook. "Know the best way to cook onions for quiche?" I inquired, with as much casualness as I could muster.

She nodded solemnly.

"Are you sure?" Eagerness to spring my surprise must have been leaking out of me like little shafts of light.

A faint smile spreading across her lips, perhaps charmed by this earnest child, she elaborated, "Very slowly, wouldn't you say? Over very low heat, for perhaps an hour or more."

"Oh, that's, uh, right," was about all I could manage to stammer through my consternation. Realizing I had brought coals to Newcastle, I soon retreated to our table. And sure enough, the adjective "fabulous" was hardly up to characterizing the quiche this obviously well-educated woman soon served.

But if my initial foray into the teaching of onion esoterica had turned out to be a deflating experience, I didn't let it deflect me from pursuing a now decades-long love affair with the whole onion family. Long before baked garlic was chic, I was serving it to my family and friends. By college, I was banking leeks in my fridge against vichyssoise cravings, punching up my salads with shallots, and always managing to find a spot to grow a lovely drift of chives.

Of course, I haven't been alone in this interest, particularly over the last several years. Lately, chefs have been exploring and reevaluating the role these vegetables should have on their menus. Enter Caesar salad garnished with sweet, golden cloves of roasted garlic; roasted and smoked onion soup; roast tenderloin of beef napped in candied shallot sauce; red onion confit; braised cippolini onions; potato and leek bouillon with thyme and goat cheese gnocchi. No sooner does a chef on the East Coast bring together artichokes, leeks, and chives in a delicate scallop soup, than a West Coast master responds with roasted garlic and potato puree to die for. Alice Waters was one of the first to wow her clientele quietly at Chez Panisse in Berkeley, California, with green garlic, and over time, interest has swelled.

As for the general public, well, we're following suit. We're whipping glorious mounds of caramelized onions into our mashed potatoes, bribing friends to bring back souvenir sacks of Maui onions, and rediscovering the charm of home-made pickled onions. Over the last ten years, sales of onions like Walla Walla Sweets and Vidalias have exploded. However, while consumers are eagerly receptive of new and better ways to incorporate onions into their personal cuisines, the main knowledge base resides with a relatively small circle of aficionados.

Of course, even that is changing as more and more cooks agree that onions— the entire collection, from leeks and garlic to the tried-and-true yellow globe—deserve an elevation in status from workhorse to truly treasured.

Alliums Abound

A Bite of Onion History

People have been growing onions, garlic, and leeks for more than five thousand years. In fact, it's speculated that onions were one of the earliest crops because they were flavorful, stored well, and could be easily transported. Additionally, onions are a hardy group, so could withstand the wrath of nature.

- In the twenty-sixth century B.C., workers building the Great Pyramid at Giza were fed a diet of onions and garlic. Much later, a "bookkeeper's" inscription was found on a wall in the pyramid which stated that these hearty laborers had consumed 1,600 talents worth of onions, radishes, and garlic. A talent was a unit of both weight and monetary value, and some have estimated that in today's dollar, 1,600 talents would be in the range of $200,000 to $2,000,000.
- During the period of the Old Kingdom (2615 to 2175 B.C.), the onion's spherical shape, with its concentric rings, was considered a symbol for the universe, representing all that it encompassed: heaven, hell, earth, and universe. In fact, throughout time, the onion has been considered sacred, and some Egyptians would swear their oaths on an onion. A basket of onions was as valued as a loaf of bread, and mourners or worshipers would often bring onions as a gift.
- Ramses IV, who died in 1160 B.C. was entombed with onions behind his eyelids. Again, there was the onion's sacred quality to be considered; however, it is also speculated that the gesture was a way to simulate eyeballs and give a lifelike appearance to the body.
- By 495 B.C., the market of Athens was selling edible plants, but most were prohibitively expensive. One of the exceptions were onions. Because they were so abundant, they were quite affordable, and hence, widely consumed.
- By the Middle Ages the three main vegetables of European cuisine were beans, cabbage, and onions.

So where did our common globe onion originate? And which cuisine was responsible for generating the initial interest? Nobody knows for sure, but it is speculated that *Allium cepa* was the result of early cultivations of a wild onion from the southwest corner or central region of Asia.

However, Waverley Root, one of the premier food historians of our time, suggests in his wonderful dictionary, *Food,* that onions are indigenous to the Western hemisphere. He even speculates that there was no single place on earth where the onion first was introduced to the kitchen, and that it came into cultivation simultaneously in a number of regions around the world.

Growing Areas and Seasonality

• Bulb onions are grown for commercial purposes in twenty-six states. Of these states, California, Texas, New York, Oregon, Michigan, Idaho, and Colorado are major suppliers. Crops are also imported from Chile, Holland, Mexico, Spain, Canada, and New Zealand.

• California produces about 90 percent of the fresh garlic in the United States from July to December. The Argentinian product arrives January to March, then Mexican garlic becomes available from April to June.

• Leeks grow best in cool to moderate climates. Commercially, California, New Jersey, Michigan, and Virginia are the main growing areas.

Selection and Storage

Bulb Onions: All varieties (fall/storage, spring/summer) should be firm and heavy, with tight, shiny skins. Avoid bulbing onions that have begun to sprout or that show any sign of mold or mildew. Also, your bulb onions should pass the "sniff test," meaning that they should have a pleasant onion smell rather than a strong odor. The fall/storage varieties should be stored in a cool, dry place and will keep for several months if the conditions are perfect (in most households, however, you should plan on using your supply within a few weeks). Store the sweet varieties of spring and summer in a cool, dark place, or even in the refrigerator. Because of their high water content, sweet onions have a short shelf life. Try to use them up within a week or so. For long-term storage, you might try a trick promoted by the Walla Walla Sweet growers: Stack your sweet onion supply inside a pair of clean pantyhose. To do so, drop an onion into each toe, then tie a knot above each one, add another onion, knot above it, and so on. Hang the collection in your garage (or any cool and dry spot) and simply clip one off as needed, starting at the bottom.

Pearl Onions: Even though they're small, they should be heavy and tight, relative to their size. They can be stored either in a cool, dark place, or in a paper bag in the refrigerator.

Leeks: Look for straight, cylindrical plants with clean bases. Avoid leeks with dried-out leaves—a sure sign they aren't very fresh. As the season heads into spring, look out for leeks that are bulbous at the root end or that have a long, pencil-thin stalk shooting up out of the center of the otherwise flat leaves. Either situation is the result of harvesting after the plants are too far along in their second spurt of growth. Such leeks will be woody, with less flavor. Store leeks, washed, in a paper bag in the refrigerator for up to two weeks.

Green Onions (Scallions): Whether they're pencil-thin or large and slightly bulbous, they should have crisp outer leaves and perky-looking roots. Pass up the slimy ones. Store green onions in the refrigerator, in either a plastic bag or a moist towel, for up to a week.

Garlic: As is the case with bulbing onions, the bulbs of mature garlic should be firm and plump, with a crisp papery outer skin. The only time not to concern yourself with a crisp, papery outer skin is if you're buying the garlic at a farmers' market where it has obviously come straight from the fields (after a brief drying-out period, of course). In such a case, I've found that the extreme moisture within the bulb is still migrating outward. Hence, the outer layer, which ultimately becomes as fragile and crisp as well-aged parchment, tends to be soft and pliable at this phase. Avoid bulbs that have a bright green sprout poking out the top, an indication of age and poor quality. Store garlic bulbs in a cool, dry, and dark place, away from moist produce.

Green Garlic: The immature phase of garlic bulbs. These young stalks, which have not yet formed into bulbs and do not even have a papery covering, are amazingly tender. The stalks should be firm, not rubbery, and the flesh will be either pure white or streaked with red on the outer layer. The wide, flat upper leaves resemble leeks, and should be fresh and crisp, colored a deep rich green. For easier storage, it's okay to trim away the upper leaves, then encase the stalks in a plastic bag or damp towel and refrigerate for up to a week.

Shallots: All varieties, be they large or small, should be firm and plump, with dry, papery skins. Avoid bulbs that have a bright green sprout poking out the top, an indication of age and poor quality. Store shallot bulbs in a cool, dry, and dark place, away from moist produce.

Tearful Orbs

The degree to which an onion can incite tears has to do with the level of sulfuric compounds it contains—the same compounds that contribute to an onion's unique flavor and keeping quality. Storage onions have a high proportion of these compounds, which makes them the most tear-inducing, strongest flavored, and best "keepers." The sulfur is absorbed from the soil up through the roots of the onion. Once the onion is cut into, the chemical is released into the air. If it reaches your eyes and nasal passages it will mingle with your body's saline solution and develop a mild form of sulfuric acid. This minor irritation is what makes you cry, of course.

Because the specialty sweet onions such as the Vidalia and Walla Walla Sweet contain very small amounts of the sulfur-containing compounds, their tear-inducing power is practically nonexistent. Hence, they are considered the mild-mannered cousins of the onion family.

Avoiding the Tears

When you ponder any number of the world's major woes, onion fumes—and the tears they cause—don't really seem very important, do they? In my kitchen, I tend to grin and bear it. If a particular orb seems exceptionally potent, I just shut my

The Shapes of Onions

Botanist Henry Jones has classified bulb onions into nine distinct shapes:

 Globe onions—round

 Spanish—the perfect round

 Flattened globes—slightly flattened at the top and bottom, giving them a more squatty look

 High globes—have a slightly elongated middle

 Flat—very squatty

 Spindle—also known as "torpedo," since they have an elongated shape that tapers at both ends

 Thick-flat—a not-quite-so-flat flat onion

 Granex—wide, flat top; round bottom

 Top—similar in shape to the Granex, but the bottom is more elongated, like a toy top

mouth, squint, and chop faster. But if you are one to avoid the discomfort at all cost, the following tips may help:

- Well-chilled onions seem to produce fewer tears.
- Often-times, avoiding the bulb end until the very end helps, since some of the tear-producing product is concentrated there.
- Slice open the bottom of a clear plastic bag so you have two openings, then chop away inside the bag—which keeps the gases from reaching your nostrils and eyes.
- Before beginning to slice or chop, light a match, blow it out, then position it under your nose by clenching the unburned end between your front teeth.

Allium Odors

There are also a long list of suggestions to help onion and garlic lovers deal with onion/garlic breath. How effective any one of them is, however, tends to depend on how serious the problem is. Not to worry, though. A bit of allium breath, after all, merely signifies that one has had a marvelous meal:

- Rinse your mouth with equal portions of lemon juice and water.
- Chew on a bit of citrus peel.
- Chew on aniseed or dillseed.
- Chew on a coffee bean or a piece of vanilla bean.
- Suck a piece of cinnamon stick or whole clove.
- Eat an apple.
- Chomp on a sprig of parsley or a mint leaf.
- To remove the scent of raw onions and garlic from your hands, rub with tomato or lemon juice.

Allium Gas

—

It's not a pleasant thought. But it's a reality. In certain people, some of the alliums, particularly onions and garlic, produce gas. But there's a dandy dietary supplement on the market that nips the problem in the bud for most folks. It's called Beano, and it's available in grocery stores, either in the pharmacy section where you find antacids and other stomach medicines, or on the health food shelves. Beano is comprised of the enzyme alpha-galactosidase. Three to eight drops on the first spoonful of potentially gas-inducing food and it leads the way to your digestive tract. As the troubling food follows, Beano goes to work. What you need to keep in mind with Beano, however, is that it becomes inactive at temperatures higher than 130°F. So you can't sprinkle it into a bubbling-hot stew. You have to wait until the food cools enough to put it in your mouth. Also, it must be taken at the beginning of the meal. If you dose yourself prior to sitting at the table, chances are the enzyme will have been digested before it has a chance to work on the garlic or onions. So Beano has to become a part of the table routine. Right there at the table. Right in front of your friends and family. Of course, since we're all plagued with similar digestive systems, chances are you'll be sharing your little vial with the whole table.

Nutrition

—

One medium storage onion (5 ounces) contains about 60 calories, 14 grams of carbohydrate, 10 milligrams of sodium, 12 grams of vitamin C, 200 milligrams of potassium, 38 milligrams of calcium, 40 milligrams of phosphorus, and 2.8 grams of dietary fiber. Onions have no fat or cholesterol and are low in sodium.

The Garlic Information Center

The Garlic Information Center is a nonprofit organization funded by grants to Cornell University Medical College. It provides technical information for scientists and health-care professionals on the latest research conducted on garlic as well as basic garlic information for the general public (including recipes, a reference list of books, and general information on garlic).

If you need further information, you can write to the center at the following address. They'll put you on their mailing list as well, so that when new information surfaces and they send out press releases, you'll be updated:

The Garlic Information Center

The New York Hospital—Cornell University Medical Center

515 East 71st Street, S 904

New York, NY 10021

After reviewing the scientific literature, they developed a list of the possible benefits of garlic as suggested by the studies:

1. *Decreases the risk of cardiovascular disease by:*
   - lowering blood cholesterol.
   - lowering blood triglycerides.
   - thinning the blood (antiplatelet).
   - lowering high blood pressure.
   - increasing circulation in the limbs.

2. *Decreases cold and flu symptoms; assists in fighting off infections by:*
   - increasing the activity of various immune cells in the body.

3. *Protects the nervous system:*
   - Memory-enhancing effects of aged garlic extract have been shown using laboratory models.

Alliums
Abound

• Anti-aging effects have been shown in animal studies.

4. *Demonstrates antimicrobial activity:*

• It has been shown to kill the yeast Candida both in test tubes and in living animal models.

• Applied topically, garlic has demonstrated antibacterial properties.

5. *Assists in preventing cancer in humans:*

• In China and Italy, garlic consumption has been significantly correlated with decreased risk of stomach cancer.

6. *Protects the body from toxins by:*

• increasing the activity of enzymes and cells that function to detoxify foreign chemicals.

• functioning as an antioxidant that destroys free radicals, which have been suggested to contribute to heart disease and cancer, as well as the aging process.

• defending cells from radiation damage.

Celebrations!

Around the globe, allium-style festivities are going on just about year-round. For example:

BERN SWITZERLAND ONION FESTIVAL—Bern, Switzerland, annually, on the last Monday in November; for information call the Swiss National Tourist Office at (212) 757-5944.

CHEZ PANISSE GARLIC FESTIVAL—Chez Panisse Restaurant, Berkeley, California; annually, on July 14th, Bastille Day. For further information call Chez Panisse at (510) 548-5525.

COSBY RAMP FESTIVAL—Newport, Tennessee; annually in early May. For further information call Tennessee Tourist Development at (615) 741-2159.

EL RENO ONION FESTIVAL—El Reno, Oklahoma; annually (the date is not firm). For further information call (405) 262-8888.

FEAST OF THE RAMSON—Richwood, West Virginia; annually in May. For further information call the West Virginia Chamber of Commerce at (304) 846-6790.

GILROY GARLIC FESTIVAL—Gilroy, California; annually the last full weekend in July ("meaning, the last full weekend without going into August," says the nice lady at the Gilroy Garlic Festival Association). For further information call (408) 842-1625.

HUDSON VALLEY GARLIC FESTIVAL—Saugerties, New York; annually; last Sunday in September. For further information call the Shale Hill Farm and Herb Gardens at (914) 246-6982.

IMPERIAL SWEET ONION FESTIVAL—El Centro, California; annually, last Saturday in April. For further information call the Imperial Sweet Onion Commission at (619) 353-1900.

LOS ANGELES GARLIC FESTIVAL—Los Angeles, California; annually in July. For further information call the L.A. Garlic Festival at (310) 275-0875, or the Los Angeles Visitor's Information Center at (213) 624-7300.

MADONNA OF THE HOLY ROSARY GARLIC FESTIVAL (formerly the Fitchburg Garlic Festival)—Fitchburg, Massachusetts; annually the first Sunday in June. For further information call Father Frank Liistro at (508) 342-1290.

MAUI ONION FESTIVAL—Maui, Hawaii; annually in August. For further information call the Kaanapali Beach Resort at (808) 661-4567.

NORTHWEST GARLIC FESTIVAL—Ocean Park, Washington; annually the third weekend in June. For further information call the Ocean Park Chamber of Commerce at (360) 665-4448.

VACAVILLE ONION FESTIVAL—Vacaville, California; annually the weekend following Labor Day. For further information, call Colleen Duke, the Vacaville Onion Festival, at (707) 448-4613.

VIDALIA SWEET ONION FESTIVAL—Vidalia, Georgia; annually in April. For further information call the Vidalia Tourism Council at (912) 538-8687

WALLA WALLA SWEET ONION FESTIVAL—Walla Walla, Washington; annually the first or second weekend of July. For further information call the Walla Walla Chamber of Commerce at (509) 525-0850.

Tears by Mail

Some of the world's specialty alliums not available in your area? No problem. Anything from a zesty French shallot to a Walla Walla Sweet is available through the mail.

Shallots

The Allium Connection
John F. Swenson
1339 Swainwood Drive
Glenview, Illinois 60025
(708) 729-4823
Beautiful imported Brittany shallots and red shallots.

Alliums
Abound

Robison Ranch

Jim Robison

P.O. Box 1018

Walla Walla, Washington 99362

(509) 525-8807

Several varieties of shallots, including the Robison Ranch varietal (jumbo and colossal).

Sweet Onions

IMPERIAL SWEET

California Imperial Sweet Onion Commission

P.O. Box 3575

El Centro, California 92244

(619) 353-1900

Call or write for further mail-order sources selling the California Imperial Sweet onion.

MAUI ONIONS

Maui Farmers Cooperative Exchange

970-B Lower Main Street

Wailuku, Maui, Hawaii 96793

(808) 242-9767

Call or write for further mail-order sources selling Maui onions.

OSO SWEET

Battle Produce

John Battle

1310 W. Bayshore Drive

Traverse City, Michigan 49684

(616) 946-9696

TEXAS 1015 SUPERSWEET

South Texas Onion Committee

P.O. Box 2587

McAllen, Texas 78502

(210) 686-9538

Call or write for further mail-order sources selling the Texas 1015 SuperSweet Onion.

VIDALIAS

Bland Farms

P.O. Box 506

Highway 169

Glenville, Georgia 30427

1 (800) VIDALIA

Available from mid-April through June; baby Vidalias available from October through December.

Vidalia Onion Committee

P.O. Box 1609

Vidalia, Georgia 30474

(912) 537-1918

Call or write for further mail-order sources selling Vidalia onions.

WALLA WALLA SWEETS

Robison Ranch

Jim Robison

P.O. Box 1018

Walla Walla, Washington 99362

(509) 525-8807

Available for shipping in late June through mid-August; baby Walla Wallas are available in the early spring.

Walla Walla Sweet Onion Commission

P.O. Box 644

Walla Walla, Washington 99362

(509) 525-0850

Call or write for further mail-order sources selling the Walla Walla Sweet.

Garlic

Sweetwater Farms (Garlic Division)

Horace Shaw

Route 1, Box 27

Weston, OR 97886

"The Gourmet Garlic Farm," plus perennial shallots, extra large chives, oriental chives, flowering alliums, wild sweet onions from the Blue Mountains of eastern Oregon. For a complete price list, send a self-addressed, stamped envelope.

Onions from Seeds, Sets, and Seedlings

Seed Savers Exchange (heirloom varieties)

R.R. 3, Box 239

Decorah, Iowa 52101

These folks are dedicated to keeping the old varieties of alliums in production. Write them for information on obtaining seeds or becoming a member.

Nichols Garden Nursery

1190 North Pacific Highway

Albany, Oregon 97321

(541) 928-9280

Mail order chives, garlic chives, and an entire array of alliums; call or write for a free catalog.

Robison Ranch
Jim Robison
P.O. Box 1018
Walla Walla, Washington 99362
(509) 525-8807
Mail order onions, garlic, and specialty shallots.

2

SPRING
INTO
SUMMER

The earth has begun to warm after a cold, dark rest, and the air has lost its winter edge. In nearby woodlands, slumbering morels have been nudged into growth by the gentle April mists, while along fertile river basins thick-piled carpets of wild onions have begun to spread. In my own garden, clumps of chives, bright green and lush, are appearing in places they never were before, threatening to invade the rutted path my wheelbarrow formed last summer from countless trips between the tomato plot and the back gate.

Not that these new chives are in jeopardy of being removed in the name of tidiness. I love the way they ramble and spread at will each spring, popping up to give life to a particularly dull corner of the garden. Indeed, if there is order to the universe, then surely chives were put on earth for a higher purpose than mere nutritional sustenance. Would Spring really be as joyful if there were no chive blossoms to be enjoyed? It's more than chance that these lovely green stalks poke through the winter-ravaged ground when they do—reassuring us that water slides, concerts in the park, and ice cream on a stick can't be far behind.

Not that fields of electric-blue bearded irises and tipsy tulips aren't equal harbingers of spring. But the chives are a symbol you can sink your teeth—and soul—into.

Typically, the onion is thought of as a hearty, tear-inciting gorilla of a vegetable, potent enough to stand up to the mightiest salsa one can devise, and therefore risky to use. But in spring, onions come on softly: my delicate chives, juicy sweet onions, green garlic, and exquisitely hued bunch onions.

The Sweets (Allium cepa)

"Yellow Granex Hybrid" doesn't exactly roll off the tongue. But once a catchy name such as Georgia's "Vidalia," has been applied, you've got an onion people tend to remember. It's definitely good for business, and several other regions of the country also have cashed in on this designer onion's recent success: Washington's Walla Walla Sweet, Maui onions, Texas 1015 Sweets, and California's Imperial Sweets. These gourmet onions have become so popular that thousands of tons of them are air-freighted cross-country to faithful fans each year.

Why onions by air? It's because the qualities that make them so uniquely desirable—high sugar and water content—also make them susceptible to destruction. When the humidity is high and the mercury reaches the mint julep range on the thermometer, mold is just around the corner. The varieties available by April, Vidalia and Texas 1015 Sweet, rarely can be found past June, and the summer Walla Walla Sweet and California Imperial Sweet are waning by late August. So don't buy a fifty-pound sack and expect everything to be peachy unless you're willing to invest a little extra time and care. These onions like to be stored in cool, dry places. They need plenty of air circulation, and suffer from crowding.

Because of its gentle nature, the sweet onion is best suited for less robust concoctions. This is where it shines. Long, slow cooking in butter turns a pile of crisp, raw rings into a decadent platter of caramelized (remember that high sugar content?) paradise, fit to accompany your finest sizzling sirloin. Baking or barbecuing them whole—with a small well hollowed out of the top for a dollop of herbed butter—is another way to take advantage of their dramatic size and delicate flavor. For a classic French treat, there's soubise ("sue-bees"), a mountain of sliced onions, and a little bit of rice, cream, and Gruyère cheese. The result, after an hour and a half in a slow oven, is smashing.

Of course, I've made my share of blunders when working with sweet onions. One really needs to hoist aboard the concept that there are distinct culinary differences between sweets and regular globes. By nature, the yellow globe is potent, with plenty of kick left after several hours in a stew pot. But expecting a mild-mannered Walla Walla or Maui onion to stand up to such treatment is unreasonable—not to mention a waste of a perfectly good onion. That was a lesson I had to learn the hard way: by pickling sweet onions (ten minutes in a boiling water bath and they were history); by stewing sweet onions (they turn to mush—if that's what you want, fine, otherwise . . .); by using them in highly seasoned dishes ("That's funny, I could swear I added an onion to this Szechwan chicken.").

Well, I finally caught on. These days, I make sure this sweet spring-into-summer commodity is treated in ways that will complement its crunchy texture and delicate flavor. That means I'm using my sweets in their raw state a majority of the time. Thanks to their mildness, you can use enough to impart a fresh, crisp texture to salads, salsas, and relishes, and to make sandwiches that just can't be achieved in any other way. That this is only possible for a few months each year makes it all the more special.

Specialty Sweet Onions
(In Order of Appearance!)

The Texas Sweet, also known as 1015Y SuperSweet, because it's traditionally planted on October 15—first appears in April and is available until June. This is a crisp onion, with just a hint of sulfur.

The Vidalia—Appears in April, and hangs on through June. The Vidalia growers have been experimenting with low-oxygen environment storage over the last few years, which has extended the shelf life, so another batch can be released in the late fall. Thanks to its catchy name and aggressive marketing, the Vidalia onion enjoys a strong following.

The California Imperial—Appears in late April, and hangs on through August.

The Arizona Sweet—Available May through June.

Walla Walla Sweet—Mid-June through August.

Maui onion—Available year-round, but difficult to come by anywhere east of the Rockies. This extremely mild, sweet onion is another type grown from Granex onion seed. It originated from varieties developed in Texas, but when planted in the volcanic soil of Maui, the effect was stunningly sweet.

OSO Sweet onion—Available November through March. This is the new kid on the block. Since it's grown south of the equator, in Chile, it comes to us during our winter-into-spring months. For the full story, turn to Chapter 5.

The Walla Walla Sweet—
Up Close and Personal

Every year, by the third week in June, Walla Walla Sweet fanciers begin flocking to market—like so many swallows—in search of their favorite onion. And every year, growers of those beloved onions from the rolling hills and gentle valleys around Walla Walla, Washington, see to it that their fans aren't disappointed.

It's a ritual that's been going on for over eighty years. Today, faithful fans around the country gobble twenty thousand–plus tons of the plump and juicy bulbs almost as quickly as growers can raise and ship them.

This globe-trotting orb's circuitous trek to the Northwest began in Italy many years ago. From there the onion traveled to Corsica, where islanders also enjoyed its sugary character. Then, around the turn of the century, when retired French soldier Peter Pieri immigrated to the Walla Walla Valley, he brought along some of the seeds from this exceptionally sweet orb.

Italian immigrant farmers quickly adopted Pieri's import. Unlike other varieties that had to be planted in the spring for a fall harvest, this onion was winter-hardy. It could be planted in the fall, survive comfortably under a blanket of winter snow, mature in the spring, and be harvested by early summer.

But the two qualities that garner high praise for Walla Walla Sweets—a mild nature and juicy character—also make them susceptible to mold, which in turn shortens their shelf life. It's a summer onion, rarely available for purchase past the latter part of August. For Walla Walla Sweet fiends, this translates into a three-month onion feeding frenzy.

Fortunately, Walla Walla Sweets are a versatile commodity to work with. One could easily graze on them weekly and never be forced to prepare them the same way twice. I love them baked; grilled; gently sautéed; stir-fried; and, perhaps the most popular way of all, raw.

Green Garlic (Allium sativum)

—

Sometimes I feel that the culinary world has reached such a level of sophistication that few surprises remain. Then along comes something like green garlic to delight and intrigue me. It's not new, of course. By definition alone—"the early stage of mature garlic, before the bulbs are formed"—it's been a potential cooking ingredient for eons.

But most cooks have been overlooking that potential until just recently. Myself included. It was my friend, the ever-vigilant fact-nut Chris Rossi, who first brought this delicate and intriguing vegetable to my attention a few years back. She had come across a description of it in Chef Paul Bertolli's fabulous cookbook, *Chez Panisse Cooking*. According to Bertolli, green garlic, when lightly cooked, has none of the hot, pungent qualities of fresh garlic cloves; and although unmistakably associated with the mature form, the flavor is much milder.

"This is something I think you should try," said Chris over coffee one day. And of course, I agreed. But that was in the fall. A bad time, it turned out, to be fiddling with green garlic if you lived in Oregon. Somewhere in the world, it was in season. But not anywhere near the Pacific Northwest. My calls to savvy chefs and specialty produce growers of the region yielded the same response: How about getting back to us in late spring or early summer?

So I waited. And when early spring turned into late spring, I called my friends Frank and Karen Morton at Shoulder to Shoulder Farms on the outskirts of nearby Philomath. Their forte is designer salad greens, which they ship to lucky chefs in restaurants around the country, but they also sell green garlic to a select few. Within hours I had a very large armload of lovely young garlic plants that had been pulled from the ground that morning, great globs of damp earth still clinging to their roots.

After a thorough scrubbing, the plants lay on my kitchen counter in all their brilliant green and pink-blushed glory. They had the look of young leeks, actually: the foliage flat and long, and the bulb ends relatively straight. When I stripped away the outer pinkish-purplish skin surrounding the bulb, the most dazzling white flesh appeared. I cut a cross section through the base of the bulb and the internal pattern hinted at the cloves beginning to form.

I trimmed off a juicy piece and nibbled. The flavor was relatively mild (for garlic!), with just a suggestion of peppery fire. Next, I chopped up a bit and gently sautéed it in a pan with a tiny bit of oil. With just the introduction of heat, the flavor turned sweet and gentle. What a wonderful spring and summer vegetable this was. It was clear that green garlic would be a permanent fixture in my kitchen throughout its seasonal life, finding its way onto my grill to be roasted whole alongside sweet onions and backyard corn, stir-fried with my sugar snap peas (and a splash of sesame oil and soy sauce), and pureed into light, creamy soups.

Although the stalk is quite fibrous, even at this young phase in the plant's life, it can also be used if finely minced. At Alice Waters's famous Chez Panisse restaurant in Berkeley, Chef Bertolli writes, they prepare a richly flavored garlic consommé by stewing together green garlic, leeks, ripe tomatoes, and poultry or lamb broth. In Spain, the mild-flavored shoots are fried and used in the various tapas.

And so I encourage you to bring this relatively new ingredient into your kitchen. Doing so may be a challenge, since it has not yet achieved wide acclaim. In fact, you're likely to get some blank stares from the average produce department manager. Your best sources include farmers' markets and garlic growers. Or call around and talk to some of your city's more knowledgeable chefs. They might offer to obtain green garlic for you through their produce brokers. Depending on where you live, local green garlic will be available anywhere from March through June. Pay attention to when your local asparagus is in season, because those young garlic shoots are zipping up through the earth at about the same time.

Chives (Allium schoenoprasum)

I think it would be perfectly lovely if we all had a healthy clump or two of chives growing in our gardens. Chives have a strong influence on one's spirit when they begin poking up through the earth each spring. It's an uplifting experience. But unless you take the time to watch the progress—from the first green tips wrestling through the mulch, to the development of plump buds that finally burst into the ultimate purple-tufted fuzzy blossom—you can't appreciate its significance.

Many of us feel we're far too busy to partake in such trivial treats. Indeed, it seems that we're all running about fifteen minutes late through life. Noses plastered against grindstones. Roses going unsmelled.

But I have six friends who know how to come up for air. The thought flashed through my mind as I was squeezing the final drops from a second bottle of Riesling into our wineglasses. At noon, two days before Easter, these women had checked their careers at my front door, and as the hour approached 2 P.M., were showing no interest in retrieving them. My answering machine was on duty; another person's beeper had been dealt with swiftly; and a third friend, after two short calls, had freed herself for another thirty minutes.

Of course, we've had plenty of practice. After all, we've been guarding these two-hour islands of sanity since 1984 when Debbie invited us to her first Christmas luncheon. The concept took hold and by the following year, Sondra, Sheri, and Rita were following suit with Valentine's Day, Halloween, and Thanksgiving lunches, respectively. By 1986, I had become Easter/Spring, and Alicia was responsible for Mother's Day. Sondra's move to Arizona a few years later precipitated a reordering of the schedule. Now Lori does Valentine's Day and Yvonne's Saint Patrick's Day.

We've become so committed to these luncheons that very few excuses warrant a valid reason for cancellation. Childbirth, perhaps. But certainly nothing as trivial as a trip to New York ("Whatta ya mean you'll be in New York meeting with your agent, Jan. YOU'RE Easter."). Lori admitted halfway through her luncheon last February that she'd been fighting a migraine for two days. Yvonne was closing a deal on a house during her Saint Patrick's Day lunch.

It's a ritual our husbands watch with fascination from afar. They are fully aware it's a "woman thing." But they're not sure exactly what that means, except that it involves a serious amount of work on the part of the hostess. And at a time in our lives when every moment of free time seems to come with a premium price tag, how can a two-hour lunch possibly be justified?

But they miss the fun parts. The exquisite food and delicious conversation. Our thoughts on cities we love and hairdressers we don't. The economy. Clarence Thomas and Anita Hill. The Wonderbra. Nothing is sacred and everything goes.

Especially the time.

But after the two hours have sped by, we slowly and reluctantly begin pulling away from the table, one by one, hurrying back to our lives. Fifteen minutes late, of course.

And so, it's because of these special ladies that I find myself out in the garden each spring, stooped over the chives, offering them tender words of encouragement: "Come on, you guys. Bloom!" About three weeks prior to my luncheon each year, I begin monitoring their progress, hoping that they'll find it in their little botanical hearts to reward my nurturing with a timely burst of blossoms. Blossoms I can use to garnish some portion of my luncheon.

This year they cooperated, and so the soup course showcased their beauty. A single flower, still attached to its slender Audrey Hepburn–style stem, floated on the surface of each serving. My friends offered the appropriate oohs and aahs. I'm always amazed at how such a simple garnish can look so stunning. And when I explained just how long I had been encouraging the chives to cooperate in time for our luncheon, everyone felt very pampered and special indeed.

But chives offer more than just a pretty face. Many people grow them in their herb gardens alongside the basil, thyme, and oregano because, unlike other members of the onion family, only the stalks are used for cooking. You leave them rooted in the ground so they'll provide years and years of pleasure. Their tender green stems offer just a hint of onion flavor, so they can be used in a variety of dishes where a mere whisper of onion is appropriate; they're particularly well suited to delicate omelettes, soufflés, light vinaigrettes, and scallop sautés. And the petals are edible as well. I like to gently pull the tufts apart and sprinkle them over pasta salads and chilled cream soups.

Garlic Chives (Allium tuberosum)

Before I'm willing to give up even one square foot of precious garden space to a vegetable I've never grown, I spend some time getting to know it from a greater distance. If it's an unusual veggie, this means tracking it down at a local farmer's market, or driving out to a specialty grower's stand. After five or six weeks of cooking with it, I know whether or not I'm willing to commit to full-time nurturing the following year.

It's probably a foolish practice, this commitment-challenged approach to backyard gardening, because to date, I have yet to meet a vegetable I haven't liked. Except for eggplants. But with eggplants, I wasn't growing them to eat. I was growing them to paint.

One vegetable under consideration a few years ago was garlic chives. This pleased my friend, RoseMarie Nichols McGee, co-owner of Nichol's Garden Nursery in the nearby city of Albany. McGee had been trying to turn me on to garlic chives for quite some time. On a number of occasions, as I'd encounter a lovely little clump of them while roaming through the nursery's various demonstration gardens, she'd point them out. "Those are garlic chives, Jan. They're WON-derful. Not garlic, really. They're a chive. But garlic flavored. Much milder, of course. Really marvelous to cook with."

Finally, instead of appealing to my culinary nature, McGee approached my practical side: "When you think of ornamental gardening, garlic chives are certainly one of the best plants to put in, because they're easy to grow, they have an attractive fragrant flower, and the stems are—as you know—edible."

The bonus, she pointed out, is that "their period of attractiveness in the garden is quite long."

So I began picking up bunches of garlic chives—also known as Chinese chives, Chinese leek, and flowering leek—every Wednesday at the local farmers' market and bringing them into my kitchen. From a distance, garlic chives do have the appearance of regular chives: they're both deep green in color, both grow in perky clumps, and both sport beautiful little pompon-shaped flowers. But garlic chive stems are flat rather than tubular, and their taste and texture are considerably stronger and tougher. And just in case you're wondering, they do indeed taste like garlic. Although many American cooks aren't yet familiar with garlic chives, they've been cultivated for centuries in China, Japan, and other Eastern countries where their uses range from culinary to medicinal.

After discovering that they added a delightful depth of flavor to soups, stir-fries, and salad dressings, I began exploring this plant's potential in a food preserver's kitchen. In China and Japan the flowers are ground and salted for long-term storage, then used as a savory spice. This brought pesto to mind, which resulted in a recipe for Garlic Chives Pesto. The chlorophyll pigment in this plant seems particularly stable, so if you make a batch, you'll see just how brilliantly hued the green puree is.

Scallions, Green Onions
(Allium cepa)

Although this style of onion is available all year long, the spring-into-summer supplies are of much higher quality, and appear in much greater abundance than at any other time of the year.

Is there a difference between a scallion and a green onion? Some people think it's a regional thing: Green onions on the West Coast are scallions on the East Coast. But doesn't that leave a very confused area around the Midwest? Within the produce industry, any onions that are harvested while the tops are still green and the bulbs are small are sold as "green onions." The scallion controversy is a non-issue. However, in some cooking circles, a scallion is considered a scallion until its bulb matures to about three quarters of an inch in diameter. *Then* it's a green onion.

For commercial purposes, white onion varieties are most often used for green onions. The most widely grown is the White Lisbon, which was developed specifically for use as a green onion. Other popular choices include Crystal Wax, Eclipse, White Sweet Spanish, Southport, White Globe, and White Portugal.

Keep in mind that botanically, green and globe onions differ only in the stage at which they're harvested. It's true that in a world of specialization, onion varieties have been bred to accentuate particular characteristics, such as durability in storage or sweetness. But all onions can be harvested fresh as green onions, or left to mature. In any case, these tender young bulbs are indispensable—the kind of staple we stock as religiously as milk, eggs, and chocolate fudge sauce.

Bunch Onions (Allium cepa)

Once the bulb of a green onion begins to swell, you've got a bunch onion. Again, it's not variety that makes a bunch onion, but maturity. Beginning in June, onion growers are thinning their crops. These juvenile onions—be they Walla Walla Sweet, Bermuda, or yellow—which have been pulled from the fields, are typically bundled into bunches and brought to local farmers' markets, where savvy shoppers waste little time tracking them down. Vidalia and Walla Walla Sweet onion growers are cashing in on the concept by marketing the thinnings from their maturing crops and selling them through the mail during the winter months (see Tears by Mail, page 15).

At this young and tender stage, bunch onion bulbs are only one to two inches across. Depending on the variety, the bulbs will vary in color from pure white to a rich purple, with thick-yet-tender stalks sporting a brilliant green. The flavor is still rather delicate—balanced squarely between what you expect from a green onion and a mature one. Thus, bunch onions are highly versatile. They're still tender and mild enough to be eaten raw, but have enough character and developing flavor to withstand a bit of roasting, grilling, or sautéing.

Welsh Onions (Allium fistulosum)

Also known as Japanese bunching onions and Chinese bunching onions, this style of green onion is widely used in Chinese and Japanese dishes, and is grown throughout the Far East. Americans know them more by the Welsh onion moniker; in Germany, they're called winter onions; in French, ciboules. Their flavor is similar to the commercially grown green onion, leaning toward a leek overtone. These are nonbulbing onions with round, hollow leaves.

Ramp (Allium tricoccum)

Also known as wild leeks, ramps are found in moist, wooded areas throughout New England, and up through southern Quebec, as far west as Minnesota, and as far south as Georgia. Ramps have a slender, white bulb at the base, from which large, wide, flat, dark green leaves extend. Although considered a specialty crop, and highly regional, they can be found in farmers' markets when they're in season. They have a strong and hearty onion flavor, and in fact, it's usually a good idea to cook them as soon as you bring them into the home so their aroma doesn't penetrate the other foods in your refrigerator. If you do choose to store them, wrap them loosely in paper towels, then place them in a plastic bag.

APPETIZERS

DEEP-FRIED
BLOOMIN' ONION MUMS

—⁘—

At Stewart Anderson's Black Angus restaurants, it's known as Wild, Wild West Onion. At Denver's Lone Star Steakhouse & Saloon, they call it Texas Tumbleweed. At the Outback Steakhouse restaurants, you'll find it on the menu as the Bloomin Onion. Throughout the Chili's Grill & Bars chain, it goes by Awesome Blossom.

By any name, it's a remarkable appetizer, with Cajun roots. Its creator? Tim Gannon, senior vice president of the Outback Steakhouse chain in Tampa, Florida, supposedly can claim that honor. Back in 1987, when he was a chef at Russell's Marina Grill in New Orleans, Gannon came across a deep-fried onion garnish that resembled a chrysanthemum in a Japanese cookbook. He spun off the concept, zipping it up with Cajun spices and deep-frying. It was an instant hit, and soon enough other New Orleans restaurants got in on the rage, then eventually, the entire country.

The version I've chosen to adapt was originally perfected in The Oregonian's FOODday test kitchen; the recipe had come to them via the Philadelphia Inquirer. In my variation, I'm opting for a regional specialty onion and one of my favorite sweets, the large, juicy Walla Walla Sweet onion. It was The Oregonian's choice as well. I've taken the seasoning to another level of zippiness, and I have you soak the onions in a bit of buttermilk first so that the coating has a chance to cling. Be warned: They're messy to make. But most agree, the results are worth it—at least once in your life.

1 gallon vegetable oil for deep-frying
6 large Walla Walla Sweet onions or other sweet onions (pick those

that are as flat at the ends as possible rather than
perfectly round onions)

1 quart buttermilk

SEASONED FLOUR:

2 cups all-purpose flour

2 tablespoons paprika

1 tablespoon garlic powder

$^1/_2$ teaspoon salt

$^1/_2$ teaspoon freshly ground black pepper

$^1/_4$ teaspoon cayenne

BATTER:

3 cups cornstarch

$1^1/_2$ cups all-purpose flour

1 tablespoon garlic salt

1 tablespoon paprika

1 teaspoon salt

1 teaspoon freshly ground black pepper

2 (12-ounce) bottles or cans beer or ale

CREAMY CHILI SAUCE:

2 cups mayonnaise

2 cups sour cream

$^1/_2$ cup bottled chili sauce

2 tablespoons white vinegar

1 tablespoon Dijon mustard

$^1/_2$ teaspoon cayenne

Heat the oil in a large, deep-fat fryer, or a deep, heavy kettle until the oil reaches
375°F. (For true success and safety, a deep-fat/candy thermometer should be
used.) Meanwhile, prepare the onions. Peel them, then cut a slice off the top to
make a flat surface. Cut the onions into quarters from the top, to within $^1/_2$ inch of

(continued)

the root base. Then cut the quarters into quarters, again being careful not to cut through the root base. (It is easiest to cut the smaller segments if you flip the onion over after first quartering it. Then insert the knife into the onion ¹/₂ inch below the root base and slice downward, holding the onion steady.)

Turn the onions back over and gently spread the slices apart to form petals. Place the prepared onions in a large bowl with the buttermilk and soak for 10 minutes.

To make the seasoned flour, in a bowl, mix together the ingredients.

To make the batter, in a large bowl, thoroughly mix together the dry ingredients. Whisk in the beer or ale; set aside for 30 minutes.

Remove the onions from the buttermilk and dip them one at a time in the seasoned flour, shaking to remove any excess. The onions should be thoroughly but lightly floured.

Dip the onions in the batter, moving them around to be sure they are thoroughly covered. Drain, petal side down, in a slotted spoon or spatula to let the excess batter drip out.

Using a long-handled slotted spoon or a strainer, and wearing oven mitts to protect against spatters, lower the coated onions gradually into the 375° oil, with the onions base side down. Fry for about 3 minutes, until light golden. (Fry one onion at a time so the temperature of the oil doesn't drop too much.) Using the long-handled slotted spoon or strainer, remove the onions from the oil and place them on paper towels. Cool slightly.

Using a knife and fork, carefully spread the petals as much as possible. With the strainer, lower the onions back into the hot oil, this time with the base side up, and the petals down. Deep-fry for another 3 minutes, or until golden brown. Remove to drain on paper towels with the petals pointing up. Keep the cooked onions warm in a 200° oven while frying the others.

To make the chili sauce, in a medium bowl combine the ingredients.

Serve the onion blossoms on a platter, either with a small cup of the chili sauce in the middle of each onion or with the sauce on the side.

Tips for "Bloomin' Mums": *The Oregonian* FOODday staff established a handy list of dos and don'ts that are worth passing on. It saved me from disaster the first time I was working with the recipe.

1. Don't attempt this with a small deep-fat fryer; if a large one is unavailable, a 10-inch-diameter, 10-quart stockpot or similar kettle will make an adequate substitute.

2. Keep an open box of baking soda handy on the counter, just in case of a fire.

3. Keep your work environment child- and pet-free since you'll be working with very hot oil.

4. Use utensils with long handles, and wear oven mitts when lowering the onions into and removing them from the oil (if you have an Oriental-style bamboo and wire strainer, this would be a perfect time to use it).

HOT ARTICHOKE DIP

There are many versions of this particular dip, but one of the tastiest can be found at the Prescott Brewing Company, in Prescott, Arizona. On a memorable spring afternoon, along with my husband and two friends from Phoenix, we dallied over frosty glasses of their best brews and this popular dip. They're particularly generous with the marinated artichokes, and the whole thing is served hot and creamy in a scooped-out loaf of bread. The next day, back at Sondra and Kerry's house in Phoenix, we managed to duplicate their creation.

YIELD: *6 TO 8 SERVINGS*

1 (8- or 10-inch) round of French bread for bread bowl, cut-up
    chunks of bread reserved from the inner portion
1 pint sour cream
$^1/_2$ cup mayonnaise
2 (6-ounce) jars marinated artichoke hearts, drained and chopped
$^1/_2$ cup freshly grated Parmesan cheese
$^1/_2$ cup finely chopped green onions (white portion only; reserve the
    green for garnish)
Assorted raw vegetables (including broccoli florets, cauliflower
    florets, carrot sticks, sweet red and green bell pepper strips)

Preheat the oven to 375°F.

To prepare the bread bowl, slice away about $^1/_2$ inch from the top portion of the bread, then cut and scoop out the insides, leaving a $^1/_2$-inch layer of bread in the bowl. The portion of bread removed to create the bowl should be cut into cubes. (For toasted croutons, they can be baked alongside the dip for the final 10 minutes, or simply served alongside the vegetables for dipping.)

In a medium bowl, combine the sour cream, mayonnaise, artichoke hearts, Parmesan cheese, and green onion. Spoon the mixture into the bread bowl and heat in the oven until the dip is very hot, 15 to 20 minutes.

Remove from the oven, garnish the top with a sprinkling of the green onion tops, and serve, surrounded by the vegetables and bread chunks.

WALLA WALLA SALSA SALSA

This salsa recipe was created during a camping trip several years ago. Since I had only a vague idea of how I wanted the recipe to turn out, I had packed along just about every ingredient I could think of that might work in a fresh salsa: Walla Walla Sweets, roasted and peeled Anaheim chiles, garlic, tomatoes, pine nuts, olives, olive oil, and a whole lot more.

And so, beneath the towering firs, with the sound of contented crawdad hunters shrieking and splashing in a nearby creek, I sat at the campground picnic table and created this salsa. When I set it out at the evening happy hour, my fellow campers went into fits of delight, devouring it in under 10 minutes. Then, while scraping the last remnants from the bowl with broken bits of tortilla chips, one of the group clowns, Bob Hogensen, christened this one-in-a-million dip Walla Walla Salsa Salsa. As its title implies, this one bears repeating. If the Walla Walla Sweet onion isn't available, use another variety of sweet onion.

YIELD: ABOUT 6 CUPS

4 large or 7 medium Anaheim chiles, roasted and peeled (see Note)

1 large Walla Walla Sweet onion (or another variety of sweet onion, such as Vidalia, Maui, or Texas 1015), diced

2 (2.5-ounce) cans sliced black olives, drained

5 Roma tomatoes, diced

1 to 2 cups diced cucumbers

$^{1}/_{2}$ cup virgin olive oil

$^{1}/_{4}$ cup white wine vinegar

2 cloves garlic, minced

$^{1}/_{2}$ to 1 teaspoon salt

Freshly ground black pepper to taste

$^{1}/_{3}$ cup pine nuts

Remove the stems, seeds, and inner membranes from the roasted chiles, then chop. In a medium-size bowl, combine the chopped chiles with the onion, olives, tomatoes, cucumbers, olive oil, vinegar, garlic, salt, and pepper. Mix well, then adjust the seasonings, adding additional salt and pepper to taste. Refrigerate for at least 1 hour (may be prepared up to 6 hours ahead). When ready to serve, stir in the pine nuts. Serve with tortilla chips.

Note: To roast the Anaheim chiles, poke each chile once with a sharp knife to avoid explosions in the oven. Place the chiles on a baking sheet and broil until dark golden on all sides, about 4 minutes total time, then place them in a plastic bag for about 10 minutes to steam loose the outer skin. Remove the chiles from the bag, and peel away the skins with your fingers.

FRESH SWEET
ONION RINGS WITH MINT

Thanks to their high water content, sweet onions are inherently crisp and juicy, and ice does a lovely job of keeping them that way.

YIELD: 6 TO 8 SERVINGS

> 1 pound (about 1 large or 2 medium) fresh sweet onions (such as
> Vidalia or Walla Walla)
> $^1/_3$ cup rice vinegar
> 1 teaspoon sugar
> 1 tablespoon chopped fresh mint leaves
> $^1/_8$ teaspoon crushed dried hot red chiles
> 1 cup small ice cubes or coarsely crushed ice
> Salt to taste

Cut the onions crosswise into $^1/_4$-inch-thick slices; separate into rings. In a bowl, combine the onion rings, vinegar, sugar, mint, chiles, and ice; cover and chill for 10 to 15 minutes, stirring occasionally. Serve with the unmelted ice; add salt.

NIDA'S CREAM CHEESE AND GREEN ONION HORS D'OEUVRE

My cousin in California always used to have this delicious, make-ahead nibble on hand at family gatherings. It was expected. And the nice thing about it is that you can prepare it a day ahead and store it in your fridge until party or picnic time. Her daughter, Ann, has taken over the hors d'oeuvre duty, but I still call it Nida's Cream Cheese and Green Onion Hors d'Oeuvre."

YIELD: *12* TO *18* SERVINGS

> 24 ounces cream cheese, softened
> 1 1/2 cups chopped green onions (use all of the white portion, about
> 2/3 of the green)
> 1 cup finely diced salami
> 6 (6-inch) sourdough French rolls, unsliced

In a bowl, combine the cream cheese, green onions, and salami. Mix well to evenly distribute the salami and onions; set aside. Cut a slice off each end of each French roll. With a serrated knife, cut a core 1 inch in diameter through each roll. Then fill each roll with the cream cheese mixture (a small spoonful at a time stuffed down into the roll with your index finger is messy, but it works best). Wrap each roll snugly in foil, then refrigerate overnight to let the flavors meld. To serve, cross-cut the still-cold rolls into thin slices and arrange on a platter.

ALTERNATE METHOD: If you don't want to take the time to stuff the rolls, you can serve the cream cheese mixture in a bowl surrounded by 1/4-inch-thick slices of baguette or French bread. People simply spread the mixture onto the bread.

The word "scallion" harkens back to biblical times, when the fresh, young onions grown in the Israeli city of Ashkelon were called *ascalons*.

Spring into Summer

In the spring and early summer months, you can gather wild garlic and wild onions just as you would green onions. When you find them, you'll know from their heady scent. They're a wonderful treat to encounter on a backpacking trip—they really dress up those freeze-dried meals.

GREEN ONION AND BUTTERMILK BISCUITS

Set them out with an array of cheeses and salami for a simple nibble.

YIELD: ABOUT *40* BISCUITS

1 cup all-purpose flour

$^{1}/_{2}$ cup yellow cornmeal

1 teaspoon sugar

$^{1}/_{2}$ teaspoon baking soda

$^{1}/_{4}$ teaspoon freshly ground black pepper

$^{1}/_{8}$ teaspoon salt

2 tablespoons cold butter, cut into small chunks

$^{1}/_{3}$ cup finely minced green onion (using all of the white and about 1 inch of the green)

$^{2}/_{3}$ cup buttermilk

Preheat the oven to 425°F. Lightly grease several baking sheets.

In a large bowl, combine the flour, cornmeal, sugar, baking soda, pepper, and salt. Using a pastry blender or your fingers, cut in the butter until the mixture is crumbly and resembles very coarse cornmeal. With a fork, gently stir in the green onion and buttermilk, mixing just until the dry ingredients are moistened and a soft dough has formed.

On a floured surface, pat and roll the dough into a 10 by 16-inch rectangle. Cut it into rounds with a 2-inch cutter and place the rounds on the baking sheets. Bake until golden brown, 12 to 15 minutes. (Note: These biscuits may be prepared, cooled, then frozen for up to 3 months.) When ready to serve, split and fill as desired. (Ham, turkey, salami, or a variety of cheeses with mayonnaise or a good mustard all make delicious fillings.)

GREEN ONION
AND GARLIC SPREAD

The onions and green garlic are roasted in butter for one hour, then puréed into a velvety, richly-flavored spread that seems to have a great affinity for toasted slices of crusty French bread.

YIELD: ABOUT 1¹/₂ CUPS

3 bunches of green onions

3 green garlic plants, each measuring about ¹/₂ inch in diameter at the
root end (including all of the white part and a portion of the
pale green stem)

4 tablespoons (¹/₂ stick) butter

¹/₄ teaspoon salt

¹/₄ teaspoon white pepper

1 French bread baguette, cut into ¹/₄-inch slices

Preheat the oven to 325°F.

Trim away the roots from the green onions, then coarsely chop the white and pale green portions, reserving the deep green stalk for another use. Coarsely chop the green garlic stalks. Arrange the chopped vegetables in the center of a large piece of aluminum foil, along with the butter, salt, and pepper. Wrap the foil around the mixture and bake for 1 hour, which makes the spread soft and creamy. When the mixture is cool enough to handle, puree it in a food processor until very smooth, adding more salt and pepper to taste.

To serve, toast the slices of French bread in a 375° oven until lightly golden, then arrange the bread on a platter around the still-warm puree. Guests simply spread some of the puree on the bread. (The puree can be made and refrigerated for up to 3 days ahead. To serve, spread the puree on the toasts and heat in a 375° oven for about 10 minutes.)

FABULOUS SPRING-INTO-SUMMER SOUPS

As spring begins to blossom northward through the United States, local produce sections expand before our eyes. The few veggies in our supermarkets have turned into a rich variety, and the seasonal cook can once again dust off recipes that had to be tucked away last December.

One of the best ways to enjoy seasonal vegetables is in light and colorful soups. From sweet onions to baby leeks, tender peas to succulent scallions and chives, vegetables fare particularly well in such enriching concoctions. Whether it's a long-simmered brew or a simple puree laced with just a hint of fresh herb, there's something particularly inviting about a bowlful of fresh vegetable soup.

So put your beautiful soup bowls into action. Stock up on fresh herbs for garnish, and an assortment of unusual breads for dipping, and you'll definitely have a handle on the season.

CREAM OF AVOCADO SOUP

— — —

YIELD: 4 TO 5 SERVINGS

2 avocados, pitted, peeled, and cut into chunks

2 (10¾-ounce) cans condensed (double-strength) chicken broth,
    undiluted

1 tablespoon chopped green onion

1 cup light cream

1 tablespoon lemon juice

Salt to taste

About ½ cup salsa (your favorite commercial brand) for garnish

Sour cream for garnish

Chive blossoms, if available, for garnish

In a blender, combine the avocado, chicken broth, and green onion. Blend until smooth. Add the cream and lemon juice, continuing to blend. Add more cream if necessary to reach the desired consistency (on the thick side). Salt to taste and chill for at least 1 hour.

When ready to serve, ladle a portion of soup into each soup bowl. Spoon about 2 tablespoons of the salsa onto the center of each serving, then top each with a dollop of sour cream. Garnish with a single chive blossom and serve.

VICHYSSOISE

This classic leek and potato soup is a marvelous way to use the tender-young leeks that find their way to market by late spring.

YIELD: 6 SERVINGS

2 tablespoons butter

6 small, young leeks, chopped (white portions only)

1 medium yellow onion, chopped

4 medium russet potatoes, peeled and chopped

4 cups chicken broth

1 ½ cups heavy or light cream

Salt and white pepper to taste

In a skillet, melt the butter and sauté the leeks and onion for 3 minutes. Add the potatoes and broth and cover; simmer for 15 minutes, or until the potatoes are tender. Place small batches of the mixture in a blender or food processor, and blend until smooth. Return to the pot, stir in the cream, and season with salt and pepper. Chill well before serving.

Two-Tone Soup

— — —

For a beautiful and delicious soup, prepare a half-recipe of Cream of Avocado Soup and a full recipe of Vichyssoise. To serve, ladle vichyssoise into soup bowls, then gently spoon a swirl of avocado soup down the center of each serving. If available, gently lay a chive blossom and stem across the top of each serving. It's beautiful.

Asparagus and Spinach Soup with Green Onions

One of spring's tastiest harbingers! I'm always on the lookout for fresh-tasting asparagus soups. I first encountered the inspiration for this one in the late Bert Greene's wonderful cookbook, Greene on Greens. Over the years I've fussed and played with it enough that Bert probably would have been very happy to disavow any responsibility for the result.

Yield: 6 to 8 servings

3/4 pound asparagus, trimmed and peeled

1 quart homemade or canned chicken broth

1 cup washed and chopped fresh spinach leaves

2 tablespoons butter

10 whole green onions (bulbs and green tops), coarsely chopped

Pinch of ground cloves

3 tablespoons cornstarch

1/2 cup heavy cream

Salt and white pepper to taste

Sour cream (optional)

Place the asparagus in a medium-size saucepan and cover with the broth. Heat to boiling over high heat; reduce the heat and simmer, covered, for 3 minutes. Remove the asparagus from the broth. Let the asparagus cool, then cut off the tips and set aside. Coarsely chop the stems and set aside.

Add the spinach to the chicken broth and cook for 3 minutes, then remove with a slotted spoon. Reserve the broth.

Melt the butter in a 2-quart saucepan over low heat. Add the green onions and sauté until wilted. Stir in the cloves, cooked spinach, and asparagus stems.

Cook over low heat for 5 to 7 minutes, or until the asparagus is tender; add the reserved broth.

Place the cornstarch in a small bowl. Slowly beat in the cream until the mixture is smooth. Whisk this into the broth and vegetable mixture, then heat to boiling, reduce the heat, and simmer gently until the mixture thickens; remove from the heat.

Cool the mixture slightly and puree it in a blender or food processor in 2 batches (be careful; hot liquid will expand). Return the puree to the saucepan and reheat over low heat. Season with salt and white pepper and stir in the asparagus tips. Serve garnished with dabs of sour cream if desired.

POTATO CHEESE SOUP

Spring is such a transitional season—some days are gloriously warm, others are cool, or downright robust—that it's a good idea to have a few soups of the hearty variety on hand. This one makes grand use of the young green onion that becomes so plentiful about now. And it has such an elegant cheese flavor, I like to pack it into a thermos and bring it along on our weekend wine-tasting excursions.

YIELD: 8 SERVINGS

1 quart homemade or canned chicken broth

$2^1/_2$ pounds potatoes, unpeeled, coarsely chopped

2 cups chopped green onions (whites and about half the green stalks)

$^1/_4$ cup soy sauce

1 quart light cream

1 teaspoon freshly ground white pepper

6 ounces Swiss cheese, grated

6 ounces Cheddar cheese, grated

$^1/_2$ cup dry white wine, beer, or dry sherry

In a heavy-bottomed pot, combine the chicken broth and potatoes. Bring to a boil, then reduce the heat and simmer for 30 minutes, or until the potatoes are very soft. Add the green onions, soy sauce, and cream, then remove the pot from the heat.

Puree the potato-broth mixture in a blender or food processor (you will have to do this in batches; when blending, fill the container only half full and cover the lid with a dish towel because the soup "spurts" quite violently as it's being blended). Return the puree to the pot. Stir in the pepper and slowly bring the soup back to a simmer.

Stir in the grated cheeses gradually, a handful at a time. Then gently whisk in the wine, beer, or sherry. Remove the soup from the heat, ladle into large soup bowls, and serve.

GREEN GARLIC SOUP

This is the perfect recipe to introduce the uninitiated to the wonders of green garlic. The white pepper and dry sherry are integral components of the flavor structure, so be sure they make it into the soup.

YIELD: *4 TO 5 SERVINGS*

1 tablespoon butter

1 tablespoon olive oil

1 2 green garlic plants, each measuring about $^1/_2$ inch in diameter at the root end (including all of the white part and a portion of the pale green stem)

$3^1/_2$ cups homemade or canned chicken broth

3 or 4 (about $^1/_2$ pound) small red potatoes, peeled and quartered

$^1/_3$ cup light cream

$^3/_4$ teaspoon salt

$^1/_4$ teaspoon white pepper

About 2 tablespoons dry sherry

Warm the butter and oil in a large, heavy pot over medium heat. Trim away the root and most of the green portion from each garlic plant, then halve each stalk lengthwise. Sauté the garlic briefly, then add the broth and potatoes; simmer until the potatoes are very tender, about 30 minutes.

Remove from the heat and cool briefly, then puree the soup in batches in a blender or food processor until very smooth. Stir in the cream, salt, and white pepper, then return to gentle heat. As the soup is rewarming, stir in the sherry, then adjust the seasonings before serving.

Chinese Pork Dumpling Soup with Hot Red Peppers and Garlic Chives

Yield: 6 servings

CHINESE PORK DUMPLINGS:

- $1/2$ pound lean ground pork
- 1 cup finely shredded Chinese cabbage
- $1/2$ cup finely grated carrots
- $1/2$ cup finely minced fresh garlic chives
- 2 tablespoons freshly grated gingerroot
- 1 tablespoon finely minced fresh cilantro
- 1 tablespoon lightly toasted sesame seeds
- 2 teaspoons soy sauce
- $1/4$ teaspoon salt
- $1/4$ teaspoon red pepper flakes
- 1 egg, lightly beaten
- 1 (12-ounce) package 3-inch square wontons

SOUP:

- 2 teaspoons corn or canola oil
- 1 teaspoon sesame oil
- $1/2$ pound Chinese cabbage (also called Napa cabbage)
- $1/4$ cup finely chopped fresh garlic chives
- 1 tablespoon freshly grated gingerroot
- 8 cups homemade or canned chicken broth
- 1 tablespoon finely chopped fresh cilantro
- 2 teaspoons soy sauce

$^3/_4$ teaspoon salt

$^1/_2$ teaspoon sugar

$^1/_2$ teaspoon red pepper flakes

To prepare the Chinese pork dumplings, in a medium-size skillet over medium heat, brown the pork; drain off any fat that accumulates and let the meat cool. Combine the cooled pork with the remaining dumpling ingredients except the wontons. To assemble the dumplings, remove 4 or 5 wontons from the package. (Keep the package sealed while working with those you have removed so the rest won't dry out.) Place the wonton skins on the counter with one corner pointing toward you. Place a rounded teaspoon of the filling slightly below the center of each one. Moisten the 2 adjacent edges of the skin with water, then fold the won-ton skin diagonally in half to form a triangle. Gently press around the filling to force out any air pockets, then gently but firmly press on the edges to seal. Finally, dampen the front of the triangle's right corner and the underside or back of the left corner. With a twisting action, bring the 2 moistened tips together, overlapping them slightly, and pinch to seal. The folded dumpling will resemble a nurse's cap. As you assemble the dumplings, place them on a baking sheet; don't let them touch. Continue until all the filling and wonton skins are used. Cover with plas-tic wrap and refrigerate if not using immediately. (Note: The dumplings may be frozen at this point, then transferred to freezer bags and stored for about 3 months.)

To prepare the soup, heat the corn and sesame oils in a large, heavy-bottomed pot or kettle. Add the cabbage, garlic chives, and gingerroot and sauté until the cabbage has wilted and the gingerroot is fragrant, about 2 minutes. Pour in the chicken broth, then add the cilantro, soy sauce, salt, sugar, and red pepper flakes. Bring the soup to a boil, then simmer gently for about 15 minutes to allow the fla-vors to develop. Add the dumplings and continue simmering very gently until the dumplings are heated through and become transparent, about 5 minutes. To serve, ladle 6 or 7 dumplings into each soup bowl, then a portion of the soup.

HOT AND SOUR SOUP

I have moved far away from the traditional Chinese Hot and Sour Soup. But over the years, this has come to be the one my family prefers. It's strong on bean curd, and completely lacking in bamboo shoots. The green onions are its backbone, their mellow-yet-oniony flavor lifting the broth from commonplace to quite extraordinary. In early summer, once the local farmers' market is up and running, I substitute the plumper, slightly heartier-flavored bunch onion for the simple green onion. The texture is a bit coarser, but the soup can certainly stand the variation.

YIELD: *8 SERVINGS*

> 7 cups homemade or canned chicken broth
>
> $\frac{1}{2}$ cup rice vinegar
>
> 2 tablespoons soy sauce
>
> 1 cup chopped green onions or bunch onions (all the white and half the green portions of about 6 onions)
>
> 1 (1-pound) block firm tofu, drained well and sliced into $\frac{1}{2}$-inch-long by $\frac{1}{4}$-inch-thick julienne strips
>
> 10 dried shiitake mushrooms, soaked and sliced into thin shreds (see Note)
>
> 3 eggs, lightly beaten

In a large pot, combine the broth, vinegar, soy sauce, green onions, tofu, and mushrooms. Bring the mixture to a boil over medium-high heat, reduce the temperature to medium-low, and simmer gently, uncovered, for about 15 minutes to give the flavors a chance to merge and develop. Adjust the seasonings, adding additional vinegar or soy sauce, if desired.

Just before serving, bring the soup back to a slow boil. While stirring the soup, slowly drizzle in the beaten eggs. They will cook quite quickly in the hot broth and blossom out into feathery strips and bits. Serve immediately.

Variation: For a spicier soup, stir in 1 to 2 teaspoons hot chile-garlic paste and a dash of sesame oil.

Note: To reconstitute the dried mushrooms, place them in a deep bowl, cover with boiling water, and let sit for about 30 minutes, or until the mushrooms are soft and pliable. To keep the mushrooms submerged as they reconstitute, place a saucer or plate on top and weight it with a heavy object, such as a can or a coffee mug.

SWEET ONION SOUP

Here's one of the many ways to enjoy those Roasted and Smoked Sweet Onions. French onion soup fans will find this to be a gentle-yet-satisfying variation on the hearty and robust classic.

YIELD: 4 SERVINGS

About 1 pound ham hocks (2 medium hocks, each sawed in half)

1 quart homemade or canned beef broth

2 cups water

$^1/_2$ cup dry red wine

5 Roasted and Smoked Sweet Onions (page 97)

About 1 tablespoon balsamic vinegar

Salt and freshly ground black pepper to taste

4 ($^1/_2$-inch-thick) slices French bread baguette

About 2 tablespoons olive oil

2 cups grated Swiss cheese

In a large, heavy pot, combine the ham hocks, broth, water, and wine. Bring to a boil, cover, and simmer until the hocks are very tender and the meat is about to fall from the bones, about 1 to 1 $^1/_4$ hours. If possible, prepare this one day ahead, cool in the refrigerator, and skim off the fat.

Lift the hocks from the pan and pull off the meat. Discard the bones, gristle, skin, and fat. Cut the meat into very tiny pieces, then return it to the broth. Chop the onions into $^1/_4$-inch cubes and add to the pot. Bring the soup to a boil and simmer uncovered until it is reduced to 5 cups, about 30 minutes; stir in the vinegar, add salt and pepper to taste.

Meanwhile, lightly brush the baguette slices with the olive oil and bake them in a 400° oven until golden, about 5 minutes. Remove from the oven and set aside.

To serve, ladle the soup into 4 preheated soup bowls. Place a toasted baguette slice on top of each serving, then top each with a portion of the cheese. If desired, place the soup bowls under the broiler just to brown the top of the cheese (make sure the bowls are ovenproof), then serve immediately.

Shrimp Chowder

If the tiny Pacific shrimp aren't available you can substitute whatever fresh variety you have in your area.

Yield: *6 to 8 servings*

3 russet potatoes, peeled and cut into thirds

4 tablespoons ($^1/_2$ stick) butter

1 large sweet onion (such as Walla Walla or Vidalia), chopped

2 cups finely chopped celery

$2^1/_2$ cups light cream or half and half

1 cup dry white wine

Salt and white pepper to taste

$1^1/_2$ pounds cooked Pacific (or other fresh) shrimp

Shrimp, parsley, and chopped green onion for garnish

Boil the potatoes until soft, then drain well and mash (you will have about 3 cups of mashed potatoes); set aside.

In a large, heavy pot over medium heat, melt the butter. Add the onion and celery and sauté until softened, about 8 minutes. Stir in the mashed potatoes and light cream, then add the wine and salt and pepper. Reduce heat to medium-low and gently reheat the soup, stirring frequently. (The soup may be prepared to this point up to 24 hours ahead and refrigerated.)

Just before serving, stir in 1 pound of the shrimp and simmer gently for 5 minutes. If the soup is too thick, thin it with additional light cream. Garnish each serving with the remaining shrimp, as well as a sprinkling of parsley and green onion.

EARLY SUMMER GAZPACHO

YIELD: 8 TO 10 SERVINGS

3 pounds ripe tomatoes, cored and coarsely chopped

2 tablespoons olive oil

2 large cloves garlic, minced

1 large cucumber, peeled and chopped

2 cups finely chopped bunch onions (if you have some baby Vidalias or young Walla Wallas, or simply very fat green onions, those are just fine)

1 large beefsteak tomato, chopped

1 large green bell pepper, seeded and chopped

2 cups vegetable cocktail juice

1 1/2 cups consommé (canned is acceptable)

3 tablespoons red wine vinegar

3 tablespoons finely chopped fresh basil, or 1 tablespoon dried

1 tablespoon Worcestershire sauce

1 teaspoon salt

1 teaspoon white pepper

2 or 3 dashes hot pepper sauce

Garnishes: 1/2 cup sour cream, diced avocado (1 to 2, depending on their size), 2 tablespoons snipped fresh chives

In a large, nonaluminum pot over medium-high heat, combine the tomatoes, olive oil, and garlic. Cover and cook at a gentle simmer for 6 minutes. Remove from the heat, let the mixture cool slightly, then puree in a food processor.

In a large bowl, combine the tomato puree with all the remaining ingredients except the garnishes. Refrigerate the mixture for at least 4 hours to allow the flavor to develop. When ready to serve, adjust the seasonings. Ladle into soup bowls, and top each serving with a portion of the garnishes, beginning with a dollop of sour cream, and ending with the chives.

Salads and Light Meals

Sweet Onion and Tomato Salad

As soon as the season's fresh, young basil plants begin to yield an adequate supply of flavorful leaves, it's time to make the pesto. Once you've accomplished this, the following salad can be assembled at a moment's notice . . . using only the freshest of summer tomatoes, of course, and the freshest and crunchiest of sweet onions.

Yield: *4 servings*

PESTO DRESSING:

    ¼ cup extra-virgin olive oil

    3 tablespoons red wine vinegar

    2 tablespoons homemade or store-bought pesto

    1 pound (about 1 large or 2 medium) fresh sweet onions (such as
        Walla Walla or Vidalia)
    1 large (about ¾ pound) firm, ripe tomato, cored and cut crosswise
        into ¼-inch-thick slices
Fresh basil sprigs for garnish
Salt and freshly ground black pepper to taste

To make the pesto dressing, in a small bowl, whisk together all the ingredients; set aside.

Cut the onions crosswise into thin slices and separate the rings into a bowl. Pour the dressing over the onions and mix gently.

On 3 or 4 dinner or salad plates, arrange equal portions of the tomato. Top with equal portions of the onions and dressing. Garnish with basil sprigs. Season with salt and pepper.

A Salad of Bunch Onions with New Potatoes

I've found that bunch onions and fresh young potatoes have a particularly nice affinity for one another, so they always find their way into my shopping basket during my early summer forays to the local farmers' market.

Yield: 4 to 6 servings

2½ pounds red or white new potatoes (marble to golf ball–sized are particularly nice if you can find them)

½ cup extra-virgin olive oil

¼ cup mayonnaise

2 tablespoons white wine vinegar

2 tablespoons fresh lemon juice

1 tablespoon chopped fresh flat-leaf parsley

About 1 cup coarsely chopped bunch onions (white and pale green portions)

2 eggs, hard-cooked, peeled, and chopped

Salt and freshly ground black pepper to taste

Cook the potatoes in a large pot of boiling water until tender, 15 to 30 minutes (depending on how large they are). Drain well and let sit until cool enough to handle. If the potatoes are larger than golf ball size, cut them into 1-inch chunks. Halve the golf ball–sized ones, leave the marble-sized ones whole.

Prepare the dressing by whisking together the olive oil, mayonnaise, vinegar, lemon juice, and parsley. Toss this dressing with the potatoes, onions, and eggs. Add salt and pepper, then refrigerate the salad for 1 to 6 hours so the ingredients can mingle and improve in flavor. If possible, let the salad sit at room temperature for about 20 minutes before serving.

Salad of Sweet Onions and Cucumbers with Sour Cream

Yield: 4 servings

$\frac{1}{2}$ cup sour cream

$\frac{1}{3}$ cup rice vinegar

1 tablespoon sugar

$\frac{1}{4}$ teaspoon salt

$\frac{1}{8}$ teaspoon freshly ground black pepper

1 large sweet onion (such as Walla Walla or Vidalia), halved
lengthwise through the root end, then thinly sliced into half-
rings

1 large cucumber, peeled and thinly sliced

In a small bowl, whisk together the sour cream, vinegar, sugar, salt, and pepper. In a salad bowl, combine the onion and cucumber with the sour cream dressing. Toss well, then refrigerate for at least 30 minutes before serving so it's refreshingly chilled (may be made up to 3 days ahead).

Pocket Delight

— — —

A melange of fresh, crunchy vegetables, grated cheese, diced egg, sunflower seeds—this really is a salad all tucked into a chewy pocket of bread, then drizzled with either of two sauces—or both.

Yield: *4 servings*

1 cup finely chopped carrots

1 cup finely chopped celery

1 cup coarsely grated Cheddar or jack cheese

3 tomatoes, cored and diced

$1/2$ cup finely chopped green onions (white and green portions)

$1/2$ cup shelled sunflower seeds

3 eggs, hard-cooked, peeled, and chopped

1 or 2 ripe avocados, seeded, peeled, and diced

4 pocket breads, halved

Alfalfa sprouts

Raita Sauce (recipe follows)

Pocket Delight Vinaigrette (recipe follows)

In a bowl, combine the carrots, celery, cheese, tomatoes, green onion, sunflower seeds, hard-cooked egg, and avocado, tossing to mix thoroughly. To assemble the sandwiches, diners fill the pocket halves with a portion of the filling, some alfalfa sprouts, and then drizzle on either one or both of the sauces.

RAITA SAUCE

Yield: *about $2^{3}/4$ cups*

1 cucumber, peeled, seeded, and chopped

$1/2$ cup finely chopped yellow onion

1 cup plain yogurt

1 cup sour cream

2 teaspoons ground cumin

Salt and freshly ground black pepper to taste

In a small bowl, combine all the ingredients. Chill for at least 1 hour before serving.

POCKET DELIGHT VINAIGRETTE

YIELD: ABOUT 1 CUP

$^1/_3$ cup red or white wine vinegar

2 teaspoons Worcestershire sauce

$^1/_2$ teaspoon salt

1 teaspoon ground cumin

$^1/_8$ teaspoon hot pepper sauce

$^1/_4$ cup extra-virgin olive oil

$^1/_4$ cup vegetable oil

$^1/_3$ cup sour cream

In a small, deep bowl, combine the vinegar, Worcestershire sauce, salt, cumin, and hot pepper sauce. Beat with a wire whisk to blend. Continue beating while you add the oils. Finally, stir in the sour cream, blend again, and adjust the seasonings. Chill for at least 1 hour before serving.

SESAME CHICKEN POCKETS

YIELD: 4 SERVINGS

5 skinless, boneless chicken breast halves

2 tablespoons vegetable oil

1 teaspoon sesame oil

1 $^1\!/_2$ tablespoons sesame seeds

1 tablespoon *each* soy sauce, sugar, ketchup

2 tablespoons red or white wine vinegar

1 teaspoon Worcestershire sauce

$^1\!/_2$ teaspoon red chili flakes

1 small jalapeño chile, seeded and finely minced

1 medium cucumber, peeled, seeded, and diced

2 medium tomatoes, diced

1 red onion, minced

$^1\!/_2$ teaspoon dried rosemary, or 1 teaspoon finely minced fresh

4 pocket breads, halved

2 to 3 cups shredded lettuce

2 cups coarsely grated Monterey Jack cheese

$^1\!/_2$ cup sour cream for garnish

Dice the chicken into $^1\!/_2$-inch pieces. In a skillet, heat the oils and sauté the chicken over medium-high heat until lightly golden, about 8 minutes. While the chicken is browning, make a well in the center of the pan and add the sesame seeds, gently stirring them occasionally, until browned. Add the soy sauce, sugar, ketchup, vinegar, Worcestershire sauce, chili flakes, and about half the jalapeño chile (add more later if you want the mixture to be even more spicy); set aside. (The mixture may be prepared to this point, covered, and refrigerated for up to 24 hours. Reheat before using, or serve at room temperature.)

About half an hour before serving, combine the cucumber, tomatoes, onion, and rosemary. To assemble the pockets, each diner fills the pocket bread halves with a portion of the chicken, the shredded lettuce, cheese, and tomato mixture. Garnish with sour cream.

Chicken Salad in Sesame and Poppy Seed Vinaigrette with Caramelized Almonds

◦ ◦ ◦

This is a delectable twist on the traditional chicken salad. The Sesame and Poppy Seed Vinaigrette really makes the recipe, so don't substitute with anything else!

YIELD: *4 SERVINGS*

SESAME AND POPPY SEED VINAIGRETTE:

$^1/_4$ cup red or white wine vinegar

1 tablespoon sugar

2 tablespoons lightly toasted sesame seeds

1 tablespoon poppy seeds

1 tablespoon coarsely chopped onion

$^1/_2$ teaspoon Worcestershire sauce

$^1/_4$ teaspoon paprika

$^1/_4$ teaspoon salt

$^1/_3$ cup vegetable oil

SUGAR-GLAZED ALMONDS:

1 scant cup sliced almonds

Several spoonfuls sugar

4 cooked skinless and boneless chicken breasts, preferably mesquite-
    grilled (see Note)

3 cups shredded fresh, young spinach leaves

2 Roma (Italian plum) tomatoes, diced

$^1/_4$ cup minced red onion

2 hard-cooked eggs, sliced

To make the vinaigrette, place the vinegar, sugar, sesame seeds, poppy seeds, onion, Worcestershire sauce, paprika, and salt in a blender or food processor. Blend until most of the sesame seeds are ground (stop the motor several times and scrape down the sides). Add the oil all at once and blend briefly once again. (For a thicker version, add the oil in a slow, steady stream while the motor is running; the dressing will thicken to the consistency of a soft mayonnaise.)

To make the almonds, in a nonstick skillet (or a skillet sprayed with no-stick cooking spray), heat the almonds over medium-high heat until golden, shaking the pan to prevent scorching, about 2 minutes. Once the almonds have browned, sprinkle on the sugar, stirring constantly, and cook until the sugar melts around the almonds. Remove from the heat and scrape the almonds out onto a sheet of wax paper to cool.

To assemble the salad, cut the cooled pieces of chicken into $1/4$-inch dice and combine with $1/2$ cup of the vinaigrette, the spinach leaves, tomatoes, almonds, and onion. Add more vinaigrette as necessary to reach the desired consistency. Divide the salad among 4 plates, garnish each one with some of the sliced egg, and serve.

Note: It's not necessary to grill the chicken over mesquite coals, but it does impart a wonderful flavor. The chickens can be grilled up to 24 hours ahead and refrigerated until you are ready to assemble the salad mixture. Alternately, you can simply broil the boneless, skinless chicken breasts in the oven, turning them once and cooking until done.

GRILLED CHICKEN SALAD
WITH GREEN GARLIC MAYONNAISE

Composed salads became popular in the early 1980s as sophisticated alternatives to the salad bar. This one, with its lovely yellow and red peppers contrasting with the salad greens, is impressive to serve. A truly exquisite French bread, if you can find it, would be wonderful along with this meal.

YIELD: *4 SERVINGS*

>   4 skinless and boneless chicken breasts (approximately 3 pounds)
>   Salt and freshly ground pepper
>   1½ cups Green Garlic Mayonnaise (recipe follows)
>   2 ribs celery, cut into 1-inch-long pencil-thin strips
>   ½ cup chopped green onions (white and green portions)
>   6 cups mixed salad greens (including several leafy varieties, a bit of
>   crunchy iceberg, and some arugula), torn into bite-size pieces
>   1 red bell pepper, seeded and sliced into rings
>   1 yellow bell pepper, seeded and sliced into rings
>   Balsamic vinegar
>   Extra-virgin olive oil

Season each breast with salt and pepper, then grill over hot coals until done, or broil, turning once. When the breasts are cool enough to handle, cut them into ½-inch chunks. This can be done up to 48 hours ahead. Cover the chicken and store it in the refrigerator.

Make the mayonnaise and set aside.

Combine the cooled chicken with the mayonnaise, celery, and green onions. To serve, arrange the salad greens equally on 4 plates. Arrange the pepper slices on top of the greens, then drizzle vinegar and olive oil over each portion. Finally, spoon on the chicken salad mixture. Serve immediately.

GREEN GARLIC MAYONNAISE

YIELD: 1½ CUPS

2 green garlic plants, each measuring about ¹/₂-inch in diameter at the
   root end (including all of the white part and a portion of the
   pale green stem)
1 whole egg
1 teaspoon fresh lemon juice
1 teaspoon Dijon mustard
¹/₄ teaspoon salt
1 cup extra-virgin olive oil

Trim away the root and most of the green portion from each of the garlic plants, then coarsely chop. Place the egg in the bowl of a food processor, along with the lemon juice, mustard, salt, and the chopped garlic. Process until the garlic is pureed and the mixture is smooth. With the motor still running, begin adding the olive oil drop by drop until you can see that an emulsion has formed and the sauce is beginning to thicken. Then increase the rate of oil addition to a slow, steady stream.

Note: If you're uncomfortable using uncooked eggs, begin with 1 ¹/₂ cups good-quality mayonnaise (such as Hellmann's or Best Foods), and process with the same amounts of lemon juice, mustard, and garlic. Omit the olive oil, eggs, and salt.

WILD RICE SALAD
WITH SMOKED SWEET ONIONS
AND SMOKED TURKEY

Francie O'Shea, a Corvallis cookbook author and restaurant owner, used to serve a delicious wild rice salad with smoked turkey. I've added the smoked sweet onions, which are a natural, and played around a bit with the vegetables.

YIELD: *6 SERVINGS*

1 cup long-grain brown rice

$^1/_2$ cup wild rice

1 teaspoon salt

3 cups homemade or canned chicken broth

$^1/_2$ pound smoked turkey breast, cubed

1 large or 2 medium sweet onions (such as Vidalia or Walla Walla),
    smoked (see Note) and diced

1 cup peeled, seeded, and diced cucumbers

$^1/_2$ cup chopped green onions (white and green portions)

$^1/_2$ cup *each* seeded and chopped green and red bell peppers

$^1/_4$ cup finely chopped fresh parsley

1 cup fresh or frozen peas

$^1/_2$ cup coarsely chopped water chestnuts

$1^1/_2$ cups mayonnaise

2 tablespoons rice vinegar

2 teaspoons Dijon mustard

$^1/_2$ teaspoon dried marjoram

$^1/_4$ teaspoon freshly ground black pepper

In a medium saucepan, bring to a boil the brown and wild rice, ¹/₂ teaspoon of the salt, and the broth. Reduce the heat to low and cook, covered, 40 to 45 minutes, or until the liquid has been absorbed and the rice is tender. Toss lightly with a fork and set aside to cool.

In an attractive salad bowl, combine the smoked turkey, onion, cucumbers, green onions, bell peppers, parsley, peas, and water chestnuts. Toss gently with the cooled rice.

In a small, deep bowl, whisk together the mayonnaise and the rice vinegar, mustard, marjoram, the remaining ¹/₂ teaspoon of salt, and the black pepper. Add the dressing to the salad and stir well, then cover and refrigerate until ready to serve.

The salad makes a perfectly lovely meal simply served on a fresh lettuce leaf garnished with a few green onion slices and toasty cheese bread. If sugar snap peas are available, they are also a delightful addition to the salad. Just throw them in along with everything else, cutting back a bit on the peppers, perhaps.

Note: To smoke the onions using a charcoal grill: Heat about 10 coals in the barbecue until they get very low, with a nice dusting of ash on their surface. Sprinkle 4 cups of wood chips that have been soaked in water for about 30 minutes (drain well before adding to the coals). Place quartered onions either directly on the grill (if the grate is narrow enough to keep the pieces from falling through; a wire fish cooker works well) or in a lightly greased shallow baking pan, and smoke/roast the onions for 45 minutes.

To smoke the onions using a gas grill: Turn the grill on to a low setting, then add the onions as directed above. Add soaked wood chips that have been packed into a small metal can or into the built-in "smoker drawer" that comes with some gas grills. Smoke/roast the onions for 45 minutes.

SWEET ONION SANDWICH

The combination of sweet onions, smoky-tasting arugula, and smooth Swiss cheese on pumpernickel creates a flavor that's unbeatable!

YIELD: 4 SERVINGS

$^1/_2$ cup sour cream

1 tablespoon Dijon mustard

8 slices dark, dense-textured pumpernickel bread

4 ounces thin-sliced Swiss cheese

12 to 16 tender arugula leaves, rinsed and crisped

1 medium (about 8 ounces) fresh Walla Walla Sweet onion (or
      another sweet onion, such as Vidalia), sliced thin

Salt and freshly ground black pepper to taste

In a cup, combine the sour cream and mustard, then slather 4 slices of the bread with a portion of the sauce. Equally distribute the cheese, arugula, and onion over the sauce, then season with salt and pepper. Spread the other 4 slices of bread with the remainder of the sauce and complete the sandwiches.

Stuffed Sweet Onions

Onions prepared this way can make exciting side dishes or entrées, depending on the stuffing.

To prepare onions for stuffing, peel them and cut a $1/2$-inch slice off the top. Slice a smaller section from the root end, just enough so the onion will stand upright without tipping over. Cook the onions in a large pot of boiling water until just barely tender, about 15 minutes; drain. Scoop out the centers, leaving a $1/2$-inch shell.

Alternatively, if you want to retain some uncooked onion, scoop out the center portion before boiling, then boil for only 5 to 7 minutes.

Onion shells can also be prepared and left raw until stuffed, or cooked in the microwave oven (see Savory Stuffed Sweet Onions, page 81).

SIMPLY STUFFED
SWEET ONIONS

Simple stuffings are a nice way to take advantage of the size and shape of sweet onions.

YIELD: *4 SERVINGS*

> 4 large sweet onions (such as Walla Walla or Vidalia)
> 3 tablespoons butter
> $1/4$ pound mushrooms, finely chopped
> 1 cup finely chopped celery
> 12 ounces well-seasoned bulk pork sausage
> 1 cup soft bread crumbs (preferably made from sourdough French
>   bread)
> $1/4$ teaspoon salt
> $1/4$ teaspoon freshly ground black pepper
> $3/4$ cup chicken broth
> $3/4$ cup dry white wine or dry sherry

Prepare the onions for stuffing as described on page 77. Trim the root end of each onion to create a flat base for it to rest on during cooking. Skin the onions and peel off any slippery membranes so you can grip them firmly when scooping out the inner flesh. Cut off the top of each peeled onion and dig into the center with a metal spoon, a grapefruit knife or spoon, or any other utensil that works for you. Scoop out the flesh, leaving a $1/4$-inch-thick shell. Chop enough of the inner flesh to measure 2 cups.

Melt the butter in a large pot, add the chopped onions, the mushrooms, and celery and sauté until softened, about 5 minutes. Preheat the oven to 400°F.

Meanwhile, in a skillet, sauté the sausage until just barely browned. With a slotted spoon, add the sausage to the vegetable mixture, along with the bread crumbs, salt, and pepper. Spoon the stuffing into the onion shells, mounding it slightly for an attractive effect.

Place the onions in a shallow, ovenproof dish or casserole that holds them snugly. Pour on the broth and wine, then cover the dish loosely with aluminum foil. Bake for 20 minutes, then reduce the oven temperature to 350° and cook for another 25 minutes. Remove the foil from the dish and continue to cook the onions, uncovered, for up to 30 minutes, until they are brown and the liquid is syrupy. Baste them frequently with the cooking liquid during the final stages to keep them moist and to create a nice glaze on the outside of the onions. Just prior to serving, pour the remaining liquid over them.

SAUSAGE-STUFFED ONIONS

YIELD: 4 GENEROUS SERVINGS

4 large sweet onions (such as Walla Walla or Vidalia)

1 pound sweet Italian sausage

1 cup coarsely grated provolone cheese

1 1/2 cups fresh Italian or French bread crumbs

2 eggs

2 tablespoons chopped fresh flat-leaf parsley

1 tablespoon chopped fresh basil

1/4 teaspoon salt

1/4 cup milk

4 slices bacon

Prepare the onions for stuffing as described on page 77, scooping out the center portion before boiling the shells. Chop enough of the raw center portion to measure 1 1/2 cups; set aside.

Preheat the oven to 350°F.

In a heavy skillet over medium-high heat, sauté the sausage until browned, about 4 minutes, breaking it into very small pieces as it cooks. Drain away all but 2 tablespoons of the fat, then add the chopped onion and continue cooking until the onion has softened, about 2 to 3 minutes. Remove the mixture from the heat and let it cool slightly. Stir in the cheese, bread crumbs, eggs, parsley, basil, and salt. Add just enough of the milk to make a moist mixture (you may need to add more, depending on the consistency of your bread).

Stuff each prepared shell with a portion of the filling, then lay a small piece of bacon over the top. Bake for 30 minutes, or until the bacon strips and exterior of the onions are golden.

SAVORY STUFFED
SWEET ONIONS

This recipe was a 1990 Vidalia Onion Festival Grand Prize winner.

YIELD: 4 SERVINGS

4 large Vidalia onions

3 ounces cream cheese, softened

3 slices bacon, cooked and crumbled

$1/4$ cup snipped fresh chives

$1/4$ cup sliced fresh mushrooms

$1/2$ teaspoon salt

$1/4$ teaspoon freshly ground black pepper

$1/2$ teaspoon garlic salt

2 drops hot pepper sauce

$1/4$ cup heavy cream

$1/4$ cup coarsely grated Cheddar cheese

Garnishes: 20 boiled shrimp, chopped fresh flat-leaf parsley

Steam the onions by wrapping each one in a damp paper towel. Microwave on High for about 10 minutes, or until tender. Spoon out the inside pulp, leaving 3 outer layers of onion. You should have a circular opening. Place the onions in a lightly greased casserole dish; set aside. Combine all the remaining ingredients except the garnish, then divide the mixture equally among the steamed Vidalias. Microwave on High for 2 or 3 minutes, until well heated. Garnish each stuffed Vidalia with 5 boiled shrimp around the top edge of the onion. Sprinkle the center with the parsley.

To prepare with a conventional oven, first prepare the onion shell for stuffing as described on page 77. Combine all of the remaining ingredients except the garnish, then divide the mixture equally among the prepared shells. Bake in a preheated 375° oven until the filling is hot and bubbly, about 20 minutes.

CHICKEN-STUFFED SWEETS

YIELD: 4 SERVINGS

4 sweet onions (such as Vidalia, Walla Walla, or Maui)

2 cups cooked and diced chicken

$^1/_2$ cup coarsely grated Monterey Jack cheese

$^1/_4$ cup freshly grated Parmesan cheese

$^1/_4$ cup fine dry bread crumbs

$^1/_4$ cup milk

1 egg, beaten

1 tablespoon chopped fresh flat-leaf parsley

$^1/_2$ teaspoon salt

1 teaspoon paprika

$^1/_4$ teaspoon dried tarragon, crumbled

$^1/_4$ teaspoon dried oregano, crumbled

Prepare the onions for stuffing as described on page 77, removing and chopping $^1/_2$ cup of the inner portion before cooking.

Preheat the oven to 350°F.

In a large bowl, combine all the remaining ingredients, including the reserved chopped onion, and mix well. Fill the prepared onion shells with the chicken mixture and arrange in a deep casserole. Bake, covered, for 15 minutes. Remove the cover and bake for 15 minutes longer, until the filling is very hot with a golden crust. Serve as a simple entrée with a tossed green salad.

Sweet Onions Stuffed with Mushroom Sauce

~ ~ ~

Yield: 4 servings

4 large sweet onions (such as Vidalia or Walla Walla)

2 tablespoons butter or olive oil

1 tablespoon fresh lemon juice

$^{1}/_{2}$ pound mushrooms, thinly sliced

1 tablespoon flour

$^{3}/_{4}$ teaspoon salt

$^{1}/_{8}$ teaspoon white pepper

1 tablespoon chopped fresh flat-leaf parsley, plus 4 fresh parsley sprigs
           for garnish

$^{1}/_{2}$ cup whole milk

1 cup heavy cream

1 tablespoon drained capers

Freshly grated Parmesan cheese

Prepare the onions for stuffing as described on page 77, removing and chopping 2 cups of the inner portion before cooking.

Melt the butter or oil in a medium-size saucepan. Add the lemon juice, reserved chopped onion, and the mushrooms, and sauté, stirring frequently, until the mushrooms are tender. Remove and reserve a few slices for garnish. Stir the flour, salt, pepper, and parsley into the mushrooms remaining in the pan, then gradually whisk in the milk and cream, stirring until the sauce is smooth and thickened. Stir in the capers, then pour the sauce into the hot, cooked onion shells. Sprinkle each with Parmesan cheese. Garnish with the reserved mushroom slices and a sprig of parsley.

ENTRÉES

PORK CHOPS
WITH SWEET ONIONS,
APPLE BRANDY, AND SAGE

In order to achieve a balance of flavor, the tart green apple—as opposed to a sweeter variety—really is essential. After more than an hour of cooking, this dish arrives at the table in the most delectably tender and flavorful state you can imagine.

YIELD: *6 SERVINGS*

6 loin pork chops, each cut $^1/_2$ inch thick

$^1/_2$ cup all-purpose flour

$^1/_4$ teaspoon dried sage

$^1/_4$ teaspoon white pepper

$^1/_4$ teaspoon salt

4 tablespoons olive oil, or as needed

1 large sweet onion (such as Vidalia or Walla Walla), halved and
        sliced

1 large tart green apple (such as Granny Smith), peeled, cored, and
        sliced

2 cups large pitted prunes, halved

1 cup canned or homemade chicken broth

$^1/_2$ cup dry white wine

$^1/_2$ cup apple brandy or Calvados

Rinse the chops in water. Combine the flour with the sage, white pepper, and salt; coat the chops lightly with the seasoned flour.

Heat 3 tablespoons of the oil in a large skillet over medium-high heat. Add the chops and brown for about 5 minutes on each side. Transfer the chops to a heavy casserole dish or Dutch oven with a tight-fitting lid and set aside.

Add the remaining tablespoon of oil to the skillet, reduce the heat to medium-low, and slowly sauté the onion until golden, about 20 minutes. Add the apple and sauté for 3 minutes longer. Spoon the onion and apple slices over the top of the chops and arrange the prunes around the sides.

Deglaze the skillet with the broth, wine, and brandy, scraping up any brown pieces that cling to the pan bottom. Bring the liquid to a boil, then pour it over the chops. Cover, and simmer over low heat until the chops are tender, 45 to 60 minutes. Check occasionally and add a little more broth if the liquid cooks down too rapidly. You should have enough sauce left at the end of the cooking time to pour over the chops just before serving.

New Potatoes, Smoky Ham, and Sweet Onion Gratin

Potatoes, ham, and onions have been going hand in hand for eons; it's a fabulous combination of flavors. For those who have lived near a supply of sweet onions—be they Walla Wallas, Vidalias, or Mauis—it's just a natural progression of thought to substitute them for the hearty yellow variety. And while you're in the mood for substituting, or simply for the sake of variety, consider using any of summer's yellow-fleshed potato varieties, such as the yellow fin or Yukon Gold.

Yield: 6 servings

2 pounds red potatoes

1 pound good quality smoked ham

About $1/3$ cup vegetable oil

1 pound (1 large or 2 medium) sweet onions, thinly sliced

Salt and freshly ground black pepper to taste

$1/2$ cup water

$1/2$ cup coarsely grated provolone cheese

Place the unpeeled potatoes in a saucepan with water to cover. Bring to a boil and simmer, uncovered, until tender, about 15 minutes. Drain, let cool slightly until easy to handle, then remove the skins, and cut the potatoes into $1/8$-inch-thick slices.

Preheat the oven to 350°F.

Trim away any excess fat from the ham and cut the meat into 1-inch pieces. Heat about 2 tablespoons of the oil in a large skillet over medium-low heat. Add half the onions and sauté gently for 15 to 20 minutes. Add half the potatoes and season with salt and pepper. Add half the ham and sauté until the potatoes are golden on both sides, 8 to 10 minutes, adding a little more oil if necessary to prevent sticking.

Transfer the mixture to an ovenproof casserole, then repeat the process with the remaining ingredients, adding them to the casserole after they have browned. Drizzle the water over the top, sprinkle on the cheese, then bake uncovered for 30 minutes, or until the water has been absorbed and the top is lightly crusted and the cheese is golden. Serve hot.

Chicago's Zinfandel restaurant is one place where you can find ramps on the menu each spring. They have a specialty known as Spring Potato Soup of Yukon Golds, Artichokes, and Wild Ramps.

Spring
into
Summer

Focaccia Bread
with Bunch Onions
and Olive Oil

Every year, when the first crop of brilliantly hued bunch onions hits the local farmers' market, this recipe is dusted off and brought to life. It's easy to assemble, and makes an easy-yet-delectable meal on those warm summer evenings when a light entrée and simple salad are perfectly satisfying.

Yield: 6 servings

$1/4$ cup olive oil

2 to 3 cups of bunch onions, thinly sliced (use entire globe plus about
$2/3$ of the green portion)

2 cloves garlic, finely minced

1 ($14^{1/2}$-ounce) can Italian-style stewed tomatoes

Salt and white pepper to taste

1 (8- or 9-inch) round of focaccia bread (these are marketed in a
"brown 'n serve" form, and are distributed nationally in most
supermarkets)

$1^{1/2}$ cups coarsely grated Cheddar cheese

$1/3$ cup freshly grated Parmesan cheese

Preheat the oven to 425°F. Lightly grease a 9-inch round cake pan.

In a skillet, heat the oil and sauté the onions and garlic just until the onions are softened, about 2 minutes. Add the stewed tomatoes and simmer until the mixture thickens, about 10 minutes. Adjust the seasonings with salt and pepper.

Place the loaf of focaccia in the cake pan. Spread half the onion mixture on top of the loaf, making sure it gets down into all of the holes on the surface. Sprinkle with half the Cheddar and Parmesan. Top with the remaining onion mixture, then sprinkle with the remaining Cheddar and Parmesan.

Bake for 20 or 25 minutes, until the top is beautifully browned and bubbly. Remove from the oven and let the loaf rest for about 5 minutes before removing it from the pan and cutting it into serving-size wedges.

ADAPTATIONS ABOUND: To the onion mixture, add any number of chopped vegetables, such as Anaheim chiles, celery, sliced olives, or mushrooms; cooked sausage also is great.

Shrimp and Sugar Snap Peas with Red Pepper and Chive Sauce

Yield: *4 servings*

4 tablespoons olive oil

$^1/_2$ cup chopped sweet onion (such as Vidalia or Walla Walla)

2 cloves garlic, chopped

$^1/_4$ teaspoon dried red pepper flakes, crushed

2 red bell peppers, seeded and cut into 1-inch dice

4 Roma tomatoes, cored, seeded, and chopped

$^1/_4$ cup homemade or canned chicken broth (chilled or at room temperature)

$^1/_2$ cup finely chopped fresh chives

About $^1/_2$ pound sugar snap peas (if unavailable, use Chinese pea pods, see Note)

1 pound raw medium shrimp, peeled and deveined, with tails intact

1 to 2 teaspoons salt

In a skillet, heat 2 tablespoons of the olive oil over medium heat and sauté the onion, garlic, and red pepper flakes for about 5 minutes, or until the onions are tender. Remove from the heat and cool, then scrape the mixture into a blender or food processor, along with the red bell peppers and the chopped tomatoes; puree, adding a bit of broth if necessary to make a fairly smooth sauce. Press the puree through a fine-meshed sieve into a saucepan. Stir in $^1/_4$ cup of the chives. The sauce can be covered tightly and refrigerated for up to 24 hours at this point.

Wash the sugar snap peas, remove the stems and strings, and set aside.

In a skillet over medium-high heat, sauté the shrimp in the remaining 2 tablespoons of oil until the shrimp turn pink and opaque, 3 or 4 minutes. Add salt to taste and sprinkle with the remaining $^1/_4$ cup of chives; remove from the heat.

While the shrimp are cooking, bring the sauce to a boil over medium-high heat.

To serve, spoon the sauce onto a serving platter, then pile the shrimp into the center and surround with the pea pods.

Note: If sugar snap peas are unavailable, use Chinese pea pods that have been steamed or blanched for 1 minute.

SIDE DISHES
AND ACCOMPANIMENTS

SIMPLY SAUTÉED

If you've never experienced a sweet onion straight from the sauté pan, after it's been delicately caramelized to a rich golden hue and gentle flavor, you simply haven't had the full experience.

YIELD: *1 TO 8 SERVINGS. IT JUST DEPENDS!*

3 sweet onions (such as Walla Walla or Vidalia)
$1/_2$ cup butter (1 stick)
Salt and white pepper to taste

Peel the onions and either slice into rings or chop, depending on what you want to use them for. Melt the butter in a large pan over medium-low heat. Add the onions, stir with a spoon to coat well, and cook gently over low to medium-low heat for about 1 hour, until the onions are thoroughly softened and a deep golden color. Stir occasionally to keep the bottom from burning. Add salt and pepper to taste before serving.

Delicious as is, or over a steak, meat loaf, or hamburger.

MASHED POTATOES
WITH SWEET ONIONS

YIELD: *6 SERVINGS*

6 tablespoons butter

2 cups chopped sweet onions (such as Walla Walla or Vidalia)

$2^1/_2$ pounds russet potatoes, peeled and quartered

1 cup milk

About $^1/_4$ teaspoon salt

Freshly ground black pepper to taste

In a small saucepan, melt the butter and gently sauté the chopped onions over medium-low heat for 25 to 30 minutes, or until the onions have softened and turned a rich golden brown; set aside.

While the onions are cooking, boil the potatoes in a large pot of salted water until tender, 15 to 20 minutes. Remove from the heat, drain well, and mash thoroughly with a potato masher.

To the onion mixture, add the milk, salt, and pepper and warm gently, then whisk into the potatoes; adjust the seasonings and serve.

A ROASTING OF WALLA WALLA SWEETS AND POTATOES

This is a simple, down-to-earth accompaniment to steak or any grilled meat. It can be assembled ahead, which makes it perfect for entertaining.

YIELD: *6 SERVINGS*

> 3 large Walla Walla Sweet onions (each approximately $3/4$ pound)
> 2 tablespoons vegetable oil
> 3 or 4 medium russet potatoes, scrubbed but unpeeled, cut into $1/4$ to
> $1/2$-inch dice (4 cups)
> $1/4$ teaspoon salt
> $1/8$ teaspoon freshly ground black pepper

Halve each onion lengthwise (through the top and root ends), then skin, peeling away any slippery membrane so that you can grip it firmly when you are scooping out the inner flesh. Dig into the center of each half onion with a metal spoon, a grapefruit knife or spoon, or any other utensil that works for you. Scoop out the flesh, leaving a $1/2$-inch-thick shell. Chop enough of the inner flesh to measure 2 cups; set aside. (Reserve the remaining onion flesh for another use later in the week.)

Heat the oil in a large nonstick skillet, add the chopped onions and potatoes, the salt, and pepper, and sauté over medium-high heat, stirring occasionally, for about 5 minutes, or just until the onion begins to soften.

Preheat the oven to 375°F. Oil a rectangular baking dish that is large enough to hold the onions and still have room to arrange some of the potato mixture around them.

Arrange the 6 scooped-out onion halves in the baking dish and spoon about $1/2$ cup of the potato mixture into each onion shell, then arrange the remaining potato mixture all around the shells, spreading it out in the pan to form a layer no deeper than about 1 inch. (Note: At this point, the mixture may be covered tightly with plastic wrap and refrigerated for up to 24 hours ahead; remove about 20 minutes before proceeding with the recipe.)

Bake for 1 hour, or until the potatoes are thoroughly cooked and deeply browned. When ready to serve, place 1 potato-filled onion half and a generous portion of the surrounding potato mixture on each of 6 dinner plates (or bring the dish to the table and serve directly from the casserole).

Simply Baked Walla Walla Sweets with Pesto

A delicious accompaniment to grilled meats or a pasta with meat and tomato sauce.

Yield: *4 servings*

2 Walla Walla Sweet onions
$^1/_2$ cup homemade or store-bought pesto

Preheat the oven to 350°F.

Slice a thin portion from the top and bottom of each onion. Then slice each unpeeled onion in half, horizontally (through the widest part). Place the onions, cut side up, in a baking dish, spread about 2 tablespoons of pesto on top of each onion, and place in the oven. Bake for about 30 to 35 minutes, or until the onions are tender and the pesto slightly browned and bubbly.

SIMPLY ROASTED AND
SMOKED SWEET ONIONS

Just when you were convinced that sweet onions suffer with too much time on the burner, along comes this fabulous offering. For the ultimate flavor experience, the onions must achieve a deep-golden hue, which translates to about an hour of grill time. However, they can be prepared on any evening when you already have the coals stoked into action, then covered and stored in the refrigerator to accompany a simple dinner of oven-roasted chicken or fish later in the week. To reheat, pop them into the oven with the roast for the last 15 minutes, or simply microwave on HIGH about 2 minutes or until heated through.

YIELD: 6 TO 8 SERVINGS

5 large or 8 medium sweet onions (such as Vidalia or Walla Walla),
    halved
$1/4$ cup extra-virgin olive oil
$1/4$ cup balsamic vinegar
2 tablespoons butter, cut into small chunks
Salt and white pepper to taste

Create a 10 by 14-inch roasting pan from at least 2 layers of heavy-duty aluminum foil by bending the edges up into 2-inch-high sides and crimping the corners to hold them in place. Lay the onions in the pan, cut side up. In a small bowl, combine the olive oil, vinegar, and butter, then pour over the onions. Add salt and pepper to taste.

Bank hot coals on 2 sides in the bottom of a barbecue grill with a lid. Place the foil pan of onions on the grill, centered between the banks of coals below. Cover the grill and bake, gently turning the onions and basting them with the pan juices about every 20 minutes, until they are deep-golden and very soft when pressed. This will take 1 to $1^{1}/_{2}$ hours. Serve them hot or at room temperature, as an accompaniment to grilled or oven-roasted fish, poultry, or beef.

ASPARAGUS AND CHIVES

What says "spring" more naturally than these two harbingers of the season?

YIELD: *6 SERVINGS*

    1 (14-ounce) can reduced-sodium chicken broth

    3 tablespoons olive oil

    $^1/_2$ cup chopped fresh chives

    1$^1/_2$ pounds very fresh asparagus, peeled and the tough fibrous lower
           portion of the stalk trimmed away

    Salt and freshly ground black pepper to taste

    Grated zest of 1 lemon for garnish

In a large skillet that is wide enough to accommodate the asparagus, bring the broth, oil, and chives to a boil. Add the asparagus, cover, and quickly return the broth to a boil. Remove the lid and simmer just until the asparagus is tender but still crisp (it will continue to cook when removed from the pot), about 7 minutes. Remove the stalks with a slotted spoon and place on a serving platter. Raise the heat and simmer the broth until it is reduced to about $^1/_2$ cup, about 3 minutes. Season with salt and pepper, then drizzle over the asparagus. Garnish with the grated lemon and serve.

BARLEY, GREEN ONION, CORN, AND RED PEPPER CASSEROLE

YIELD: 6 SERVINGS

2 tablespoons olive oil

1 large red bell pepper, seeded and chopped

3 cups of green onions, chopped (all of white and half of the green portion)

1 1/2 cups barley

2 (14 1/2-ounce) cans homemade or canned chicken broth

2 cups fresh or frozen corn (if not local, in-season corn, use frozen)

1/2 cup sliced fresh basil

Salt to taste

1/2 teaspoon white pepper

In a heavy-bottomed, medium-size saucepan, heat the oil and sauté the bell pepper and 2 cups of the green onions over medium-high heat for about 5 minutes. Add the barley, stirring to coat the grains with olive oil, and sauté for another minute. Add the chicken broth, bring the mixture to a boil, stirring once or twice, then reduce the heat, cover, and simmer until the barley is tender, about 40 minutes. Stir several times during the cooking to keep the barley from sticking. Add the corn and heat through for 5 minutes. Gently stir in the basil and remaining green onions. Let the dish sit for another 2 or 3 minutes to heat the onions; season with salt and the pepper and serve.

For more ways to cook with sweet onions, track down the recipes using OSO Sweet Onions in Chapter 5.

Spring into Summer

A Springtime Risotto
with Chives, Prosciutto, and Watercress

— — —

Yield: *4 servings*

6 cups homemade or canned chicken broth

1 cup dry white wine

2 tablespoons butter

2 tablespoons olive oil

$^1/_2$ cup finely chopped shallots

2 cups uncooked arborio rice (see Note)

3 ounces very thinly sliced prosciutto, julienned into $^1/_4$ by
2-inch strips

$^3/_4$ cup freshly grated Parmesan cheese

Salt and freshly ground black pepper to taste

$^1/_2$ cup chopped fresh watercress leaves

$^1/_3$ cup snipped fresh chives

In a medium-size saucepan over medium heat, bring the chicken broth and wine to a simmer; reduce the heat and keep the liquid just below a simmer.

In a heavy saucepan, melt the butter with the oil over medium heat. Add the shallots and sauté, stirring constantly, until the shallots have softened, about 3 minutes. Stir in the rice until well coated and cook for a moment, then add about $^1/_2$ cup of the hot broth, stirring constantly, until all of the liquid has been absorbed. Continue adding $^1/_2$ cup portions of the broth to the rice, stirring constantly, and waiting until the liquid has been mostly absorbed before adding the next amount.

Be sure to keep stirring so the rice won't stick and will cook evenly. About 25 minutes into this process, most of the liquid should have been added to the rice and the rice should be very tender, but still retain a firm center.

Remove the rice from the burner, then stir in the prosciutto and Parmesan cheese and gently stir. Adjust seasonings at this point, adding salt and pepper, then gently stir in the watercress and chives.

Note: This is really the rice you want to use. Arborio has shorter, fatter grains with a starch content that is very high, and a firm center that retains a bit of firmness even after cooking (as long as you don't overcook it). Additionally, arborio rice has an outer coating that falls away during cooking and helps turn this dish into a creamy wonder. You can track it down at specialty food stores and well-stocked supermarkets.

Risotto with Cheese and Spring Onions

— —

Yield: *4 servings*

2 tablespoons olive oil

1 tablespoon minced garlic

3 cups thinly sliced leeks (white and pale green portions only)

1 cup chopped sweet onions (such as Vidalia, Walla Walla, or another sweet variety)

10 green onions, chopped (keep the white and green portions separate)

³/₄ teaspoon salt

¹/₂ teaspoon white pepper

2 cups uncooked arborio rice (see Note, page 101)

About 6 cups homemade or canned hot chicken broth

¹/₂ cup dry white wine

3 tablespoons snipped fresh chives

2 tablespoons butter

¹/₃ cup freshly grated Parmesan cheese

Chives blossoms, if available, for garnish

In a heavy saucepan, heat the oil and gently sauté the garlic and leeks over medium-low heat for about 5 minutes. Add the sweet onions and the white portion of the chopped green onions and cook for another 5 minutes. Add the salt and pepper, raise the temperature to medium, add the rice, and continue cooking and stirring, for another 5 minutes, or until the grains are glossy but not browned.

Meanwhile, in a saucepan, bring the chicken broth to a boil, then reduce the heat and keep it just below a simmer.

Add the white wine to the rice and cook, stirring constantly, until the wine has been absorbed. Now begin adding the hot broth, a ladleful at a time, stirring and simmering between additions until the liquid is nearly absorbed. Keep the rice and broth simmering at all times if possible. Continue stirring in the broth a ladleful at a time, until the rice releases its outer layer, turns creamy, and the grains are firm but not hard in the center. This will take about 20 minutes.

When ready to serve, stir in 2 tablespoons of the chives and the reserved green portion of the chopped green onions. Stir in the butter and Parmesan, adjust the seasonings, then spoon the rice into the center of a lovely bowl or platter. Garnish with the reserved tablespoon of chives and the chives blossoms.

GRILLED MUSHROOMS AND BUNCH ONIONS WITH SESAME OIL

Shiitake mushrooms have a strong, unique flavor. However, they are also quite expensive. You may decide to substitute oyster mushrooms or cultivated white mushrooms for this recipe.

YIELD: *4 TO 6 SERVINGS*

1 ½ pounds medium-to-large shiitake mushrooms

1 2 bunch onions (each measuring about ½ inch at the root end)

¼ cup sesame oil

Salt and freshly ground black pepper to taste

1 tablespoon toasted sesame seeds

Trim the bottom portion of the stem from each mushroom. Trim the roots from the bunch onions and peel away their outermost layer. Trim the leaves so the onions measure about 8 inches long.

Brush the mushrooms and onions with some of the oil. Grill them over medium-hot coals, turning them once and cooking until lightly browned on both sides, about 5 minutes. Arrange the grilled vegetables on a platter, then season with salt and pepper. Sprinkle with the toasted sesame seeds and serve.

FRESH SWEET ONION RELISH

Use this fresh and crunchy relish as an accompaniment to any roasted or grilled meat, chicken, or fish.

YIELD: ABOUT 3 1/2 CUPS

    About 2 cups chopped sweet onions (such as Walla Walla or
           Vidalia)
    $^1/_2$ cup chopped red bell pepper
    $^1/_2$ cup chopped yellow bell pepper
    $^1/_3$ cup balsamic vinegar
    $^1/_4$ cup extra-virgin olive oil
    $^1/_4$ teaspoon salt
    $^1/_4$ teaspoon chopped fresh oregano

Combine all of the ingredients in a bowl. Refrigerate the mixture for at least 1 hour so all of the flavors can meld. This will keep, refrigerated, for up to 3 days.

SOUTHWEST VINEGAR

— — —

YIELD: ABOUT 6 CUPS

7 sprigs fresh cilantro

10 to 12 fresh jalapeño peppers, unseeded, halved lengthwise

10 to 12 cloves garlic, halved lengthwise

3 whole green onions

1 lime, thinly sliced

10 to 12 sun-dried tomato halves (not packed in oil)

1 teaspoon black peppercorns

About 6 cups white wine vinegar, more if needed

Lightly bruise the cilantro stems by gently pounding them with the handle of a chef's knife. Stuff the cilantro into a 1.5-liter wine bottle (I've found that a chopstick performs this task beautifully) along with the jalapeño peppers (if still too chubby after halving lengthwise, halve again), garlic, green onions, lime, sun-dried tomatoes, and peppercorns. Through a funnel, pour enough of the vinegar into the bottle to fill it. Cover the bottle loosely with plastic wrap or foil and let stand at room temperature away from direct light for at least 2 weeks, to allow the flavor to develop. At room temperature this vinegar will keep indefinitely, but after 6 months or so the onions, cilantro, and dried tomatoes will look pretty weary.

Garlic Chives Puree

This puree is brilliantly hued a luscious green, and the flavor is both unique and familiar. Use it just as you would a traditional pesto—tossed with freshly cooked pasta, as a dip with French bread or raw vegetables (stir in a little sour cream or mayonnaise for a milder flavor), or to season any other sauce.

Yield: 1 cup

2 cups coarsely chopped garlic chives
$^1/_3$ cup extra-virgin olive oil
$^1/_4$ cup fresh basil leaves
$^1/_4$ cup lightly toasted pine nuts (optional)
1 tablespoon freshly squeezed lemon juice
Scant $^1/_4$ teaspoon salt
$^1/_2$ cup freshly grated Parmesan cheese

Place the garlic chives, olive oil, basil leaves, pine nuts (if used), lemon juice, and salt in a blender or food processor. Process until smooth. Scrape the puree from the container and whisk in the Parmesan cheese. Adjust the seasonings and oil to taste. Spoon into a jar, cover, and refrigerate. This will keep, refrigerated, for about 2 weeks, or frozen, for several months.

Garlic Chives Vinegar

— — —

Yield: about 1½ pints

1½ cups coarsely chopped garlic chives
3½ cups rice vinegar

Place the garlic chives and vinegar in a clean, dry jar and screw on the lid. During the day, place the jar in a sunny location, indoors or outside, and let it stand for about 10 days, or until the vinegar has become infused with flavor from the garlic chives.

Strain the vinegar through several layers of cheesecloth, squeezing the cloth gently to release even more flavor; discard the garlic chives. Decant the strained vinegar into attractive jars, and to each jar add several long stems of garlic chives (preferably ones with a flower bud on their tip). Seal with corks or caps and store in a cool, dark place. This flavored vinegar will keep indefinitely.

GARLIC CHIVES BUTTER

A fabulous and handy seasoner for garlic bread, sautéed scallops, or freshly baked rolls. It will keep for several weeks in the refrigerator, or up to 6 months in the freezer.

YIELD: *1 CUP*

1 cup (2 sticks) butter, softened

$1/3$ cup finely chopped garlic chives

1 teaspoon freshly squeezed lemon juice

Salt, white pepper, and dry mustard to taste (all are optional)

In a bowl, cream together the butter, herbs, and seasonings. Shape as desired and chill (for 1 month) or freeze (for 6 months).

GARLIC CHIVES
PRESERVED IN PARMESAN

I learned this trick from an Italian friend who grows lots and lots of basil. She discovered long ago that Parmesan, in contact with basil, keeps the basil in fairly good condition. And since many of her recipes pair the two anyway, it seemed a natural. It works equally well with the garlic chives.

> Garlic chives
> Freshly grated Parmesan cheese

Place a handful of garlic chives in your food processor and chop coarsely. Add an approximately equal amount of Parmesan cheese and run the motor briefly just to mix. Scrape the mixture into a clean container, cover, and refrigerate. The chives will store this way for about 1 month.

A few of the many uses: Sprinkle over a platter of pasta (works equally well with cream, wine, or tomato sauces); sprinkle on top of buttered French bread before broiling; stir into omelettes; sprinkle over a platter of sautéed vegetables; combine with sour cream for a vegetable dip.

Green Garlic Pickle

Chop up this delectable condiment and add it to a tossed green salad, chicken salad, or pasta salad. It's heavenly with steamed potatoes, and even makes a tasty appetizer. The taller the jar, the prettier the pickle.

Yield: about 2 quarts

- 2 pounds green garlic, dark green tops removed
- 2 teaspoons pickling salt
- 2 teaspoons whole mustard seed
- About 20 whole black peppercorns
- 2 fresh or dried chile peppers, bruised, or $\frac{1}{2}$ teaspoon red pepper flakes
- 3 cups distilled white vinegar
- 2 cups water
- 1 tablespoon sugar

Cut the garlic stalks so that they fit in a quart-size jar with about 1 inch of head space. Wash the garlic well, dry, then arrange in the jars. You should have filled 2 quart-size jars. To each jar, add 1 teaspoon pickling salt, 1 teaspoon whole mustard seed, 10 peppercorns, and either 1 fresh or dried chile or $\frac{1}{4}$ teaspoon red pepper flakes.

In a nonaluminum pot, bring the vinegar, water, and sugar to a boil, stirring until the sugar is dissolved; remove from the heat. Ladle the hot vinegar solution into the jars, filling them to within $\frac{1}{2}$ inch of the top. Wipe the jar rims with a clean, damp cloth. Attach the lids. Let the closed jars cool to room temperature, then refrigerate for at least 3 weeks before using. It will keep for at least 3 to 4 months.

3

SUMMER
INTO
FALL

If there's one time of year when it's darned near impossible to wreck a meal, it has to be summer. Summer, when the overwhelming array of colorful, flavorful produce assaults your lucky senses at every turn. Summer, when the trunk of your car after a trip to the farmers' market resembles the produce section at Harrods Food Hall—but a day later you're kicking yourself for not picking up "just a few more peppers and corn." Summer, when the only mistake you can make in the kitchen is to underutilize or overcook what nature has so generously provided. Summer, when the best thing you can do is very little, such as bringing a few exquisitely flavored vegetables together on the same platter, then let the commingling of flavors and textures work its magic on your lucky palate.

Indeed, this is the time of year when understatement is the best statement, and wowing a hungry crowd is as easy as grilling half a big ol' sweet onion with a zesty glob of pesto on top.

So roast those peppers, boil that corn, steam those green beans, and toss a bounty of salad greens. It's that simple. It's that good.

The Onions of Summer

Merging into the fast lane of summer produce are all of the wonderful varieties of garlic and sweet, subtle shallots. Perhaps you've been tolerating the diminishing quality of shallots over the late winter, because, well, let's admit it, shallots aren't the bread-and-butter ingredient that garlic is. So when quality goes, you more or less patiently wait until the good stuff appears again.

But remember how frustrating it became last spring trying to find a decent head of garlic? Most shopping excursions yielded nothing better than a few dried-out cloves from a half-dozen heads—at a ridiculous price, no less.

And then the long, warm, days of July arrived, and before your eyes, a miracle occurred. You spotted the grower's table ten yards in front of you: Fresh-from-the-field garlic had finally arrived at the local farmers' market.

"I just picked it last night. It hasn't been aged yet," cautions the grower as you scoop up an armload of heavenly scented bulbs with long stems and leggy leaves still attached, great globs of dirt cling to the roots, and the moisture within the bulbs is all but oozing out. Certainly, you'll be setting these fine plants out to dry in the backyard at some point in the week. But not tonight. Tonight you'll be smashing open a head or two, prying through the still-damp sheaths surrounding the precious cloves, and mincing the lot into a wonderful mound of zesty, garlicky goodness. At this stage it's not as punchy strong as it will be. It's just richly flavored and full of aroma. And so sweet. That's new crop garlic at its prime.

Garlic (Allium sativum)

Garlic Varieties

Considering the fact that garlic has been growing all over the world for thousands of years, the vast number of horticultural varieties is not so surprising. Nor is the fact that you can't get all of the horticulturists to agree on exactly how many varieties exist. Estimates range from thirty to over three hundred, with many authorities insisting there's no real definable way to distinguish between most of the different varieties, even though they may differ from one another in very specific ways, such as flavor or color. To complicate matters further, exactly the same variety is often known by a wide range of common names. Just as the same cut of beef is a filet mignon in New York City and a chateaubriand in San Francisco, exactly the same variety of garlic may be grown and known by several common names in different countries.

The exception to this rule seems to be the botanical variety called Ophioscorodon, commonly known as rocambole, or serpent garlic. It's quite distinctive in construction, so you will know if you've ever encountered it. The cloves are much plumper than your average garlic clove, and they're arranged around the flower stalk much like the segments of a tangerine.

The "serpentine" description comes from rocambole's coiled, looping stems, also referred to as "scapes." Aside from the fact that it is a garlic of wonderful cooking quality, its exotic appearance makes it a marvelous addition to your backyard vegetable garden. However, you will rarely find it in nurseries under its botanical name; the key description to look for is "top setting," a phrase that refers to the fact that after the light purple flower buds fade, a cluster of baby bulbs, known as bulbils, develop. These are edible, of course—fresh in salads, or even pickled—but if left on the plant, they can actually be used to propagate the next season's plants. In nurseries, they are often sold as "rocambole seeds," which they aren't, since true seeds are seldom produced by this plant.

Your Basic, Tried-and-True, Bread-and-Butter Garlic Cultivars

In California, where thousands and thousands of acres of precious farming soil are dedicated to garlic, there are three common varieties, or cultivars. They are:

California Late—This one is considered California's most valuable commercial garlic variety, particularly in the Gilroy and Salinas Valley areas. It is a very good storage garlic, the one you're most likely to be seeing well into winter, with a strong flavor; high solid content; and firm, smooth bulbs. The outer paper covering is white.

California Early—Maturing about one month earlier than California Late, it has greater yield than the Late, but doesn't store as well, due to its higher moisture content. Its outer paper covering is off-white, with occasional traces of purple veining.

Creole—Being heat tolerant, this is one of California's main varieties and has become the mainstay in the state's warmer regions, such as the Imperial and Palo

Verde valleys. It has become an important crop in Louisiana, Mexico, and South America, as well. It matures about one month earlier than California Early. This variety is rather inconsistent in its flower production. Sometimes it sends up a seed stem that grows as high as three feet and develops a glorious flower at the top. Other times the stem never emerges. Go figure! The Creole is the variety that is filled with bulbs of various sizes, all rather randomly arranged, with some cloves on the small side and ganged up in the sheathing material with one or more other cloves.

Beyond those three, there are . . .

Chileno—Also known as Chilleno, this is simply a new-and-improved version of the Creole. The bulbs are larger, better shaped, and less likely to be disorganized within the head.

Chilean—Some speculate that this is a descendant of the Spanish Rojo. Strains of this variety are popular in Spain, India, Japan, and Formosa. It's classified as an early variety, which makes it desirable, but it is a little more sensitive to its environment. The bulbs are somewhat flat, with a white color, and the exterior of the cloves are shaded dark pink to deep wine. Like those of the rocambole, the cloves are much plumper than your average garlic clove, and they're arranged around the flower stalk much like the segments of a tangerine.

Egyptian—This fast-maturing plant has large white bulbs containing a collection of small elongated cloves encased in white skin. It is another extremely heat-tolerant variety, so is found throughout California's desert regions and southern interior valleys.

Italian—This variety is also known as artichoke garlic because its cloves are arranged much like an artichoke's leaves.

Spanish Rojo—This drought-tolerant variety is extremely pungent in flavor, with a rich, beautiful red color. Most agree that it originated in Spain, and in fact, you'll be hard-pressed to find a true Spanish Rojo in the United States.

Elephant garlic—More and more people are finally becoming aware of the fact that Elephant garlic isn't actually garlic at all, even though it does have a mild garlic flavor. It is a completely separate species of allium, more closely related, actually, to the leek.

Need a healthy slave? In ancient Egypt, fifteen pounds of fresh garlic would get you just that.

Shallots (Allium ascalonicum)

Considered an elegant member of the onion family, the shallot is perhaps more precious than the other bulbed alliums—at least based on its price. Per pound, they rank right up there with boned chicken breasts and top sirloin. Although a bit zesty in the raw, a shallot quickly becomes refined and mild with a bit of roasting, providing diners with just a subtle reminder that, yes indeed, there is a bit of onion here.

So why cook with them when the taste is so fleetingly delicate? The answer is that shallots have a truly lovely flavor, and because they are so tender, they cook quickly. This makes them the perfect candidate for those last-minute sauces chefs are so fond of throwing together to crown a fillet or chop.

Garlic Sparks (Allium dynamiteus)

One of the best parts of being on the road is the opportunity to encounter a new specialty food that hasn't yet found its way to my tiny corner of the world.

So there I was, a while back, standing in the middle of a cute little gourmet food store in Sedona, Arizona, perusing the shelves. Amongst the vast display of designer salsas, relishes, and marinades fighting for my attention, one little jar reached out and grabbed my eye. It was called Garlic Sparks, and right away I knew I had to pick it up and read all about it. Below the catchy title was a brief description: "Crunchy Bits of Hot Roasted Spice."

The ingredients list included roasted garlic, blanched garlic, virgin olive oil, and parsley. All kinds of things I love, so a $4.50 jar of Garlic Sparks was purchased and brought home to Corvallis. What a coup! That little jar of crunchy-chewy garlic morsels has been in constant use ever since.

Indeed, this product was so unique I just had to learn more about it. So I tracked down the company, called Immediate Gratifications, conveniently located in Capitola, California—a stone's throw from Gilroy, the nation's "garlic capital"—and spoke with its founder, Andra Rudolph.

Rudolph said that she got into the specialty food business in 1994, and at the point of our conversation, a mere twelve months later, had already placed her unique commodities in over 350 stores around the country. "At this year's Fancy Food Show," she added, "the buyer for Marshal Fields (a nationally renowned retail operation in Chicago) came to our booth and said we were one of the hottest things happening."

It probably didn't hurt matters, she speculated, that Immediate Gratifications had just been mentioned in *Gourmet* magazine's new-product section.

Rudolph stated that she's always been interested in food, but I suspect it's her eighteen years as a marketing and design professional that caused her products to turn so many heads so quickly. A product can be fabulously flavored, but out in the real world where thousands of them are vying for attention, it's the name and packaging that hook the consumer. Hence, such catchy monikers as Garlic Sparks, Blackened Mayonnaise, and Roasted Garlic Garlic Pâté.

"I'm a one-woman show," she said. "My friend Roger Barnes, who's the chef, is actually down in the basement right now labeling jars." Barnes, a Lockheed physicist-turned-restaurant consultant, developed the formulas for Rudolph's product line, as well as a collection of recipes using them.

Of the ten items carrying that Immediate Gratifications label, its those Garlic Sparks that seem to be particularly popular. No surprise to me. To keep up with the demand, Rudolph has had to move to larger roasting facilities.

"I sent two cases to a grocer in San Diego, and a week later he called and said, 'The Sparks are flying, send four more cases,' and that is so encouraging!"

Zipping Through a Pile of Garlic

How to peel it in no time: Need to peel several heads' worth? The speediest approach is to peel away the outer papery skin, then place the heads on a cutting board and press down firmly with the broad side of a chef's knife, a not-too-precious cookbook, or a heavy cleaver, until the heads break apart. To peel away the skins from individual cloves, simply whack them with the broad side of the chef's knife, then peel away the cracked skin.

Garlic mushroom: This is a handy gadget you'll encounter at well-supplied gourmet cooking stores. It's a little wooden utensil shaped like a mushroom. Hold the rounded head of the "mushroom" in your hand, place the flat bottom on top of the garlic head and press down firmly; the cloves fall away in an efficient and effortless manner. Similarly, to break open an individual clove, simply press down on the clove with the flat base of the garlic mushroom and the skin cracks away quickly and effortlessly.

Roasted Garlic

It's true. When baked at a moderate temperature for about an hour, garlic becomes relatively harmless—from a dragon-breath perspective—and actually achieves a mild, almost buttery texture and flavor. But until a short time ago, not many home cooks knew just how wonderful these rich-and-golden morsels were, either as an offering all unto itself when placed in the vicinity of French bread and butter, or as a savory ingredient in dishes ranging from mashed potatoes to stir-frys and vegetable sautés.

Well, like many cooks who have fallen head over heals in love with the process over the last few years, I've worked out some variations on the roasted garlic theme. All of these variations, however, can really be broken into three categories: roasting whole heads, roasting halved heads, or roasting individual cloves. I'm not sure which treatment I prefer; they produce considerably different results, gastronomically speaking. When the head is roasted intact, the cloves have the most mild and tender disposition. Roasting individual cloves, on the other hand, produces more intense results. But from the standpoint of simplicity, roasting the individual cloves has one advantage: They are easier to peel after roasting since the crisp peelings easily flake away.

Whatever the method, you can do the roasting several days ahead, so the garlic will be on hand for all those wonderful dishes in which it can be used, including spinach or Caesar salads, grilled foods, rustic breads, pizzas, focaccias, and pasta dishes (particularly those with chicken or cream sauces).

OVEN-ROASTED GARLIC—WHOLE HEAD: For an appetizer, it's best to figure 1 whole head per person. To prepare, preheat the oven to 350°F. Remove the outer skin covering each head of garlic. An easy way to do this is to make a superficial cut all around the circumference of the head about $1/2$ inch from the base; the outer skin will peel off easily, exposing the cloves, but leaving them intact. Slice off about 1 inch from the top so that a bit of the innards are open.

Set the garlic heads in a baking dish, root end down. Top each head with a dab of butter, then sprinkle each with a bit of olive oil. Cover loosely with foil and bake for 30 to 60 minutes, depending on the head's size. The cloves will be soft when pressed, but don't overcook or they will taste bitter.

OVEN-ROASTED GARLIC—WHOLE HEAD (BUZZED VERSION): As delightful and delicious as roasted garlic cloves are, well, they're a bit messy. Particularly at parties when friends are juggling a drink and conversation as well. Trying to wrangle the tender morsels of garlic out of their sturdy skins can lead to disaster. A far more graceful approach than forcing diners to squirt a tender clove of garlic from the firm grasp of its outer peel (I've observed attempts that have resulted in the Incredible Flying Garlic Act) is to offer them heads that look as if they've been given that popular NBA hairstyle, the buzz cut.

To achieve this look, cut each head of garlic in half horizontally prior to roasting. Since diners will simply pluck the tender morsels from a relatively stable base, they won't be wrestling with individual cloves. And since you bake the halves cut side down, in little puddles of olive oil, the cloves will brown and caramelize, which makes them deliciously rich in flavor and texture. The only trick is to achieve the perfectly browned exterior without scorching.

Preheat the oven to 350°F. Prepare the heads by cutting them in half horizontally (through the plumpest portion of the cloves), keeping each half intact. Don't worry if you have to snuggle some of the cloves back into their skins, that's to be expected. Place the heads, cut side down, in a baking pan (preferably), layered with a bit of olive oil. Be sure and leave about $1/2$ inch of breathing room around each half. Bake the garlic, uncovered, for 25 to 40 minutes (depending on the size and age of the heads), until the cloves are a rich golden brown on the bottom. (Garlic juices will be oozing around the edges of each clove.)

The garlic may be served hot, warm, or chilled. The cloves may be roasted up to 24 hours ahead, then rewarmed gently in the oven or microwave before serving. Serve with crusty chunks of *very* fresh French bread.

OVEN-ROASTED GARLIC—INDIVIDUAL CLOVES: Preheat the oven to 400°F. To separate whole cloves from the head, place the head root side down on a firm cutting surface. Place a flat heavy object (such as a cast-iron skillet) on top of the head and press down firmly (the head will try to scoot out from beneath your press, so some counterjiggling and pressing will be necessary). The cloves miraculously disengage from the root and center stem into a papery pile. Place the cloves in a baking dish with 1 tablespoon olive oil per head of garlic, stir to coat each clove in oil, then bake, uncovered, for 20 to 30 minutes, or until the cloves are richly browned and soft. Remove from the oven and cool. At this point, the skins are crisp and can easily be peeled. You can roast and peel the cloves several days ahead. Depending on how you plan to use them, the cloves can be re-heated in a 350° oven, microwaved, or left chilled.

ROASTED GARLIC FROM THE GRILL—WHOLE HEAD: Prepare the grill. Using heavy-duty foil, cut a square large enough to accommodate the number of heads to be roasted. Slice off about 1 inch from the top of each head so that a bit of the innards are open. Set the garlic heads in the center of the foil, root ends down. Top each head with a dab of butter, then sprinkle each with a bit of olive oil. Cover loosely with foil and roast over a bed of hot coals for 30 to 60 minutes, depending on the size. The head should be soft when pressed, but don't overcook, or it will taste bitter.

ROASTED GARLIC FROM THE GRILL—INDIVIDUAL CLOVES: Prepare the grill. To separate the whole cloves from the head, follow the directions for oven roasting (see above). Using heavy-duty foil, cut a square large enough to accommodate the number of cloves to be roasted. Place them onto the center of the foil and mold the foil loosely around the garlic, leaving the package open at the top. Drizzle with about 1 tablespoon olive oil per head, season with salt and pepper, then place on the grill over a bed of hot coals. Cover the barbecue with its lid and roast the garlic for about 30 minutes, or until the cloves are richly browned and soft. Remove from the grill and cool. At this point, the skins are crisp and can easily be removed. Serve warm or at room temperature. These can be prepared and refrigerated several days ahead. Depending on how you plan to use them, the cloves can be reheated in a 350° oven, microwaved, or left chilled.

A SIMPLE OFFERING WITH ROASTED GARLIC CLOVES: As a simple make-ahead appetizer, roasted garlic cloves are marvelous. Up to several days before the party, roast and peel the cloves in one of the manners described above. A few hours before your guests arrive, simply skewer each clove with a toothpick, then anchor the pointy end of each pick into a cube of fresh mozzarella.

Roasted Shallots

Their more delicate nature notwithstanding, shallots, too, lend themselves to a wide range of flavor and texture possibilities when roasted. . . .

OVEN-ROASTED SHALLOTS—WHOLE: Preheat the oven to 350°F. Slice away about $^1/_2$ inch from the stem end of each bulb. Place the bulbs in a baking pan and drizzle them lightly with a bit of olive oil. Be sure to leave about $^1/_2$ inch of breathing room around each bulb. Bake uncovered for 35 to 45 minutes (depending on the size and age of the bulbs), until the bulbs are a rich golden brown on the bottom and extremely soft.

OVEN-ROASTED SHALLOTS—HALVED: Preheat the oven to 350°F. Leaving the outer skins on, halve each bulb lengthwise. Place the halves, cut side down, in a baking pan layered with a bit of olive oil. Be sure to leave about $^1/_2$ inch of breathing room around each half. Bake the shallots, uncovered, for 25 to 40 minutes (depending on the size and age of the bulbs), until they are a rich golden brown on the bottom.

OVEN-ROASTED SHALLOTS—VARIATIONS ABOUND: Follow the directions above for oven-roasted shallots, halved, but sprinkle the shallots with an herb or two of your choice. During the last few minutes, drizzle them with some balsamic vinegar and then crank up the temperature to about 400° and let them sizzle away.

ROASTED SHALLOTS FROM THE GRILL—WHOLE: Prepare the grill. Cut a square of heavy-duty foil large enough to accommodate the number of bulbs to be roasted. Slice off about $^1/_2$ inch from the top of each bulb so that a bit of the innards are open. Set the shallots in the center of the foil, root ends down. Top each head with a dab of butter, then sprinkle each with a bit of olive oil. Cover loosely with the foil and roast over a bed of hot coals for 30 to 60 minutes, depending on the size of the shallots. The heads should be soft when pressed, but don't overcook or they will taste bitter.

ROASTED SHALLOTS FROM THE GRILL—HALVED: After halving the shallots, follow the directions above for Roasted Shallots from the Grill—Whole.

ROASTED GARLIC SPREAD

— — —

This is not—I repeat NOT—as marvelous a concoction as Immediate Gratifications Roasted Garlic Garlic Pâté. But since I'm not making my living as an industrial spy, this is as close as I could come to re-creating their masterpiece. If you can't locate a jar of the real thing at a specialty food shop near you, this will do in a pinch.

YIELD: ABOUT *1¹/₂ CUPS*

6 medium-large whole heads of garlic (³/₄ pound)

¹/₂ cup chopped fresh flat-leaf parsley

¹/₄ cup red wine vinegar

¹/₃ cup olive oil

1 tablespoon soy sauce

1 teaspoon Blackened Seasoning (see Note)

¹/₂ teaspoon hot pepper sauce

Preheat the oven to 225°F. Separate 4 of the whole heads of garlic into individual cloves. Peel away the outer papery skin. Then set the heads on a stable surface, root ends down. Place a heavy, flat object (such as a hefty cookbook) on top of each head and simply press down firmly. This causes the heads to collapse apart into individual cloves. The 4 heads will equal about 2 cups of cloves. Next, peel all the cloves by pressing firmly down with the wide side of a chef's knife (position the blade away from you). Give the side of the blade a firm-but-controlled whack with your hand (your goal is to crack the skins and slightly crunch the cloves). Treat all the cloves in this manner, then go back and simply remove the loosened skins.

Separate the remaining 2 heads into individual cloves and set them aside without peeling them.

Garlic and shallots are perennials: As long as a portion of the plant is left in the ground, they'll come back year after year after year.

—

Summer into Fall

(continued)

Arrange the peeled-and-crunched cloves in a 10-inch pie dish (or a casserole dish of similar dimensions). Stir in the remaining ingredients except unpeeled garlic. Place the dish, uncovered, in the oven, and roast slowly for $3^1/_2$ to 4 hours (that's right, 4 hours), stirring and turning the mixture every half hour or so to keep an eye on the process. Even though it seems like a very long time to roast garlic, the low temperature keeps everything under control and really does create a fabulously sweet and rich flavor. After the 3-hour mark, you want to watch closely to make sure the mixture doesn't burn. Remove the dish and let the mixture cool.

Meanwhile, boil some water in a 2-quart pot and drop in the unpeeled garlic cloves. Simmer for 1 minute; remove from the heat and run under cold water to stop the cooking. Peel the cloves (the blanching makes this easy) and chop them coarsely.

Combine the roasted garlic mixture with the blanched garlic cloves. Scrape the mixture into the workbowl of a food processor and process in 2 or 3 very short bursts to chop the garlic without pureeing it. Scrape the spread into a container, cover tightly, and refrigerate for several hours or overnight to allow the flavors to meld. At that point, taste and adjust the seasonings, adding more of the Blackened Seasoning, vinegar, olive oil, or hot pepper sauce if you like. When ready to use, bring the spread to room temperature for the best flavor.

Note: Blackened Seasoning is a commercially prepared spice blend. Paul Prudhomme markets a brand under the name Louisiana Cajun Magic. You could blend your own, using, in equal proportions, spoonfuls of sweet paprika, salt, onion and garlic powders, ground red pepper, white pepper, black pepper, dried thyme leaves, and dried oregano leaves.

Roasted Garlic Crunchies

～　　　～　　　～

They aren't Garlic Sparks—that snazzy, garlicky creation of Immediate Gratifications. But, if you can't locate a jar in your local market, these are worth making. They will keep in your refrigerator for months at a time, and are extremely handy to have around for flavoring vinaigrettes, mashed potatoes, pasta sauces, or green salads (just toss them in with the lettuce and vegetables).

Yield about 1¹/₄ cups

1 recipe Roasted Garlic Spread (see above)

Preheat the oven to 400°F.

Smooth the Roasted Garlic Spread on the bottom of a 10-inch glass pie plate or shallow casserole. Roast for about 1 hour, stirring frequently until the mixture caramelizes and darkens and becomes quite firm (with a few spots remaining on the chewy side). With a slotted spoon, scoop the crunches onto paper towels to cool. When cool, refrigerate in a tightly sealed container, such as a glass jar.

APPETIZERS AND SOUP

CROSTINI WITH ROASTED GARLIC, ARUGULA, AND TOMATO

Crostini is Italian for "small toasted breads." This is a classic combination in which the crispy slices are topped with a blend of flavors and textures that will delight your guests.

YIELD: *24 CROSTINI*

3 heads of garlic, roasted (pages 120–21)

1 French bread baguette, sliced into 24 (½-inch-thick) rounds

About ½ cup extra-virgin olive oil

2 cloves garlic, minced

About 24 arugula leaves, washed and trimmed

3 to 4 medium tomatoes, sliced ¼ inch thick (you will need 24 slices)

Freshly grated Parmesan cheese; or fresh mozzarella, sliced

Preheat the oven to 350°F.

Peel away the skins from the cloves of roasted garlic and set aside.

Arrange the bread slices on a baking sheet. Combine the olive oil with the minced garlic and brush the mixture on top of each bread slice. Bake until the bread begins to brown lightly, about 12 minutes, then remove from the oven and cool. (Note: The bread slices can be roasted up to 24 hours ahead; after cooling, cover with paper towels or store in paper bags; or freeze until needed.)

When ready to serve, arrange the crostini (bread slices) on a platter. Cover each slice with a leaf of arugula, then top with 1 or 2 cloves of roasted garlic and a slice of tomato. Sprinkle with freshly grated Parmesan or a slender slice of fresh mozzarella and serve.

Simple
Roasted Garlic Puree

This baked garlic puree, a simple little concoction that goes well with raw vegetables and chunks of French bread, is much more robust and zesty than the spread I patterned after Immediate Gratifications Roasted Garlic Garlic Pâté, and it comes together in a much shorter time. Since it stores well in the fridge for weeks, I'm always dipping into it when I need a tasty garlic flavor in salad dressings, soups, stews, or vegetable sautés.

Yield: about $1^1/2$ cups

5 heads of garlic

7 tablespoons olive oil

Salt and freshly ground black pepper to taste

$1/4$ to $1/2$ teaspoon crushed red pepper flakes

1 teaspoon soy sauce

Using the garlic, olive oil, and salt and pepper, prepare the roasted garlic using one of the methods described on pages 120–21. Let the heads cool, reserving the olive oil that the heads were baked in. With kitchen shears, gently cut the cloves away from the base (5 heads of garlic will yield approximately 60 cloves). Gently snip the pointed tip of each clove and squeeze out the soft bulb of garlic (the cooked cloves will be soft but firm enough to hold together). Place the cloves in a blender or food processor with the red pepper flakes, soy sauce, and 3 tablespoons of the reserved olive oil. Blend until the mixture is pureed but still slightly grainy.

Serve the puree with chunks of French bread and fresh vegetables. The puree will keep for weeks in the refrigerator. To store, pour a thin layer of olive oil on the surface (stir the olive oil into the puree when ready to serve).

Variation: Add fresh or dried basil to the puree instead of or in addition to the soy sauce and crushed red peppers.

Seasoned
Raw Garlic Puree

A handy seasoner to have on hand for brushing onto prawns, halibut, chicken, ribs, or hamburger during grilling. Also great for whisking into a homemade salad dressing, or to season stir-fried vegetables or scallops, or fresh-cooked pasta.

YIELD: ABOUT *1/2* CUP

20 large cloves garlic, peeled

2 tablespoons olive oil

1 tablespoon soy sauce

1 tablespoon Worcestershire sauce

1 tablespoon Dijon mustard

2 teaspoons honey

$1/8$ teaspoon cayenne

Place all of the ingredients in a blender or food processor and process until smooth. Scrape the contents into a small container, cover tightly, and store in the refrigerator. This will keep its flavor and potency for up to 2 months.

Roasted Garlic Puree

A kinder-richer-lustier version of the previous garlic puree. This one stands alone as a dip, spread, or additive for anything from French bread or vegetables to baked potatoes, pasta, or risotto.

Yield: about ¹/₂ cup

20 large garlic cloves, roasted and peeled (see pages 1 20–21)

¹/₄ cup olive oil

1 tablespoon soy sauce

1 tablespoon Worcestershire sauce

1 tablespoon Dijon mustard

2 teaspoons honey

¹/₈ teaspoon cayenne

Place all of the ingredients in a blender or food processor and process until smooth. Scrape the contents into a small container, cover tightly, and store in the refrigerator. This will keep its flavor and potency for up to 2 months.

MUFFULETA
GARLIC-OLIVE RELISH

This is a marvelous concoction, with roots in New Orleans, where the muffuleta sandwich—a hearty combination of Italian-style meats and cheeses, slathered with a rich olive and garlic relish—was created decades ago. However, this is also a wonderful mixture in its own right. Simply place the relish in a bowl alongside slices of a crusty baguette for a simple appetizer.

YIELD: *1 CUP*

$1/2$ cup coarsely chopped pimiento-stuffed olives

$1/2$ cup coarsely chopped pitted black olives

$1/4$ cup chopped red onion

$1/4$ cup minced fresh flat-leaf parsley

2 tablespoons balsamic vinegar

1 tablespoon minced garlic

1 teaspoon drained and rinsed capers

$1/4$ teaspoon dried oregano, crumbled

$1/4$ teaspoon freshly ground black pepper

$1/3$ cup extra-virgin olive oil

Place the olives, onion, parsley, vinegar, garlic, capers, oregano, and pepper in a food processor. Pulse the mixture until the ingredients are finely chopped. Add the olive oil and continue processing until the mixture is thoroughly chopped but not pureed. This will keep in the refrigerator for at least 2 weeks.

LAMB AND SAUSAGE SOUP

For comfortable, casual entertaining, few dishes can surpass a substantial soup. Only the simplest accompaniments are needed—a green salad, good bread, and perhaps dessert. This hearty soup of lentils, lamb shanks, and plump garlic sausage is served in wide bowls, to be eaten with knife and fork as well as a spoon.

YIELD: 6 TO 8 SERVINGS

1 3/4 cups lentils (12-ounce package)

2 medium carrots, coarsely chopped

2 medium onions, chopped

9 cups water

4 lamb shanks

3/4 pound meaty ham hocks

About 1 1/2 cups dry red wine

6 to 8 garlic sausages (or perhaps a bratwurst)

Salt to taste

Sort the lentils and remove any debris. Rinse and drain the lentils; place them in an 8- to 10-quart pan and add the carrots, onions, and water. Bring to a boil, then add the lamb shanks, ham hocks, and 1 cup of the wine. Reduce the heat, cover, and simmer gently until the meats are very tender when pierced, about 2 1/2 hours. If you wish, lift out the meats; when cool enough to handle, remove the skin, bones, and fat. Tear the meat into bite-size pieces and return it to the soup. (At this point, you may cover and refrigerate the soup for up to 2 days.)

Skim (or lift out) and discard the fat from the soup. Bring the soup to a simmer. Add the sausages (whole or thickly sliced) and simmer for about 20 minutes more. Ladle the soup into large bowls and add about 1 tablespoon of wine to each serving, if desired. Season with salt.

SALADS
AND LIGHT MEALS

CAESAR SALAD WITH
ROASTED GARLIC CLOVES

The first time I was treated to roasted garlic cloves in my Caesar salad was a few years ago in San Francisco. I've been a fan of this particular garnish ever since and use it with my own Caesar salad.

If you want a dynamite Caesar salad remember to use only the very crisp and tender center portions (the heart) of the romaine lettuce. This means that for a salad serving more than 4 people, you'll have to buy 2 or more heads. Reserve the dark green outer leaves for another night's meal.

YIELD: *8 SERVINGS*

4 large heads of romaine lettuce, bright green inner leaves only

FRESH CROUTONS:

1 loaf sourdough or French bread

$^1/_3$ cup butter

1 teaspoon Worcestershire sauce

$^1/_4$ teaspoon dry mustard

DRESSING:

1 egg, coddled (see Note)

$^1/_4$ cup fresh lemon juice

1 tablespoon minced fresh garlic

1 tablespoon Dijon mustard

2 teaspoons Worcestershire sauce

Several dashes hot pepper sauce

4 anchovy fillets

$^3/_4$ cup extra-virgin olive oil

Salt and freshly ground black pepper to taste

1 cup freshly shaved (somewhere between shredded and grated)
        Parmesan cheese

3 heads of garlic, separated and roasted (see pages 120–21)

Preheat the oven to 350°F.

Wash the lettuce leaves, dry them thoroughly, then break into 2- to 3-inch long pieces; chill well.

To make the croutons, cut the bread into $^3/_4$-inch cubes, crust and all. Cut enough to measure about 4 cups. Melt the butter, Worcestershire, and dry mustard in a pan. Place the bread on a cookie sheet and, with a spoon, drizzle the butter mixture over the cubes, making sure each chunk gets a healthy dose of butter. Bake for about 15 minutes, or until golden. The croutons may be stored in a plastic bag for several days.

For the dressing, in a medium-size bowl (or in the salad bowl if you're doing this at the dinner table), combine the egg, lemon juice, garlic, mustard, Worcestershire, and hot pepper sauce. Whisk until well blended. Add the anchovy fillets and mash into a paste with a fork (you may mash the anchovies separately and then add them to the lemon juice mixture, if you prefer). Slowly add the olive oil, whisking well.

The salad may be prepared to this point up to 1 hour before serving. When ready to serve, add the lettuce leaves to the salad bowl and sprinkle them generously with salt and freshly ground pepper. Toss with most of the dressing. Add the Parmesan and fresh croutons and toss until all the lettuce and croutons are evenly

(continued)

coated, adding more dressing if necessary. Sprinkle with the roasted garlic cloves and serve immediately.

Note: To coddle an egg, first bring it to room temperature by running it under hot water for a moment (otherwise it might crack when coddled). Place it in a mug and pour boiling water over it; allow it to stand for 1 minute.

Variation: For those concerned about using undercooked eggs because of possible salmonella poisoning, here's an egg-free Caesar salad. Prepare exactly as described above, but omit the coddled egg; increase the olive oil to 1 cup, and add 1 scant tablespoon good-quality commercially made mayonnaise (homemade mayonnaise uses raw eggs, which is what you're trying to avoid).

Robison Ranch
Vinaigrette Dressing

Shallot growers Jim and Jane Robison of Walla Walla, Washington, offer this house specialty.

YIELD: ABOUT *1* CUP

> 3 tablespoons minced shallots
>
> 1/4 cup raspberry vinegar
>
> 1/2 cup olive oil
>
> 1 teaspoon seasoned salt
>
> 2 teaspoons Dijon mustard
>
> 1/2 teaspoon Worcestershire sauce
>
> 2 tablespoons water
>
> Juice of 1/2 lemon (2 tablespoons)
>
> 1 teaspoon sugar

In a bowl, combine the shallots, vinegar, olive oil, seasoned salt, mustard, Worcestershire sauce, and water; mix well and refrigerate.

Remove from the refrigerator 20 minutes before serving. Before tossing with salad greens, add the lemon juice and sugar and mix well again.

SHRIMP IN
LEMON-GARLIC VINAIGRETTE

YIELD: 6 SERVINGS

1 pound large raw shrimp, in their shells

2 tablespoons whole peppercorns

2 teaspoons salt

2 quarts boiling water

LEMON-GARLIC VINAIGRETTE:

6 cloves garlic, finely minced

$^1/_3$ cup lemon juice

$^1/_3$ cup olive oil

1 tablespoon minced fresh flat-leaf parsley

1$^1/_2$ teaspoons minced fresh thyme

$^1/_2$ teaspoon grated lemon zest

$^1/_2$ teaspoon salt

$^1/_4$ teaspoon freshly ground black pepper

2 cups finely minced celery

18 tomato slices

2 large, ripe avocados, peeled and seeded, each sliced into 12 slices

Add the shrimp, peppercorns, and salt to the pot of boiling water and simmer just until the shrimp turn bright orange and become opaque, 2 or 3 minutes. Drain well and, when cool enough to handle, remove the shells, keeping the tails intact, if possible.

To make the vinaigrette, in a bowl, whisk together all the ingredients; adjust the seasonings.

Place the shrimp in a bowl with the celery, add the vinaigrette, toss well to coat the ingredients evenly, and refrigerate for at least 1 hour but not more than 3 so the flavors will meld but not get weary. If possible, give the mixture a stir every now and then. When ready to serve, arrange 3 tomato slices on each of 6 salad plates. Spoon equal portions of the shrimp over each serving, then top each salad with 4 avocado slices.

THE ETYMOLOGY
OF "GARLIC"

According to
Martin Elcort, in
*The Secret Life of
Food*, the word
"garlic" comes
from the Old
English and
means "spear
leek." During
the Middle
Ages, bald men
were called
pilgarlics (peeled
garlics).

Linguine with Scallops, Sun-Dried Tomatoes, and Roasted Garlic Garlic Pâté

*This recipe—featuring Immediate Gratifications Roasted Garlic Garlic Pâté—was cre-
ated by the company chef, Roger Barnes.*

Yield: *2 to 3 servings*

9 ounces fresh linguine

8 ounces medium sea scallops

$^1/_2$ cup flour

1 tablespoon olive oil

3 to 4 ounces (about $^1/_2$ cup) chicken broth, white wine, or a
    mixture of both

3 to 4 tablespoons Immediate Gratifications Roasted Garlic Garlic Pâté
    (if unavailable, see Note)

1 tablespoon chopped fresh thyme

8 to 10 sun-dried tomatoes, diced

Salt and freshly ground black pepper to taste

1 tablespoon chopped fresh basil

1 tablespoon chopped fresh flat-leaf parsley

Parmesan, Romano, or asiago cheese, freshly grated

Prepare the pasta according to package directions; drain, rinse, and set aside.

Dredge the scallops in the flour, shaking off any excess. Heat the olive oil in
a medium skillet. Place the scallops in the skillet and sauté until they begin to turn
white. Add the broth/wine, deglazing the pan by keeping it on the heat while you
stir and scrape up any cooked-on bits of food; simmer until the liquid is reduced
and thickened slightly, about 3 minutes. Add the Roasted Garlic Garlic Pâté,

thyme, and sun-dried tomatoes, and heat thoroughly until the sauce clings to the scallops, about 3 more minutes. Season with the salt and pepper.

Add the cooked pasta, the basil, and the parsley, stirring to incorporate completely. Serve with one of the fresh grated cheeses.

Note: If you can't obtain a jar of the Roasted Garlic Garlic Pâté, you could substitute the Roasted Garlic Spread (page 125).

CHEESE TORTELLINI WITH SHALLOT-MUSHROOM SAUCE

YIELD: 4 SERVINGS

2 tablespoons olive oil

1 cup finely chopped shallots

2 cups thinly sliced mushrooms

$^1/_2$ cup canned condensed (double-strength) chicken broth

$^1/_3$ cup dry white wine

1 cup whole milk

2 tablespoons all-purpose flour

2 tablespoons water

$^1/_4$ teaspoon white pepper

1 pound fresh cheese tortellini

About $^1/_2$ cup freshly grated Parmesan cheese

In a large skillet over medium heat, warm the olive oil and sauté the shallots and mushrooms until the shallots begin to brown and the mushrooms are quite dark, about 10 minutes. Stir in the broth and wine and simmer gently, uncovered, for 10 minutes. Stir in the milk, then create a flour paste by combining the flour and water and whisk this into the sauce. Continue stirring until the mixture begins to thicken slightly. Season with the pepper and set aside.

Drop the tortellini into a large pot of rapidly boiling water and cook just until al dente. If the tortellini are fresh, this will only take 3 to 4 minutes; dried, about 15 minutes. Drain the tortellini, rinse briefly under warm water, then drain well again. Return the tortellini to the pot, add the sauce, and toss gently to coat. Sprinkle on some of the Parmesan and toss again. Serve, providing additional Parmesan at the table.

ENTRÉES

EASY SHRIMP SAUTÉ

Shallot grower Jim Robison has found that the shallots in this simple sauté are the perfect complement to the delicate-tasting shrimp.

YIELD: 6 SERVINGS

 2 tablespoons butter

 1 tablespoon olive oil

 1 1/2 pounds (26 to 30) peeled raw medium-size shrimp

 2 tablespoons minced garlic

 2 tablespoons minced shallots

 3 to 4 sun-dried tomatoes, drained and chopped

 1 tablespoon dried herb mixture (basil, thyme, parsley, marjoram,
      pinch of oregano)

 Salt and freshly ground black pepper to taste

 1/2 cup white wine

 Fresh sprigs flat-leaf parsley for garnish

In a heavy skillet over medium-high heat, warm the butter and oil. Sauté the shrimp, and as the undersides begin to turn pink, after about 2 minutes, add the garlic, shallots, tomatoes, herb mixture, and salt and pepper. Turn the shrimp, and, after 1 to 2 more minutes, when both sides blush to pink and become opaque, remove from the heat and divide among 6 warm au gratin dishes or plates. *Do not overcook or the shrimp will be tough.* Deglaze the pan by adding the white wine and scraping up any small bits; boil for a few minutes to reduce the sauce. Pour a portion of sauce over each serving of shrimp and garnish with fresh parsley sprigs.

BROILED SALMON FILLET WITH CREAMY MUSTARD-SHALLOT SAUCE

Another one of the specialties of Washington state shallot grower, Jim Robison.

YIELD: *8 SERVINGS*

$3^1/_2$ tablespoons unsalted butter

$^1/_4$ cup minced shallots

$^3/_4$ cup dry white wine

$^3/_4$ cup bottled clam juice

$^1/_2$ cup heavy cream

2 heaping tablespoons coarse-ground Dijon mustard

Salt and white pepper to taste

1 (3-pound) salmon fillet, whole or cut for individual servings

Prepare the sauce first (it takes 10 to 15 minutes). In a saucepan, over medium-high heat, melt 2 tablespoons of the butter and sauté the shallots until golden, about 3 minutes. Be careful not to scorch the shallots. Add the wine and clam juice. Bring to a boil and reduce until the liquid barely coats the pan but the shallots are still moist, about 7 to 8 minutes. Whisk in the cream and mustard, then reduce to a thickened consistency, stirring often, about 4 minutes. Whisk in the remaining butter a little at a time until smooth. Season with salt and pepper. Set the sauce aside on low heat or in a double boiler (or reheat gently just before serving).

To prepare the salmon, preheat the broiler and cover a cookie sheet with foil. Spray with a nonstick cooking spray. Remove any skin from the fish; season it with salt and pepper, then spray with nonstick cooking spray or brush lightly with the remaining butter. Place the fish on a cookie sheet and broil for 3 minutes on the side that had the skin and 2 minutes on the flesh side. The fish should be very moist with a lovely, light crust on the top. Adjust the distance of the pan from the broiler element depending on the thickness of the fish. Be careful not to overcook it. To serve, place 2 to 3 tablespoons of sauce on each dinner plate, then arrange a portion of the salmon on top. A nice accompaniment, suggest the Robisons, is a serving of spinach, shiitake mushrooms, and Chinese pea pods sautéed in butter with minced shallots and garlic.

Chicken with a Heap of Garlic

— — —

James Beard gets the credit for introducing American cooks to the traditional French dish incorporating a large quantity of garlic cloves with roasted chicken. All these many years later, numerous adaptations abound. In my updated version, I've reduced the amount of oil by quite a bit, and upped the ante on garlic by 10 cloves—since we're no longer gasping at the concept of 40 cloves. Also, instead of dry vermouth, which was more of a staple when martinis were in fashion, my recipe calls for a blend of dry sherry and white wine.

Yield: *8 servings*

4 heads (about 50 cloves) of garlic, unpeeled

16 pieces of chicken (a combination of legs, thighs, and breasts)

$^1/_3$ cup olive oil

4 ribs celery, cut into 2-inch-long, slender strips

1 large sweet onion (such as Walla Walla or Maui)

1 tablespoon chopped fresh tarragon, or 1 scant teaspoon dried

$^1/_4$ cup dry sherry

$^1/_4$ cup dry white wine

Salt and freshly ground black pepper to taste

Preheat the oven to 375°F. Lightly oil a 6-quart casserole.

Separate the heads of garlic into cloves (see page 122). Drop the cloves into a pot of boiling water and simmer for 1 minute. Remove the cloves, rinse under cold water until they're cool enough to handle, drain again, and peel.

Place the chicken pieces in a dish and drizzle with the oil, turning each piece to coat it thoroughly. Place the celery, onion, tarragon, and garlic cloves in the bottom of the casserole. Add the oil-coated chicken, then drizzle with the sherry and white wine. Sprinkle with a bit of salt and pepper, then cover the casserole tightly with a sheet of aluminum foil, sealing it well so the steam won't escape. Bake for $1^{1}/_{2}$ hours. When ready to serve, take off the foil, being very careful not to burn yourself from the steam, and remove the casserole from the oven. Serve the chicken with the roasted garlic cloves.

LOTS OF GARLIC
PORK STEW

— — —

YIELD: *6 SERVINGS*

3 tablespoons olive oil

2 pounds boneless pork loin, cut into 2-inch cubes

1 large yellow onion, chopped

12 cloves garlic, peeled and halved

2 pounds Roma tomatoes, peeled, cored, seeded, and chopped

1 (8-ounce) can tomato sauce

3/4 cup dry white wine

1/2 cup sliced pimiento-stuffed olives

1 (4-ounce) can diced green chiles

Salt and freshly ground black pepper to taste

In a large heavy pot or Dutch oven over medium-high heat, heat the oil. Add the pork, a portion at a time so that the temperature won't drop, and brown well on all sides, about 4 minutes. Once browned, lift the meat out with a slotted spoon and repeat with the remaining meat. Once all the meat has been browned, set it aside, then add the onion to the pot and sauté until it is limp and lightly golden, about 5 minutes. Return the meat to the pot, along with the garlic, tomatoes, tomato sauce, wine, olives, and chiles. Bring the liquid to a boil, cover, reduce the heat, and simmer until the meat is tender, about 1 hour. Remove the lid, increase the temperature, and boil the stew until the sauce has reduced and thickened slightly, about 5 minutes. Adjust the seasonings, adding salt and pepper.

SIDE DISHES AND
ACCOMPANIMENTS

ROASTED POLENTA
WITH SHALLOTS

I learned from Michael Chiarello, renowned chef-owner of the acclaimed Tra Vigne restaurant in Napa Valley, that the secret to a smooth and creamy polenta is semolina. Semolina, in combination with the traditional cornmeal, provides the velvet touch. Since then, I keep a premixed batch of equal parts cornmeal and semolina in a plastic container, so when I have a polenta attack, I'm ready to go.

Polenta is especially wonderful with roasted or grilled chicken, shrimp, and pork; however, one of my favorite presentations brings together polenta and sautéed mushrooms.

YIELD: ABOUT *8* SERVINGS

3 cups chicken broth (canned is okay)

1 cup finely chopped shallots

3 cups half and half

$1/4$ teaspoon white pepper

1 cup polenta or yellow cornmeal

1 cup semolina

$3/4$ cup freshly grated Parmesan cheese, plus extra for baking

$1/2$ cup grated Swiss cheese

Combine the chicken broth with the shallots in a medium-size heavy-gauge pot.

Bring the mixture to a boil and simmer for 10 minutes. Whisk in the half and half and white pepper, bring the mixture back to a boil, then gradually whisk in the polenta and semolina. Continue cooking over medium-low heat, stirring constantly. After about 5 minutes, as the polenta thickens to the proper consistency it will begin to pull away from the sides of the pan (and the bursting bubbles will be quite volcanic—both in temperature and character). Remove it from the heat and stir in the Parmesan and Swiss cheeses.

Spread the polenta to an even thickness of about ³/₄ inch on a lightly greased jelly-roll pan measuring at least 11 by 14 inches. Refrigerate the polenta until cool, then cover it with plastic wrap and refrigerate for up to 48 hours (Note: The polenta could also be frozen at this stage for up to 6 months—cut it into desired shapes first, freeze on trays for about 1 hour, then gently stack the pieces, wrap them tightly, and return to the freezer; thaw before proceeding with the recipe.)

When ready to serve preheat the oven to 475°F. Lightly oil a baking sheet. Cut the polenta into the desired shape—squares, rectangles, or diamonds. Place the pieces on the baking sheet, sprinkle generously with additional Parmesan cheese, and bake until the polenta is nicely golden, about 10 minutes.

Roasted Garlic Crunchies Variation: Prepare the polenta as directed above, omitting the shallots, up to the point where it thickens and begins pulling away from the sides of the pan. Remove from the heat and stir in ¹/₄ cup Roasted Garlic Crunchies (page 127), and the Parmesan and Swiss cheeses. Continue with the recipe as directed.

NIPS AND SPUDS
WITH CRISPY SHALLOTS

~ ~ ~

Crispy shallots are a popular garnish these days on potatoes. Nips and spuds are the Scottish collaboration of two great vegetables made better when joined together in this dish.

YIELD: *8 SERVINGS*

1 cup peanut oil

$^1/_2$ cup (1 stick) unsalted butter

1 $^1/_2$ cups flour

$^1/_3$ cup cornstarch

2 pounds large shallots (preferably those weighing about 3 ounces each), peeled and sliced into thin rounds

2 pounds russet potatoes

1 $^1/_2$ pounds yellow turnips (also known as rutabagas)

1 tablespoon salt, plus extra to taste

1 cup heavy cream

White pepper to taste

Chopped fresh flat-leaf parsley for garnish

In a large, heavy-bottomed saucepan, heat the oil and $^1/_4$ cup of the butter over high heat until the mixture begins to smoke. In a medium-size bowl, combine the flour and cornstarch. Coat the shallots with the flour, then, when the oil is hot, reduce the heat, add the shallots, and cook, stirring occasionally, until the shallots are a lovely golden brown, about 4 to 5 minutes. Scoop the shallots from the hot oil with a slotted spoon and let them drain on several layers of absorbent paper towels. Transfer the shallots to paper toweling and set aside in a warm place for up to 3 hours. (Note: If desired, the shallots may be prepared up to 24 hours ahead and refrigerated; reheat in a 400°F. oven before serving).

Peel the potatoes and yellow turnips and cut each one into about 8 pieces. Place in a large pot of water with the tablespoon of salt, cover, and simmer over medium-high heat until very tender, 35 to 40 minutes. Drain well and puree in batches in a food processor until very smooth. Transfer the puree back to its pot.

Meanwhile, heat the heavy cream with the remaining $1/4$ cup of butter in a saucepan over medium heat until the butter has melted, then remove from the heat. Gradually whisk the butter and cream mixture in the puree until it reaches the desired consistency (it should be soft but not runny). Adjust the seasonings with salt and white pepper. Spoon the mixture into a serving bowl and garnish with the crispy shallots and chopped parsley.

ROASTED POTATOES
AND GARLIC

YIELD: *6 SERVINGS*

2 pounds red or white new potatoes, cut into 2-inch chunks or
    wedges
20 to 30 large cloves garlic, peeled (page 1 2 2)
1 tablespoon chopped fresh rosemary
2 tablespoons olive oil
Salt and freshly ground black pepper to taste

Preheat the oven to 350°F. and lightly grease a shallow baking dish.

Place the potatoes and garlic in the baking dish. Combine the rosemary with the olive oil and drizzle over the potatoes and garlic, tossing the vegetables to coat each piece with some of the oil. Season with salt and pepper and bake for 45 minutes to 1 hour, or until the potatoes and garlic are golden and tender. Turn the potatoes several times during the cooking so they brown evenly.

Garlic-Roasted Potatoes
with Marinated Artichokes

~ ~ ~

Yield: 4 to 6 servings

2 (6-ounce) jars marinated artichoke hearts

1 1/2 pounds red or white boiling potatoes, cut into 1/2-inch slices

1 head of garlic, separated into cloves and peeled (page 122)

1 tablespoon fresh rosemary, gently crushed

Salt and freshly ground black pepper to taste

Preheat the oven to 400°F.

Drain the artichoke hearts, reserving the marinade. Halve the larger artichoke pieces so they are all about the same size; set aside.

Pour the marinade into the bottom of a 9 by 13-inch baking dish. Add the potatoes, artichoke hearts, and garlic and toss them with the marinade until thoroughly coated. Sprinkle the rosemary on top of the vegetables, add a bit of salt and pepper, then cover the pan with foil and bake for 15 minutes. Remove the foil and continue baking until the potatoes and garlic are tender and beginning to brown, about 45 to 50 minutes. Adjust the seasoning and serve.

carry cloves into the ring for extra protection.

Garlic has also been used to heal everything from the plague to scurvy. The Greeks would coat themselves in garlic oil before gathering poisonous roots. And in World Wars I and II, garlic was placed on bandages and wrapped around wounds to prevent infection.

~

Summer

into

Fall

MASHED POTATOES
WITH ROASTED GARLIC

YIELD: *6 SERVINGS*

> 5 heads of roasted garlic (page 1 21)
> 2¹/₂ pounds russet potatoes, peeled and quartered
> 6 tablespoons butter
> 1 cup whole milk
> Salt and freshly ground black pepper to taste

Peel the garlic cloves, then put them in the work bowl of a food processor and process in short spurts in order to obtain a puree that still has visible chunks of roasted garlic; set aside.

Boil the potatoes in a large pot of salted water until tender, 1 5 to 20 minutes. Remove from the heat, drain well, and mash thoroughly with a potato masher.

Meanwhile, in a small saucepan, combine the pureed garlic with the butter and milk and warm gently over medium heat, stirring once or twice. Whisk the garlic mixture into the potatoes, adjust the seasoning with salt and pepper, and serve.

Southwest Chile Mashed Potatoes with Corn, Cumin, and Shallots

YIELD: 6 CUPS

1 1/2 pounds (3 large) russet potatoes, peeled and diced

1/3 cup butter

1/2 cup minced shallots

6 cloves garlic, peeled and minced

3/4 cup whole milk

2 1/2 cups fresh corn kernels (3 ears)

1 tablespoon chili powder

1 tablespoon chopped fresh cilantro

2 teaspoons ground cumin

Salt and freshly ground black pepper to taste

Place the potatoes in a large pot of salted water. Bring to a boil and simmer until the potatoes are tender, about 20 minutes; drain thoroughly.

Meanwhile, in a small saucepan over medium heat, melt the butter. Add the shallots and garlic and sauté gently for about 10 minutes. Add the milk, bring the mixture to a boil, then remove from the heat. Add the corn, chili powder, cilantro, and cumin; stir well to thoroughly combine, and set aside.

After draining the potatoes, return them to their pot and mash until quite smooth. Stir in the shallot mixture and season with salt and pepper.

A Mash of Potatoes, Cauliflower, and Shallots

Yield: *4 to 6 servings*

1 pound russet potatoes, peeled and quartered

About ¹/₂ pound cauliflower, trimmed and cut into several chunks

¹/₂ cup chopped shallots

4 tablespoons (¹/₂ stick) butter

Salt and freshly ground black pepper to taste

2 eggs, beaten

1 ¹/₂ cups grated Swiss or Cheddar cheese

¹/₄ cup freshly grated Parmesan cheese

Preheat the oven to 350°F. Lightly grease a 1 ¹/₂-quart baking dish.

Simmer the potatoes and cauliflower in a large pot of salted boiling water until very tender, about 15 to 20 minutes; drain well.

Meanwhile, in a skillet, sauté the shallots in the butter until softened, about 5 minutes.

Mash the potatoes and cauliflower with the shallots and salt and pepper. Adjust the seasonings and stir in the eggs and 1 cup of the grated Swiss or Cheddar cheese. Turn into the baking dish and bake for 30 minutes. Sprinkle with the remaining ¹/₂ cup of Swiss or Cheddar cheese combined with the Parmesan cheese, return to the oven, and bake for an additional 15 minutes or until browned on top.

CHINESE LONG BEANS
WITH LOTS OF GARLIC

Perhaps you've encountered the exotic-looking Chinese long beans, which look like over-grown green beans, and wondered how you could possibly use them. They're a natural with garlic.

YIELD: *4 SERVINGS*

$^3/_4$ pound Chinese long beans (or regular green beans)

2 tablespoons peanut oil

5 large cloves garlic, peeled and cut into thin slivers

$^1/_2$ teaspoon salt

$^1/_4$ teaspoon red pepper flakes, crushed

$^1/_4$ cup homemade or canned chicken broth

1 teaspoon soy sauce

Cut the beans into desired lengths (about 2 to 3 inches). Heat the oil in a wok or a large, heavy-bottomed skillet over high heat. Add the garlic and stir-fry for just a brief moment, then add the beans and salt and continue stir-frying for 1 minute. Add the pepper flakes, then pour in the broth and soy sauce and continue cooking, stirring occasionally, until the liquid has reduced to a glaze. This will take about 8 minutes. Serve immediately, or cool to room temperature.

Dry-Fried Green Beans
with Szechwan Garlic Pickles

A Hunan specialty with a twist. Be sure to use very high heat so the beans cook quickly and achieve a crisp-yet-tender perfection.

Yield: *4–6 servings*

  1 quart peanut oil

  1 1/2 pounds tender young string beans, trimmed

  1 teaspoon sesame oil

  1 1/2 cups finely chopped green onions (use both white and green
       portions)

  1/2 cup chopped Szechwan Garlic Pickles (recipe follows)

  1/3 cup homemade or canned chicken broth

  2 tablespoons dry sherry

  1 tablespoon soy sauce

  1 tablespoon sugar

Heat the oil in a large wok over high heat until it is very hot. Add the string beans and cook, stirring carefully to avoid splatters, just until tender and beginning to turn slightly golden. With a slotted spoon or a Chinese brass wire skimmer, remove the beans from the oil to a strainer. Remove the wok from the heat and let the oil cool slightly until it is safe to handle, then pour it from the wok into a metal container (the oil may be refrigerated to be used again) or discard it.

Reheat the wok over high heat, then add the sesame oil. When the oil is hot, add the green onions and stir-fry briefly, about 20 seconds. Add the Szechwan Garlic Pickles, chicken broth, sherry, soy sauce, and sugar and continue cooking until the sauce begins to boil. Stir in the beans and cook just until the beans are heated through and the sauce has thickened slightly, about 3 minutes. Serve immediately.

SZECHWAN GARLIC PICKLES

YIELD: ABOUT 7 HALF-PINTS

2 pounds garlic heads, separated into cloves but unpeeled (page 122)

$^1/_3$ pound fresh ginger, peeled and thinly sliced

1 cup pickling or kosher salt

2 cups white or red wine vinegar

1 cup dry white wine

$2^1/_2$ tablespoons mustard seed

7 dried red chiles

Put the garlic in a large nonaluminum saucepan with enough water to cover. Place over medium heat and bring to a boil; boil for 2 minutes, then drain thoroughly. When cool enough to handle, peel each clove without crushing.

Transfer the cloves to a nonaluminum bowl. Add the ginger and salt with enough water to cover; refrigerate this mixture for 2 days. Drain the garlic mixture and rinse thoroughly in cold water. Drain again.

Combine the vinegar, wine, and mustard seed in a medium nonaluminum saucepan and bring to a boil; keep hot.

Divide the ginger and garlic evenly among 7 half-pint jars, adding 1 chile (if unavailable, use about a teaspoon of dried chili flakes per jar) to each jar. Ladle the hot brine into 1 jar at a time, leaving $^1/_2$-inch headspace. Wipe the jar rim with a clean, damp cloth and attach the lid. Fill and close the remaining jars.

Refrigerator storage: Store the sealed jars in the refrigerator for at least 4 weeks before using to allow the flavor to develop. The pickles will keep for up to 3 months.

For long-term storage: Use canning jars with 2-piece canning lids. After the lids have been placed on the jars, process in a boiling water canner for 15 minutes. Remove from the canner and let sit, untouched, in a draft-free place overnight. Check to make sure the jars are sealed (the lids will remain convex in the center when pushed down with your finger), then store in a dark, cool, dry pantry.

Green Bean Sauté
with Elephant Garlic

This happens to be an excellent way to use those huge cloves. With the long cooking process, the slices become sweet, flavorful, and even milder than in their raw state.

YIELD: *6 servings*

1 1/2 pounds green beans, French cut

2 teaspoons olive oil

1/2 teaspoon sesame oil

1/2 cup sliced elephant garlic (approximately 8 cloves)

3 cups homemade or canned chicken broth

1/2 teaspoon soy sauce

1/4 teaspoon freshly grated ginger

1/8 teaspoon white pepper

1 tablespoon Dijon mustard

Drop the beans into a large pot of boiling water and, when the water returns to a boil, cook, uncovered, for 3 minutes. Drain the beans immediately and plunge into cold water to set the color and stop the cooking process. (Note: You can prepare the beans to this point up to 3 days ahead. Sprinkle them with a bit of garlic salt, drizzle them with olive oil, then cover tightly and refrigerate.)

When ready to proceed with the recipe, heat the olive and sesame oils in a large, nonaluminum skillet over medium heat. Add the garlic and sauté for about 1 minute. Add the chicken broth, soy sauce, ginger, and white pepper and simmer until reduced by half, about 15 minutes. Whisk in the mustard, then add the green beans, and cook, uncovered, for another 5 minutes, just until the beans have reheated and absorbed the flavors from the broth.

ZESTY ITALIAN VINEGAR

Collect beautiful bottles all year long so you can make beautiful gifts for friends and family during the holiday season. It takes a while for the vinegar to achieve it's ultimate flavor, so early fall is a great time to start. Good for salads, or simply drizzled over a platter of sliced tomatoes.

YIELD: ONE *1.5*-LITER BOTTLE

8 sprigs fresh oregano

8 stems (with small leaves) fresh basil

5 sprigs fresh rosemary

4 sprigs flat-leaf parsley (a large-leaved variety)

2 sprigs sage

1 whole green onion (with roots intact), part of the green trimmed to
fit the bottle

6 cloves garlic, halved

1 tablespoon whole peppercorns (any combination of colors will do)

1 tablespoon sugar

1 teaspoon whole mustard seed

About 6 cups white wine vinegar

Place all of the ingredients except the vinegar into a 1.5-liter wine bottle. Through a funnel, pour enough of the vinegar into the bottle to fill it within $\frac{1}{2}$ inch of the rim. Cork the bottle and store for at least 2 weeks in a dark, cool place.

Tomato, Garlic,
and Herb Vinegar

A very beautiful display of herbs and veggies mingling in vinegar. Delectable when used in salad dressings, sprinkled over poor boy sandwiches, or in a number of zesty sauces.

Yield: One 1.5-liter bottle

10 large sprigs fresh rosemary

6 large leaves fresh basil

4 large sprigs fresh oregano

12 cloves garlic, peeled and halved

10 sun-dried tomatoes (not packed in oil), halved

1 teaspoon black peppercorns

5 cups white wine vinegar, or more as needed

Lightly bruise the stems of the herbs by gently pounding them with the handle of a chef's knife; press the garlic halves with the back of a spoon to crush lightly. Place the herbs, garlic, tomatoes, and peppercorns in a 1.5-liter wine bottle. (Note: You may have to roll up the tomatoes to make them fit through the opening.) Using a funnel, pour the vinegar into the bottle, filling it to within $1/2$ inch of the rim. Cork the bottle and let stand at room temperature away from direct light for at least 2 weeks.

ROASTED
GARLIC-SHALLOT SAUCE

A simply wonderful sauce for pasta.

YIELD: ABOUT 2¼ CUPS

10 cloves garlic, roasted and peeled (page 122)

5 shallots, roasted and peeled (page 124)

1 cup dry white wine

2 cups heavy cream

$^1/_4$ teaspoon salt

$^1/_4$ teaspoon white pepper

Combine the garlic, shallots, and wine in a medium-size saucepan. Bring to a boil and simmer until reduced by three quarters, about 20 minutes. Lower the heat to medium, add the cream, salt, and pepper and simmer gently for about 20 minutes. Cool slightly, then transfer the mixture to a blender or food processor and puree; taste and adjust the seasonings. Serve immediately, or cover and refrigerate for up to 2 days.

Until the middle of the eighteenth century, Siberia's tax collector was paid in garlic.

Garlic in Oil

It's always right about now—when the harvests of new-crop garlic and fresh, flavorful basil hit the local markets—that I begin to get the calls: How do you make garlic- and herb-flavored oil?

Certainly, it's a reasonable request. Both ingredients produce a deliciously flavored oil. However, it's just such ardor that forces me to address the issue many cooking professionals don't like to face: The United States Department of Agriculture is nervous about the entire concept of flavored oils. It's not a popular stance for them to have taken in light of all the snazzy recipes that have spun off from the simple act of uniting a fine-quality oil with a fistful of fresh herbs and garlic. But they're concerned because some flavored oil preparations—including those containing fresh garlic and herbs—under the right conditions, may lead to botulism.

Most of us, upon hearing the word "botulism" think of home-canned green beans. Very few think of gourmet-flavored oils. But the USDA says the potential is there; not so much because of the oil, but because of the low-acid, high-moisture ingredients that are added. They recommend that when oil is combined with fresh herbs, fresh garlic, or fresh chiles, the mixture should be refrigerated. For storage at room temperature, the oil should be strained to remove all of the solids.

With these concerns in mind, I developed the following procedure for making infused oil. It's considered safe by USDA standards and produces an absolutely heavenly concoction.

GARLIC-INFUSED OIL

Ready-up the French bread. This stuff was made for dipping! The added bonus is that your neighborhood will smell absolutely marvelous during the process.

YIELD: *3 CUPS*

    2 to 3 heads of garlic (enough for about 30 cloves)
    3 cups virgin olive oil

The speediest way to handle the garlic heads is to peel away the outer papery skin, then place the heads on a cutting board and whack them with the broad side of a chef's knife or cleaver until they break apart. Similarly, whack each clove to crack it open, then simply peel away the skin. Put the cloves in a food processor and process until finely minced. Scrape the minced garlic into a pan, add the oil, and heat over medium heat until you begin to see a few tiny bubbles starting to drift up from the bottom of the pan. Reduce the heat to low, and let the oil and garlic "stew" at this low temperature for 2 hours. Don't let the oil come anywhere near a simmer or the garlic may develop a bitter flavor (I keep it at around 170°F.).

After 2 hours, remove the pan from the burner and let it cool to room temperature for about 30 minutes. Pour the oil through a fine-meshed sieve lined with multiple layers of cheesecloth, into clean jar(s), and cap. The well-strained oil may be stored at room temperature indefinitely, but if you don't use it within a month or so, consider keeping it in the fridge to keep it from going rancid. It will get cloudy, but will clear up when returned to room temperature. (Note: It is very important to keep all garlic bits out of the oil in order to store it safely at room temperature.)

Use the flavored oil when sautéing or grilling poultry, in a simple vinaigrette, or when preparing a marinade or sauce. For a quick and traditional Italian appetizer, simply pour a little oil into a saucer and serve it with chunks of Italian bread and fresh vegetables.

(continued)

Summer
into
Fall

Chile-infused Variation: Prepare as previously described, adding 2 cups finely minced chiles in place of the garlic (consider combinations of bell peppers, medium-hot, and hot peppers, or single varieties).

Herb-infused Variation: Prepare as previously described, adding 2 cups loosely packed, coarsely chopped herbs in place of the garlic. What would be some particularly flavorful herbs to use? The most popular, of course, is basil, which makes a sweet and richly flavored oil that can be used in a number of ways—from vegetable or meat sautés to vinaigrettes and pasta dishes. It also turns the oil a lovely pale green. Less adaptable, culinarily speaking, but equally delicious would be oregano, or a combination of oregano, thyme, and basil. Chives or garlic chives also makes delicious oils, but their delicate flavor is overpowered by most other herbs, so I don't advise blending.

INDIAN SPICE OIL

Take your Garlic-Infused Oil for a spin to the other side of the globe. This powerfully fla-vored oil adds a tang to marinated or sautéed food, and is also ideal for barbecued steak or chicken.

YIELD: ABOUT 3 CUPS

1 teaspoon garam masala (available in well-stocked spice sections or
       stores specializing in East Indian cooking)
$^1/_2$ teaspoon ground coriander
$^1/_2$ teaspoon ground cumin
$^1/_2$ teaspoon chili powder
$^1/_2$ teaspoon ground turmeric
2 teaspoons dried fenugreek leaves
2 whole cloves
3 cups Garlic-Infused Oil (page 167)

Put all the powdered spices in a small bowl and mix well. Divide the spice mix-ture equally and spoon them through a funnel into 2 washed and dried bottles. Di-vide the fenugreek leaves and cloves between the bottles.

Divide the oil between the 2 bottles, filling them to within $^1/_8$ inch of the top (if that takes a bit more oil than called for in this recipe, that's okay). Cover the bottles, shake gently to distribute the spices, and store in a cool, dark place for 1 to 2 weeks before using to allow the flavors to develop. (Note: Since all the sea-sonings are dry, you don't need to refrigerate this oil.) Whenever you think of it, give the bottles a gentle shake. Once aged, strain the oil into fresh bottles through a funnel lined with double or triple layers of cheesecloth. Seal and label the bot-tles. It may be safely stored at room temperature indefinitely, but the oil will stay fresher for a longer period of time if refrigerated.

Garlic Sauces
from Around the World

—

Could a cookbook featuring garlic be complete without recipes for these classic garlic-rich sauces from around the world?

AIOLI

—

Aioli is a specialty of Provence, a southern province of France bordering the Mediterranean. For those uncomfortable using raw eggs, an eggless version follows.

YIELD: ABOUT 1 CUP

> 8 cloves garlic, peeled and pressed through a garlic press
> 1 egg yolk
> ¼ teaspoon salt
> 1 cup olive oil
> Juice of 1 lemon

In the work bowl of a food processor, combine the pressed garlic, egg yolk, salt, 3 tablespoons of the oil, and the lemon juice. Blend until smooth. With the motor still running, add the remaining oil, drop by drop, until the sauce is thick.

Eggless Aioli

—— —— ——

This version is not only faster to assemble than the classic version, it's also a little zippier, and doesn't rely on raw egg. Please use a very fine-quality mayonnaise, such as Best Foods or Hellmann's.

YIELD: ABOUT 1 CUP

    1 cup fine-quality mayonnaise
    8 cloves garlic, peeled and pressed through a garlic press
    $1/_2$ teaspoon white wine Worcestershire sauce (Lea & Perrins produces
           one)
    Several dashes Tabasco sauce

Whisk together the mayonnaise, garlic, Worcestershire sauce, and Tabasco. Taste and adjust the seasonings, then cover and refrigerate for up to 1 week.

If you'd really like to immerse yourself in the garlic mystique, drop by the Stinking Rose Restaurant in San Francisco. Named for the garlic bulb, this popular establishment is completely decked out in garlic motif, memorabilia, and culinary offerings. Garlic potato chips? They've got them. Garlic wine? You guessed it.

—

SKORDALIA

— — —

This is a classic Greek garlic sauce. You'll find it served as a spread for appetizers, accompanying fried fish and roasted meats, and even as a vegetable topping. Garlic is always at the heart of its preparation, but in some parts of Greece, the sauce is prepared without the bread.

YIELD: ABOUT 3 CUPS

4 slices firm-textured whole wheat bread, crusts removed, soaked in
water
$^1/_2$ cup mashed potatoes (1 potato)
7 cloves garlic, peeled and pressed through a garlic press
$^1/_2$ cup finely chopped almonds
1 cup olive oil
$^1/_3$ cup fresh lemon juice, or more, to taste
Salt to taste

Squeeze the bread to remove the excess water. Place the bread, potatoes, garlic, and almonds in the work bowl of a food processor and process until the mixture is smooth. With the motor running, add the olive oil at a slow and steady pace, almost drop by drop. Once the mixture has thickened, add the lemon juice in a steady stream. Now adjust the seasonings, adding salt, and more lemon juice, if desired.

Adobo Caribbean
Garlic Sauce

YIELD: ABOUT $2/3$ CUP

10 cloves garlic, peeled
1 tablespoon chopped fresh oregano
1 tablespoon chopped fresh marjoram
3 tablespoons extra-virgin olive oil
$1/2$ cup white wine vinegar
Salt to taste

Combine all of the ingredients except the salt in a blender and blend until smooth. Adjust the seasonings by adding salt. Scrape the mixture into a jar, seal, and refrigerate for several hours before using. This will keep, refrigerated, for several months.

HARISSA (GARLIC AND HOT CHILE)

A specialty of Tunisia, harissa is a very hot chile pepper paste sold in tubes. A little dab gives a big boost.

YIELD: GENEROUS $1/3$ CUP

$1/3$ cup red pepper flakes mixed with 1 tablespoon paprika

2 tablespoons Roasted Garlic Puree (page 131), or 6 garlic cloves,
    finely minced

1 tablespoon minced fresh cilantro

$1/2$ teaspoon ground coriander

1 teaspoon ground caraway

1 tablespoon water

About 2 tablespoons olive oil, plus extra for jar

In a food processor, process all the ingredients to make a thick paste (more water and olive oil may be needed). Pack tightly in a small jar and top with olive oil to cover. Harissa keeps in the refrigerator for 6 months or more.

Nahm Jeem Gratiem

In Thai cooking, this hearty and sweet-hot garlic sauce is fabulous with all sorts of deep-fried foods, particularly spring rolls, as well as any grilled or roasted meat.

Yield: about 1½ cups

1 cup sugar
½ cup water
½ cup rice vinegar
2 tablespoons finely minced garlic
½ to 1 teaspoon salt
1 tablespoon chili-garlic sauce (found alongside other condiments in the Oriental specialty food section of most markets)

In a small saucepan, combine the sugar, water, vinegar, garlic, and ½ teaspoon of the salt. Bring the mixture to a boil and stir until the sugar is dissolved. Reduce the temperature slightly and simmer until the sauce has reduced slightly and thickened to the consistency of a light syrup, about 20 minutes. Remove the sauce from the heat and stir in the chili-garlic sauce. Cool to room temperature, then store in the refrigerator for up to 5 days.

Jim's Garlic-Shallot Marinade for Steak, Pork Tenderloin, or Chicken Breasts

From shallot grower, Jim Robison, another specialty. . . .

YIELD: ENOUGH FOR *2* PORK TENDERLOINS OR *8* TO *10* CHICKEN BREASTS

3 tablespoons soy sauce

3 tablespoons sugar

6 tablespoons (3 ounces) sour mash bourbon or dark rum

1 teaspoon salt

4 to 5 cloves garlic, smashed or chopped

2 to 3 tablespoons minced shallots

1 tablespoon grated fresh ginger

About $2^1/_4$ pounds of steaks, pork tenderloins, or chicken breasts

Hot dry mustard (optional)

Toasted sesame seeds (optional—see Note)

In a small bowl, mix together the soy sauce, sugar, bourbon, salt, garlic, shallots, and ginger. Place the marinade in a self-closing plastic bag with the meat of your choice and refrigerate overnight for steaks and pork tenderloins, or 5 to 6 hours for chicken breasts. This is enough marinade for 4 steaks, 2 small tenderloins, or 8 to 10 chicken breast halves.

Remove the marinated meat from the refrigerator and drain for 20 to 30 minutes before cooking. Discard the marinade. Grill the meat on both sides to the desired degree of doneness.

For chicken breasts, the Robisons use high heat only: Salt the pieces lightly before grilling, and take the meat from the grill when it is still soft to the touch.

Use the pork tenderloins as hors d'oeuvres: Slice and serve them with hot dry mustard mixed to the proper consistency with cold water. Serve with toasted sesame seeds (dip a slice of tenderloin first in the mustard, then in the sesame seeds).

Note: To toast seeds, spread them in the bottom of a skillet over medium-high heat and toast, shaking gently, until the seeds begin to turn golden and some of them begin to "pop."

4

Fall
into
Winter

For this lover of autumn, there's a color that represents the season as clearly as a date on the calendar. It's a soft, fuzzy gold—like glimmering waves of heat drifting up from a distant beach—a gentle and alluring image that reflects the welcome pulling-up on the hand brake of summer's wild ride.

These faintly warm days always end with a nip in the air. The harvest season is coming to an end and winter's dormancy is approaching the back door. There's now time to contemplate fireside chats, crisp white linens, silver service, and long-simmering stews. For every one reason it's sad to leave the sunny days behind, I'll give you five for moving on—beginning with that brisk evening air, harvest moons, and fresh-squeezed apple cider.

Even kitchen activities have a different feel and are accomplished at a more leisurely pace. And although there's not quite the vast array of August bounty to fill the produce bins, there are still many offerings, including the tail end of the sweet and hot pepper crop, an impressive array of tomatoes and potatoes, and a new collection of onions.

The sweet, tempered varieties of summer are dwindling, of course. The heartier, more robust onions that replace them will take us through winter. For Nature designed them to be the keepers that tide us over until the fresh sweet onions of spring come again.

The Bulb Onions
of Autumn into Winter
(Allium cepa)

I have a friend who hates onions. It's a real problem for her, as a food professional. Lurking invisibly in so many innocent-looking delicacies, and with so much popular support, onions make bad enemies. But, for the most part, it's a private battle.

Only once, to my knowledge, did her aversion to onions turn public. On a tour of the British Isles one summer, Mary opted for a pub lunch. As it was a typically cold and foggy day, she gratefully accepted a seat in front of the fireplace. Lunch came, and there, planted squarely in the middle of her Plowman's Special, was a large pickled onion. What to do?

Not wanting to seem the Ugly American by disdaining such a national treasure, but most certainly wanting to rid her plate of the offending orb, she surreptitiously took aim with her index finger and flicked it into the fire.

Lunch went well for about five minutes, before that spurned onion burst from the flames in feisty retaliation with a mighty "POW!"

Mortified silence followed.

Of course, Mary isn't alone in her aversion to hearty globe onions, the least-delicate alliums. However, if like me, you are one of the overwhelming majority pursuing a love affair with this marvelous vegetable in all its varieties and forms of preparation, the season holds delectable promise.

All-purpose yellow globe—This onion is the workhorse in the kitchen, the one called upon most frequently to perform a wide range of tasks. Lower in water content than its spring and summer counterparts, the yellow globe is good for storage and is, therefore, more likely found throughout the year than any other in the family. These onions have a strong flavor which makes them the right candidate for long-term cooking, such as in stews and soups.

Spanish Sweet onions—This large yellow storage onion is known for its large, spherical shape and mild, sweet flavor. Its higher water content makes it a little less hot and slightly more crisp than the yellow storage onion. In the Pacific Northwest, these onions are referred to as Spanish Sweets, but they are not to be confused with the Walla Walla Sweet, which is strictly a spring-into-summer onion. The Spanish Sweet onion will keep into March, if treated well.

Red onion—Although most people think of "Bermuda" onion as *the* red onion, that particular variety died out in 1985. The red onion is similar in character to the Spanish onion—slightly sweet, with a crisp character. Although the red onion is a vibrant addition to uncooked dishes, its red pigment is unstable under heat and nonacid conditions, which means that the color is lost during cooking (or turns a bluish-greenish color), unless a bit of vinegar, wine, or lemon juice is added.

Cippoline—Pronounced "chi-po-li-nee," an Italian import, this zesty little white onion is traditionally pickled in Italy. It is becoming increasingly more available in the States; however, you're still likely to have a hard time tracking it down; Frieda's Finest Produce Specialties, Inc., based in California, is one reliable source.

Pearl onions—Generally speaking, any white bulb onion you encounter that measures no larger than $1\frac{1}{4}$ inches in diameter is considered a pearl onion. People always seem to want white pearl onions; however, yellow or red would also be considered "pearls" as long as they measured up size-wise.

Boiling onions: Like the pearl onion, the boiling onion is determined by its size. To be considered in this category, the bulb must be just about golf-ball size. Typically, they're white, although on occasion you'll encounter red or yellow ones as well.

White storage onions—Although hot and strong in flavor, these are milder than the yellow storage onion, with a slightly "cleaner," "crisper" character

A Pickled Pearl

Because of my Great-aunt Joey's fondness for Gibsons, I discovered at an early age the delectability of the cocktail onion. If I had ever actually experienced one that had been floating about in a puddle of Tanqueray, my zeal for this zesty orb would probably have waned early on. But Joey always fished a few out from the tall, sleek jar and presented them to us young people on a lovely blue Wedgwood saucer.

I've been partial to pickled pearl onions ever since. But only in the last few years did I consider making my own. With a lifetime of field research under my belt, it's been a bit of a breeze. After all, I do know what makes a dandy cocktail onion.

So what makes a pearl onion? As mentioned previously, any bulb onion that measures no larger than $1\frac{1}{4}$ inches in diameter falls within the category. However, white is the preferred color, and when it comes to size, the smaller ones I feel make the best pickling candidates, so I'm always looking for those in the $\frac{1}{2}$- to $\frac{3}{4}$-inch range.

But there's more than size to consider. To become a cocktail onion, the fresh specimen should contain a delightful sweetness, with only a tiny bit of sharp onion flavor kicking in after you've munched on one.

Growers who produce pearl onions for a living have a very special way of cultivating perfect specimens. Instead of spreading $3\frac{1}{2}$ pounds of seeds over one acre to obtain 40,000 pounds of grown-up storage onions, growers in the pearl onion industry are known to use about 70 pounds of seed per acre (some Idaho growers have been known to use up to 110 pounds!). This makes for really crowded growing conditions, so try as they might to do otherwise, the onions will remain small.

Some growers swear by specific varieties, as well—ones known to produce a wonderful flavor even in a small package. Such varieties are Snow Baby and Purplette. Still other growers blend the two concepts: They pick "short day" varieties with excellent flavor, such as Wonder of Pompeii, Crystal Wax, Eclipse, and Barletta, which prefer only twelve hours of southern sun, then grow them close together in the "long-day" northern states, at a time when the onions will get fifteen to sixteen hours of light. This causes them to bulb up before they attain full size.

Some say that you can tell a hard winter is in the making if the fall onions have produced a lot of layers.

APPETIZERS

ONION RINGS

— — —

This is your basic-but-delicious fried onion ring recipe. The slightly sweet and smoky malt vinegar complements the hearty yellow onion remarkably well.

YIELD: 4 APPETIZER OR SIDE DISH SERVINGS

Vegetable oil for deep-frying

2 cups all-purpose flour

1 tablespoon Hungarian paprika

$^1/_2$ teaspoon salt, plus extra to taste

$^1/_2$ teaspoon freshly ground black pepper, plus extra to taste

2 eggs, lightly beaten

1 cup whole milk

2 to 3 large yellow onions, cut into $^1/_2$- to $^3/_4$-inch-thick rings

$^1/_4$ cup snipped fresh chives

$^1/_4$ cup malt vinegar

Fill a deep, large, heavy-bottomed skillet with oil to a depth of 4 inches. Heat the oil over medium heat until it reaches 350°F. on a deep-fat/candy thermometer.

While the oil is heating, combine the flour, paprika, $^1/_2$ teaspoon salt, and $^1/_2$ teaspoon pepper in a large bowl. In another bowl, whisk together the eggs and milk. Dredge the onion rings in the flour mixture, shaking to remove the excess. Dip the flour-coated rings into the egg mixture. Then, using a slotted spoon, lift the rings from the egg batter, allowing the excess liquid to drain off. Transfer the moistened rings back to the seasoned flour and coat well. Shake off the excess flour, then place the rings on a cookie sheet and allow the coating to dry for about 15 minutes at room temperature.

Carefully place a few of the rings into the hot oil and cook until golden, 3 to 5 minutes. Do not cook too many onions at once or the temperature of the oil will drop and you will have soggy onions. Remove the cooked rings from the oil and drain them on paper towels. Keep the cooked rings on a paper towel–lined platter in a 200°F. oven while cooking the remaining rings. To serve, mound them in the center of a platter and season them lightly with salt and pepper. Sprinkle with the chives and pass the vinegar at the table for diners to drizzle on.

Red Onion
and Blue Cheese Spread

Red onions and blue cheese have a natural affinity for one another. In our little town of Corvallis, there's a popular café, Burton's, that has always offered a simple yet wonderful dressing based on this combination. It's considered the house dressing. Several years ago, with my husband at my side (since he's really the blue cheese fan in our house), we managed to duplicate the dressing. Not such a major sleuthing job since it's nothing more than chopped red onions, crumbled blue cheese, corn oil, and red wine vinegar. It's now The Dominguez House Dressing as well.

With that accomplishment under our belts, we've advanced to more sophisticated spin-offs, such as this elegant spread featuring toasted bits of Oregon walnuts, gently warmed extra-virgin olive oil, and coarsely chopped black olives. I like to serve it with lightly toasted baguette rounds. And when I think to include a platter of our homegrown grapes—still warm from the late afternoon sun—guests are always shocked at how delightfully they complement the spread.

YIELD: ABOUT $2^{1}/_{2}$ CUPS SPREAD

$^{1}/_{2}$ cup extra-virgin olive oil

$^{1}/_{2}$ cup chopped red onion

$^{1}/_{2}$ cup chopped toasted walnuts (see Note)

$^{1}/_{4}$ cup pitted and coarsely chopped kalamata olives

1 large clove garlic, minced

$^{1}/_{2}$ cup crumbled blue cheese

Freshly ground black pepper to taste

1 French bread baguette, sliced into $^{1}/_{4}$-inch-thick rounds, lightly toasted

1 bunch of sweet table grapes (optional, but delicious)

In a small saucepan over medium heat, gently warm the olive oil with the onion, walnuts, olives, and garlic. Do not bring the oil to a boil. Remove from the heat and cool for a moment. Place the blue cheese in an attractive serving bowl, then pour the warm oil mixture over the cheese and stir gently. Add pepper to taste, then let the mixture cool to room temperature.

To serve, arrange the toasted baguette rounds and the grapes on a platter and serve alongside the spread.

Note: To toast the nuts, spread them in a single layer on a baking sheet and toast in a 350° oven until lightly golden, about 4 minutes.

Red Onion and Roasted Garlic Spread

This is a fabulous seasoner for soups, sautés, or stir-frys. But where it really shines, of course, is simply as a spread for fresh and crusty French bread. Don't let the amount of onions and garlic concern you—the flavors mellow with the lengthy roasting time.

Yield: about 2 cups

3 heads of garlic, the papery outer skin rubbed off

$^{1}/_{2}$ cup extra-virgin olive oil

4 red onions, chopped

2 tablespoons red wine vinegar

$^{1}/_{2}$ teaspoon Worcestershire sauce

2 tablespoons chopped fresh thyme

About $^{1}/_{4}$ teaspoon salt

Freshly ground black pepper to taste

Preheat the oven to 350°F.

Slice off about $^{1}/_{2}$ inch from the top of each garlic head. Place the heads, root end down, in a large square of aluminum foil. Drizzle the heads with $^{1}/_{4}$ cup of the olive oil, then wrap them loosely, leaving the foil slightly open at the top for a bit of steam to escape. Roast the heads until the bulbs are tender when pressed, 45 to 60 minutes.

Meanwhile, in a large, heavy-bottomed skillet, heat the remaining oil and sauté the chopped onions over medium heat until the onions are softened and turning slightly golden, about 10 minutes. Midway through the process, stir in the vinegar and Worcestershire sauce. When the onions are cooked, set them aside to cool.

Remove the roasted garlic from the oven and loosen the foil; set aside until cool enough to handle. Reserve the oil in case it is needed later to soften the puree.

Squeeze out the cooled cloves, then add them to the work bowl of a food processor along with the sautéed onion and oil mixture, the thyme, salt, and pepper. Process to a smooth puree, adding a bit of the reserved oil from the roasted garlic if necessary. Taste and adjust the seasoning. Scrape the mixture into a container, cover tightly, and refrigerate for up to several weeks.

Caramelized Shallot and Sun-Dried Tomato Tart

The fieriest of shallots mellow to a rich, sweet flavor with just gentle heat. You'll love this tart.

YIELD: 8 TO 10 SERVINGS

> 2 tablespoons olive oil (preferably the oil from the sun-dried tomatoes)
> 1 pound shallots, peeled and chopped, to measure 1 quart
> 2 green onions, minced (include all of the white and half the green portions)
> 1 teaspoon dried basil, plus fresh basil leaves for garnish
> 1/4 teaspoon salt
> 1/4 teaspoon white pepper
> 1/3 cup finely chopped sun-dried tomatoes (packed in oil, well drained)
> 3 eggs
> 1/2 cup light cream
> 1 (11-inch) quiche crust, partially baked (page 207)

In a large, heavy skillet over medium-low to low heat, warm the oil and gently sauté the shallots, green onions, basil, and salt until the shallots are a rich golden brown and very soft and tender. This will take at least 20 to 30 minutes, and you should stir the mixture occasionally to keep the shallots from burning. Remove the onions from the heat, stir in the white pepper and sun-dried tomatoes, and let the mixture cool.

Preheat the oven to 400°F.

In a bowl, whisk together the eggs and cream, then stir into the cooled shallot mixture. Pour into the tart shell and bake for 20 to 25 minutes, or until the tart is set and a knife inserted into the center comes out clean. Let the tart cool to room temperature and then cut it into appropriate-size chunks or wedges. Arrange the pieces on a lovely platter, garnish with a few healthy sprigs of basil, and serve.

SOUPS

SIMPLE MINESTRONE

— — —

YIELD: *6 TO 8 SERVINGS*

2 tablespoons olive oil

1 cup chopped yellow onions

1 cup diced carrots

1 cup diced celery

2 cups peeled and diced potatoes

3 cups shredded cabbage

1 (16-ounce) can Italian tomatoes, diced, including juice and liquid
     from the can

3 cups assorted chopped vegetables, including zucchini, broccoli, and
     green beans or peas

6 cups homemade or canned beef broth

1 1/2 cups canned or cooked white beans

Salt and freshly ground black pepper to taste

In a skillet, heat the oil and sauté the onions until softened, about 3 minutes. Add the carrots and celery and cook for 2 to 3 minutes more. Add all the remaining ingredients except the white beans, salt, and pepper; cover, and cook over low heat until the soup is thick, 2 to 3 hours. Add the beans and simmer for an additional 15 minutes. Taste and adjust the seasonings, adding salt and pepper.

FLORENTINE ONION SOUP

YIELD: *4 TO 6 SERVINGS*

$^1/_4$ cup extra-virgin olive oil

4 pounds yellow onions, peeled, halved lengthwise, then thinly sliced

2 teaspoons sugar

$^1/_2$ teaspoon salt

$^1/_4$ teaspoon white pepper

1 (750 ml) bottle dry white wine, such as Sauvignon Blanc, dry
       Riesling, or Chardonnay

1 quart homemade or canned beef broth

1 tablespoon finely chopped fresh basil, plus fresh sprigs for garnish

1 teaspoon finely chopped fresh oregano

$^1/_2$ teaspoon finely chopped fresh thyme

4 cups very stale Italian bread chunks (about $^1/_4$ pound)

Freshly grated Parmesan cheese

In a large, heavy pot or Dutch oven over medium heat, warm the olive oil and gently sauté the onions for 3 minutes. Cover tightly, reduce the heat to medium-low, and cook, stirring occasionally, for about 30 minutes, or until the onions are very soft and just beginning to turn golden.

At this point, uncover the pot, increase the temperature slightly, and continue cooking for another 30 to 40 minutes, or until the onions are a rich, deep golden brown. Add the sugar, salt, and pepper and continue cooking and stirring until the sugar melts. Stir in the wine, broth, chopped basil, oregano, and thyme, bring to a boil, then reduce the heat and simmer gently for about 20 minutes. Add the bread to the soup and continue cooking, uncovered, until the bread softens and disinte-

Remember, cooking converts the sulfur compounds in onions into sugars, which explains why they mellow and sweeten.

Fall
into
Winter

grates, 20 to 25 minutes longer. Be sure to stir the soup occasionally to keep it from sticking to the bottom of the pot. (Note: The soup may be prepared to this point up to 24 hours ahead.)

When ready to serve, reheat gently over medium-low heat. Make sure to give the soup a stir with a wire whisk to thoroughly incorporate the bread. Adjust the seasonings and ladle a portion into each soup bowl. Sprinkle each serving with Parmesan cheese and garnish with a sprig of fresh basil.

ITALIAN
VEGETABLE-SAUSAGE SOUP

A delicious accompaniment to the Garden Salad (page 204).

YIELD: *8 SERVINGS*

>   ³/₄ pound sweet Italian sausage, removed from its casing and cut into
>   1-inch chunks
>   2 medium yellow onions, chopped
>   3 cloves garlic, minced
>   1 (16-ounce) can Italian tomatoes, undrained
>   6 cups homemade or canned beef broth
>   1¹/₂ cups dry red wine
>   2 teaspoons dried basil
>   ¹/₂ teaspoon dried thyme
>   4 ribs celery, sliced
>   1 green bell pepper, chopped
>   3 white new potatoes, cubed
>   1 cup uncooked macaroni pasta
>   ¹/₂ teaspoon salt, or more to taste
>   ¹/₄ teaspoon freshly ground black pepper, or more to taste
>   Freshly grated Parmesan cheese

In a large pot, brown the sausage and drain the fat. Add the onions and garlic and cook until the onions are limp, about 5 minutes. Stir in the tomatoes, breaking them up with a spoon. Add the broth, wine, basil, and thyme. Simmer uncovered for about 30 minutes. Add all the remaining ingredients except the Parmesan, and simmer for another 25 minutes, or until the potatoes are tender. Ladle into bowls, sprinkle each serving with Parmesan cheese, and serve. For a light supper, simply serve with hot French bread and a large tossed green salad.

CRAB BISQUE WITH
ROASTED YELLOW ONIONS

YIELD: 6 SERVINGS

$^1/_2$ cup (1 stick) butter

2 medium yellow onions, roasted as described on page 228, and
    chopped

1 medium carrot, finely minced

$^1/_2$ rib celery, finely minced

1 tablespoon flour

1 tablespoon chopped fresh flat-leaf parsley

1 teaspoon commercial seafood seasoning (available at the fish counter
    of most supermarkets)

$^1/_4$ teaspoon celery salt

$^1/_8$ teaspoon white pepper

1 quart whole milk, heated

3 to 4 tablespoons Madeira or dry sherry

$^1/_2$ pound cooked fresh crabmeat

Salt and additional white pepper to taste

In a medium-size saucepan over medium-high heat, melt the butter. Add the onions, carrot, and celery, and sauté until soft, about 4 minutes. Reduce the heat to medium and add the flour, whisking constantly until smooth. Cook for 5 minutes over medium heat, whisking frequently to keep the flour from scorching. Stir in the parsley and seasonings, then gradually whisk in the warm milk, stirring constantly. Add the Madeira, crabmeat, and salt and additional white pepper to taste, and simmer gently for 15 to 20 minutes; do not boil. Serve hot. If the bisque is thicker than desired, stir in additional milk or cream to thin it.

SPLIT PEA VEGETABLE SOUP

YIELD: 6 TO 8 SERVINGS

1 cup dried split peas

4 cups homemade or canned chicken broth

2 tablespoons vegetable oil

1 cup chopped yellow onions

$1/4$ cup chopped fresh flat-leaf parsley

2 carrots, diced

2 ribs celery, chopped

$1/4$ head green cabbage, chopped

$1/4$ cup tomato sauce

4 to 5 cups water

1 cup uncooked rice

Salt and freshly ground black pepper to taste

Tabasco or other hot pepper sauce to taste

2 tablespoons freshly grated Parmesan cheese for garnish

In large pot, cook the split peas in the chicken broth until soft, about 25 minutes. In a medium-size skillet, heat the oil and sauté the onions until limp, about 3 minutes; add the parsley and cook for a few more minutes. Add the onion mixture to the split peas, along with the remaining vegetables, tomato sauce, and water. Cover and cook over medium heat for about 1 hour, then stir in the rice and cook for about 20 more minutes, stirring frequently, until the rice is tender. If the soup gets too thick, add more water or broth. Taste and adjust the seasonings with salt, pepper, and Tabasco. Garnish each serving with Parmesan cheese.

Hearty Taco Soup

YIELD: *6 SERVINGS*

$^1/_2$ pound extra-lean ground beef

1 green bell pepper, diced

1 cup chopped yellow onion

3 cups homemade or canned beef broth

1 (16-ounce) can peeled tomatoes, chopped, with their juice

1 (15-ounce) can pinto beans, drained

1 (15$^1/_4$-ounce) can whole kernel corn

4 teaspoons chili powder

2 teaspoons ground cumin

3 cloves garlic, minced

$^1/_4$ teaspoon cayenne

Salt and freshly ground black pepper to taste

About 1$^1/_2$ cups crumbled tortilla chips

$^1/_2$ cup grated part-skim mozzarella cheese

Brown the meat in a large pot and drain well. Add the green pepper and onion and continue cooking until the onion is softened, about 3 minutes. Add the broth, tomatoes and juice, beans, corn, chili powder, cumin, garlic, and cayenne. Cover and simmer for 30 minutes. Taste and adjust the seasonings, adding salt and pepper. Place a portion of the tortilla chips into each of 6 bowls. Add the soup, and top with the grated cheese.

Do you doubt the health benefits of onions? In the early 1800s, during an outbreak of infectious fever in London, the dying civilians were aided by both English and French priests. The French, whose diets were rich in onions and garlic, suffered no ill effects from the exposure, while

---

SALADS
AND LIGHT MEALS

WINTER SALAD
OF ORANGES, FENNEL,
RED ONIONS, AND AVOCADOS

YIELD: 6 SERVINGS

$^1/_2$ fennel bulb, sprigs reserved for garnish

1 red onion

2 ripe avocados (preferably Haas variety)

3 oranges

FENNEL VINAIGRETTE:

$^1/_3$ cup freshly squeezed lemon juice

3 tablespoons rice vinegar

2 tablespoons chopped fresh chervil

1 tablespoon chopped fresh fennel leaves

$^1/_2$ teaspoon salt

2 tablespoons sour cream

3 tablespoons olive oil

1 small head of butter lettuce (or other soft-leaved variety), broken
   into bite-size pieces

Trim away the leaves and stalks from the fennel bulb as well as any brown or tough outer layers. Reserve at least 6 nice sprigs of the feathery leaves for the garnish, if desired. Working lengthwise (through where the stalks and root end would be), cut the bulb into julienne strips. Halve the onion lengthwise through the stem and root ends, then cut each half into julienne strips, working in the same direction. Peel and seed the avocados, then slice lengthwise into ¼-inch-thick strips.

Place the prepared fennel, onion, and avocados in a lovely salad bowl. Cut one of the oranges in half crosswise through its mid-section and juice it. Add the juice to the bowl and toss to thoroughly coat with the ingredients. Refrigerate the salad until ready to serve, but not more than 1 hour.

To make the vinaigrette, in a small bowl, whisk together the lemon juice, vinegar, chervil, fennel, and salt. When well combined, whisk in the sour cream and oil. Taste and adjust the seasonings.

Cut away the peel and white pith from the remaining 2½ oranges and slice them into ¼-inch-thick rounds; set aside.

When ready to serve, arrange a bed of salad greens on each of 6 plates. Arrange 2 or 3 orange slices on each, then spoon a portion of the fennel mixture over the oranges. Drizzle with a bit of the dressing, and garnish each plate with a feathery sprig of fennel. Pass the remaining dressing to diners at the table.

many of the English healers (who never ate onions or garlic) died. At other times in history Alexander the Great, General Ulysses S. Grant, General George Patton, and Captain Cook all insisted their men eat onions.

Fall into Winter

SHRIMP AND CARAMELIZED ONION SALAD WITH CITRUS-JALAPEÑO VINAIGRETTE

YIELD: 6 SERVINGS

2 tablespoons olive oil

2 large yellow onions, chopped

CITRUS-JALAPEÑO VINAIGRETTE:

Juice of 1 *each* orange, lemon, and lime

1 teaspoon *each* minced orange, lemon, and lime zest

1 clove garlic, minced

1 jalapeño pepper, seeded and minced

$^1/_2$ teaspoon salt

Freshly ground black pepper

$^2/_3$ cup extra-virgin olive oil

4 cups mixed salad greens (arugula, romaine, butter leaf)

20 cherry tomatoes, halved

1 yellow bell pepper, seeded and cut into thin rings

1 Haas avocado, peeled and sliced $^1/_2$ inch thick

1 pound medium raw shrimp, peeled, deveined, and tails removed

1 large, uncooked ear of corn, shaved, or $^1/_2$ cup frozen kernels

$^1/_3$ pound good-quality white Cheddar cheese, crumbled

In a medium skillet over medium-low heat, heat the oil and cook the onions until they are soft and tender, about 20 minutes; set aside to cool thoroughly.

To make the vinaigrette, in a bowl, combine the fruit juices and add the zests, garlic, jalapeño, salt, and several good cranks of pepper. Mix well with a wire whisk. Slowly add the oil, whisking gently but constantly; adjust the seasonings. Set aside.

Place the greens on a large platter or 4 individual plates. Place the tomatoes, bell pepper rings, and avocado slices in a large bowl. Add enough of the Citrus-Jalapeño Vinaigrette to coat the vegetables.

In a large sauté pan filled with about $^1/_2$ inch of lightly salted water simmer the shrimp for $1^1/_2$ minutes. Add the corn kernels and cook for an additional 30 seconds; remove with a slotted spoon and drain well. Add the hot shrimp and corn to the bowl with the vegetables and vinaigrette; toss well to evenly coat the ingredients. Drain and arrange the mixture on the bed of greens. Sprinkle with the cheese and the caramelized onions and serve immediately, passing around the remaining vinaigrette at the table.

Bay Scallop Salad
with Red Onions,
and Tarragon Vinaigrette

— —

YIELD: *6 SERVINGS*

¼ cup olive oil

1 pound bay scallops, rinsed and patted dry

1 small red onion, thinly sliced

1 clove garlic, minced

1 red bell pepper, julienned

1½ cups fresh peas (see Note)

2 tablespoons rice wine vinegar

2 tablespoons minced fresh basil

1 tablespoon *each* minced fresh thyme and chives

Salt and freshly ground black pepper to taste

TARRAGON VINAIGRETTE:

¼ cup red or white wine vinegar

1 teaspoon Dijon mustard

1 teaspoon minced fresh tarragon, or a scant ½ teaspoon dried

1 clove garlic, minced

¼ teaspoon salt

⅓ cup *each* extra-virgin olive oil and another vegetable oil, such as canola or corn oil, or ⅔ cup olive oil

1 head of butter lettuce, leaves separated and washed

⅓ cup coarsely grated fresh Parmesan cheese

½ cup toasted pine nuts for garnish (see Note, page 319)

In a large skillet over medium-high heat, warm 2 tablespoons of the oil and sauté the scallops for 2 minutes, stirring constantly; remove the scallops from the pan and set aside.

Add the remaining 2 tablespoons of oil to the pan and sauté the onion and garlic for about 2 minutes. Add the red pepper and peas, and cook for another minute, stirring frequently. Add the vinegar, herbs, salt and pepper, and the reserved scallops. Stir to combine, then remove from the heat. Set aside.

To make the vinaigrette, in a small container, combine all the ingredients except the oil. Stir in the oil; taste and adjust the seasonings.

Break the lettuce into large, bite-sized pieces and toss with enough of the Tarragon Vinaigrette to coat the leaves. Add the cheese and toss again. Divide the lettuce mixture among 6 individual plates. Serve the scallop mixture on the bed of greens, garnishing each serving with pine nuts.

Note: Prepare fresh peas by blanching them for 20 seconds in boiling water. If using frozen baby peas, simply thaw them in a strainer under cold running water and use.

Garden Salad

YIELD: *4 SERVINGS*

$^1/_2$ head of iceberg lettuce, thoroughly washed and broken into pieces

$^1/_2$ head of curly-leaved lettuce, thoroughly washed and broken into
  pieces

1 green bell pepper, seeded and chopped

$^1/_2$ medium cucumber, peeled and diced

1 red onion, sliced into rings

2 or 3 Roma tomatoes, diced

$^1/_2$ cup *each* shredded carrot, sliced black olives, sliced pickled banana
  peppers or Hungarian wax peppers cut into $^1/_4$-inch thick
  rings

GARDEN SALAD VINAIGRETTE:

$^1/_3$ cup olive oil

2 tablespoons red wine vinegar

1 tablespoon fresh lemon juice

$^1/_2$ teaspoon salt

$^1/_2$ teaspoon sugar

$^1/_2$ teaspoon dried oregano leaves, crumbled

2 cloves garlic, minced

$^1/_4$ teaspoon freshly ground black pepper

In large salad bowl, combine all of the ingredients except the vinaigrette; chill well.

To make the vinaigrette, in a small bowl, whisk together all the ingredients.

When ready to serve, drizzle the salad with enough dressing to thoroughly coat the leaves, or pass the dressing at the table.

Roasted Pepper Salad
with Feta and Shrimp

Yield: 4 to 6 servings

1 cup plain yogurt

$1/4$ teaspoon dried oregano, crumbled

1 small clove garlic, minced

3 green bell peppers, rinsed and dried

3 red bell peppers, rinsed and dried

2 yellow bell peppers, rinsed and dried

1 red onion, cut into thin rings

2 tablespoons olive oil

2 tablespoons red or white wine vinegar

Salt and freshly ground black pepper to taste

8 inner leaves of romaine lettuce

1 pound raw medium shrimp, boiled about 3 minutes, peeled, and
    deveined

$1/2$ pound feta or fresh goat cheese, coarsely crumbled

$1/2$ cup Greek olives

3 small green onions, finely chopped (all of the white and half of the
    green portions)

Combine the yogurt, oregano, and garlic in a food processor or blender and puree.

Preheat the broiler. Pierce each pepper near the stem with a sharp, thin knife. Arrange the peppers on a broiler pan and roast on all sides until blistered (but not charred), about 4 minutes. Transfer them to a plastic or paper bag, close tightly, and set aside for 15 minutes. Slip off the skins and discard the stems and seeds. Slice the peppers into thin strips and transfer them to a large bowl, along with the

(continued)

onion rings. Add the olive oil and vinegar and toss gently until blended. Add salt and pepper and toss gently again.

Arrange the lettuce leaves in a fan pattern on a serving platter. Mound the peppers in the center and drizzle some yogurt dressing over the top. Scatter the cooked shrimp, cheese, olives, and green onions around the peppers. Serve with the remaining yogurt dressing.

Smoked
Onion-Provolone Quiche

In earlier times, Italians preferred their provolone well-matured and heavily smoked. Not so these days. The modern version has a more delicate smoky flavor, which gently complements the smoked onions in this delectable tart.

YIELD: *8 SERVINGS*

QUICHE CRUST:

> 1 ¹/₂ cups all-purpose flour
>
> ¹/₄ teaspoon salt
>
> 6 tablespoons cold butter
>
> 3 tablespoons vegetable shortening, cut into small chunks
>
> 1 egg
>
> 3 tablespoons ice water
>
>
> 1 ¹/₂ cups shredded provolone cheese
>
> 6 slices bacon, diced
>
> 3 medium onions, quartered, smoked (see Note, page 75), and diced
>
> 1 ³/₄ cups light cream
>
> 4 eggs
>
> 2 tablespoons flour
>
> ¹/₂ teaspoon salt
>
> ¹/₂ teaspoon white pepper
>
> ¹/₂ teaspoon *each* dried basil and thyme
>
> ¹/₄ teaspoon cayenne

SMOKEHOUSE ONIONS USING A CHARCOAL GRILL

Heat about ten coals in the barbecue until they get very low. Sprinkle four cups of wood chips over the coals and when they begin to smoke, place quartered globe onions on the grill and cook them covered for 1 hour.

To make the crust, in a large bowl, mix the flour with the salt. Using a pastry blender or 2 knives, cut the butter and vegetable shortening into the flour until it

(continued)

resembles coarse meal. (Food processor method: Place the flour and salt in the work bowl of a food processor and pulse briefly; add the cut-up pieces of butter and shortening and pulse a few more times until the dough resembles coarse meal.)

In a small bowl, whisk together the egg and ice water. Stirring with a fork, add only enough of this to the flour/butter mixture for the dough to start holding together. (Food processor method: As you pulse the machine, add only enough of the egg/ice water mixture through the feed tube for the flour/butter mixture to start holding together.)

Collect the pastry and form it into a ball on a lightly floured board. Gently press the ball into a flat circle about 1 inch thick, cover it with plastic wrap and chill for at least 20 minutes before rolling it out. (The pastry can be refrigerated overnight at this point or frozen for later use.) When ready to use, sprinkle the work surface with more flour and roll the pastry into a circle 1/8 to 1/4 inch thick. It should be about 16 inches in diameter. Lightly butter a 10-inch pie or quiche tin. Place the crust in the pan and press gently to line the inside without stretching the dough. The edges of the pastry will hang evenly over the rim and drape down to the counter. Tuck the excess dough under to form a thick edge. Crimp the edges decoratively with your fingers or a fork. Refrigerate the crust while you proceed with the recipe.

Preheat the oven to 350°F.

Evenly distribute the shredded cheese over the bottom of the prepared crust, then refrigerate again.

Sauté the bacon in a small skillet until crisp. Remove the bacon with a slotted spoon and pour off all but 2 tablespoons of the bacon drippings. Add the onions to the skillet and continue sautéing over medium heat until lightly golden, about 10 minutes. Remove from the heat and cool slightly.

Sprinkle the bacon and onions over the bottom of the quiche shell. In a bowl, whisk together the cream, eggs, flour, salt, pepper, basil, thyme, and cayenne. Gently pour the cream mixture into the quiche (you may have a little extra cream mixture; stop filling about 1/2 inch from the top edge). Place the quiche on the lowest shelf of your oven and bake until the custard is set, 40 to 45 minutes. Remove from the oven and let it sit for 10 minutes before serving.

QUICHE CALIFORNIA

Unlike the classic Quiche Lorraine, from which this has spun away, the Quiche Califor-nia contains caramelized onions, Swiss cheese, and marinated artichoke hearts, as well as a hearty dose of prosciutto. The combination of flavors and textures is really wonderful—in fact, my Easter luncheon group gave it a unanimous thumbs up.

YIELD: *8 SERVINGS*

2 tablespoons butter

2 cups chopped yellow onions

3/4 cup finely chopped prosciutto

2 (6-ounce) jars marinated artichoke hearts, drained and chopped

1 (10-inch) unbaked quiche crust, well chilled (page 207)

1 1/2 cups coarsely grated Swiss cheese

3 eggs

1 1/2 cups light cream

1/2 teaspoon salt

In a large, heavy bottomed skillet over medium-low heat, melt the butter. Add the onions and sauté gently for 30 to 40 minutes, or until the onions turn a light caramelized gold and turn very sweet. Remove the pan from the heat, stir in the prosciutto and artichoke hearts and set aside.

Preheat the oven to 425°F.

Sprinkle the bottom of the crust with half the cheese (placing some of the cheese on the bottom tends to help keep the crust from becoming soggy). Then spread on the onion/prosciutto mixture and the remaining cheese. In a bowl, whisk together the eggs, cream, and salt, then gently pour this mixture into the quiche, leaving about 1/2 inch between the filling and the top of the crust (you

(continued)

may have a bit of the cream mixture left over). Bake the quiche for 15 minutes, then reduce the temperature to 325° and continue baking for 40 minutes, or until the quiche is a rich golden brown and a knife inserted in the center comes out clean. Remove from the oven and let stand for at least 10 minutes before serving. Serve hot or at room temperature. The quiche may be prepared up to 24 hours in advance and reheated gently in the oven or microwave before serving (but the crust won't be quite as perky and flaky).

Stuffed Onions—
A Spectacular Feast

I still remember the night my oldest son came face to face with his first stuffed onion. It was a big one—intact, and sporting a rich, golden glaze from an hour of roasting in the oven. A crusty, plump filling of sausage, sourdough French bread, and herbs spilled out the top from its steamy interior.

In a word, Brandon summed up my feelings for stuffed onions: "Wow!"

Stuffed onions look impressive and taste wonderful. They're a great make-ahead item and a simple way to vent the creative urge we rarely have time to satisfy in the kitchen.

Within reason, just about anything you ferret from the fridge and pantry can be fashioned into an amazing filling. For starters, consider leftover meats, any kind of rice, cooked pastas, pesto, legumes, nuts, cheeses, minced vegetables, apples, bread crumbs—even salsas.

The amount of preparation to ready a container for a filling varies from recipe to recipe. In the Onion Spectacle that hooked Brandon, for instance, very little was done to the onion before stuffing. First I trimmed the roots to create a flat base for each onion to rest on during cooking. Next I cut off the top, peeled away the outer skin, and scooped out all but two or three layers of the flesh. I chopped a portion of the scooped-out flesh, sautéed it in butter, and added it to the filling.

Because the onions were going to be cooking for at least an hour in a simmering pool of broth and wine, there was no reason to blanch the shells first. But if the cooking time for your recipe is less than 35 minutes or so, you may want to give the orb a head start by precooking it in boiling water or broth for a few minutes. (See page 77 for instructions on preparing onions for stuffing.)

That's all there is to it. It's up to you what filling you use, and whether your stuffed veggies will be an entrée or an elegant side dish. The following recipes will give you some ideas for how to come up with creations of your own.

ONION SPECTACLE

This is the one that captured my son, Brandon's, attention.

YIELD: *4* ENTRÉE OR *8* SIDE-DISH SERVINGS

> 4 large yellow onions
>
> 3 tablespoons butter
>
> $1/4$ pound mushrooms, chopped
>
> 1 cup finely chopped celery
>
> 12 ounces well-seasoned bulk pork sausage
>
> 1 cup soft bread crumbs (preferably made from sourdough French
> > bread)
>
> $1/4$ teaspoon salt
>
> $1/4$ teaspoon freshly ground black pepper
>
> $3/4$ cup homemade or canned chicken broth
>
> $3/4$ cup white wine or dry sherry

Preheat the oven to 400°F.

Trim the root of each onion to create a flat base. Skin the onions and peel off any slippery membrane so that you can grip them firmly when you are scooping out the inner flesh. Cut off the top of each peeled onion and dig into the center with a metal spoon, a grapefruit knife or spoon, or any other utensil that works for you. Scoop out the flesh, leaving 2 or 3 layers to form a solid shell.

Set the shells aside and finely chop enough of the scooped-out flesh to measure 2 cups. Melt the butter in a large pot, add the chopped onions, mushrooms, and celery and sauté until softened, about 3 minutes. Meanwhile, in a skillet, sauté the sausage until just barely browned, about 4 minutes. With a slotted spoon, add the sausage to the vegetable mixture, along with the bread crumbs, salt, and pepper; mix lightly but thoroughly. Spoon the stuffing into the onion shells, mounding it slightly for an attractive effect.

(continued)

Place the onions in a shallow, ovenproof dish or casserole that holds them snugly. Pour the broth and wine around the base of the onions, then cover the dish loosely with aluminum foil. Bake for 20 minutes. Remove the foil from the dish and continue to cook the onions, uncovered, for up to 30 minutes, until they are brown and the liquid is syrupy. Baste them frequently with the cooking liquid during the final stages to keep them moist and create a nice glaze on the outside. To serve, pour the remaining liquid over them. If serving as a side dish, cut each onion in half after baking.

Note: If the onions are well chilled before scooping out the flesh, they'll be less likely to cause your eyes to tear.

BRAISED STUFFED ONIONS

YIELD: 4 ENTRÉE SERVINGS

4 large yellow onions

3 tablespoons olive oil

$1/2$ cup chopped mushrooms

$1/2$ pound lean ground raw chicken

$1/2$ cup ground cooked ham

1 egg yolk, lightly beaten

1 tablespoon chopped fresh basil, or 1 teaspoon dried

1 tablespoon chopped fresh flat-leaf parsley, plus extra for garnish

2 tablespoons dry white wine

Juice of $1/2$ lemon

3 tablespoons freshly grated Parmesan cheese

$1/2$ teaspoon ground cumin

Salt and freshly ground black pepper

$1/2$ cup homemade or canned chicken broth

2 medium tomatoes, peeled, seeded, and chopped

Cut the onions in half lengthwise through their root ends; scoop out all but 3 layers of flesh and chop enough of the flesh to measure $1 1/2$ cups. Set the shells aside.

Heat 1 tablespoon of the oil in a medium skillet over medium heat. Add the chopped onions and the mushrooms; sauté until golden, about 4 minutes. Remove from the heat. Place the chicken and ham in a large bowl and mix lightly. Add the onion and mushroom mixture, the egg yolk, basil, parsley, wine, lemon juice, Parmesan, cumin, and salt and pepper to taste; mix well.

Fill the onion halves with the meat filling. Heat the remaining 2 tablespoons of oil in a large, heavy-bottomed skillet over medium-low heat. Add the onions,

(*continued*)

filled side up. Pour the chicken broth around the onions and sprinkle the tomatoes over and around them. Heat the sauce to boiling; reduce the heat, cover, and simmer over medium to medium-low heat for about 20 minutes. Transfer the onions to a serving platter with a slotted spoon and keep them warm. Raise the heat under the saucepan and boil the liquid until reduced and thickened slightly, about 4 minutes. Pour this over the onions and sprinkle with the chopped parsley.

ENTRÉES

BUTTERFLIED
BARBECUED LAMB

I learned this recipe from my mom. She learned it from a friend, Doris Ashman. We've all been making it for about a zillion years, if you combine our kitchen time. And it's always a hit. Even with folks who are only lukewarm on lamb. The onions are the featured attraction: 4 of them, thinly sliced, then left to marinate with the lamb in a zesty soy and herbed vinaigrette. While the lamb is grilling, you slowly sauté the onions in some of the marinade until they are tamed to a caramelized mound of decadence.

YIELD: *6 SERVINGS*

1 6-pound leg of lamb, butterflied and trimmed of fat (see Note)

2 cups of your favorite bottled herb and garlic vinaigrette

$1/2$ cup soy sauce

4 yellow onions, thinly sliced

1 recipe of Armenian Noodles and Nuts (recipe follows)

Be sure to trim away the entire blanket of fat that normally surrounds a leg of lamb. Combine the salad dressing with the soy sauce. Place the lamb in a large container or plastic bag. Add the soy sauce mixture and the onions and spread these evenly over the entire surface of the lamb. Marinate in the refrigerator for 1 2 to 24 hours, turning the lamb occasionally so it remains evenly coated.

(continued)

Broil the meat in the oven or over a hot bed of coals for 15 to 20 minutes, basting often. Turn and continue grilling for another 15 to 20 minutes, continuing to baste occasionally. Meanwhile, drain the onions from the marinade and cook them uncovered in a large frying pan over medium heat for about 20 minutes.

Allow the meat to "rest" for 5 minutes before cutting it across the grain into thin slices. Serve with the sautéed onions and Armenian Noodles and Nuts.

Note: "Butterflied" is another term for boned. Once a lamb has been boned, it is thin enough to cook on a grill, just as you would a thick steak or London broil. If you have never boned a leg of lamb, talk with your butcher. He or she will either do it for you, or at least teach you how. If you have a decent, sharp knife in your kitchen, it won't be difficult. Once the lamb has been boned, trim away the blanket of fat as well.

ARMENIAN NOODLES AND NUTS

YIELD: *6 TO 8 SERVINGS*

2 tablespoons vegetable oil

2 tablespoons butter

1 cup uncooked long-grain white rice

2 ounces vermicelli, broken into $^1/_2$-inch pieces

$^1/_4$ cup pine nuts

2 cups homemade or canned chicken broth

In a heavy pot, heat the oil and butter and brown the rice, vermicelli, and pine nuts. When golden, add the broth. After the mixture has come to a boil, reduce the heat to low, cover, and cook for 25 minutes, until the liquid is absorbed and the rice is tender.

Braised Lamb Shanks
with Caramelized Onions

Yield: 6 servings

3 tablespoons olive oil

6 lamb shanks, each sawed into 2-inch lengths (let the butcher do it!)

$^1/_2$ cup flour

$^1/_4$ teaspoon salt

$^1/_4$ teaspoon freshly ground black pepper

6 yellow onions, thinly sliced

3 to 4 large cloves garlic, minced

$^1/_4$ cup chopped fresh flat-leaf parsley

2 teaspoons minced fresh oregano

3 cups homemade or canned beef broth

1 cup dry red wine

2 cups pitted and chopped Italian black olives

In a large, heavy pot or Dutch oven, heat the oil over medium-high heat. Dredge the lamb in the flour, salt, and pepper, shaking off any excess, then add it to the pot and brown on all sides for about 8 minutes. Remove the lamb shanks and set aside.

Add the onions and garlic to the pot and sauté until the onions have softened, 3 to 4 minutes. Place the browned lamb shanks on top of the onions, add the parsley, oregano, beef broth, and wine and bring to a boil. Reduce the heat, cover, and simmer for 1$^1/_2$ to 2 hours, or until the lamb shanks are very tender.

Remove the lamb from the pan and let the sauce cool. Skim off as much fat and oil as possible, then puree the onions and sauce in a food processor. Return the sauce to the pan, stir in the olives, and simmer for 5 minutes. Adjust the seasonings, then pour the sauce over the lamb shanks and serve.

Bulb onions are "biennial": They grow and store food in the bulb the first year and will flower the second year; then their lifespan is over.

Fall
into
Winter

Turkey and Pork Terrine

Delicious as an entrée, of course, but my favorite use for this excellent concoction is as picnic fare. Or cross-country-skiing fare. Or tailgate fare. Your food processor makes preparation a snap—and it can be done days in advance.

Yield: *6 to 8 servings*

1 pound boneless raw turkey breast, cut into 1-inch chunks

1 large yellow onion, coarsely chopped

3 tablespoons chopped fresh flat-leaf parsley

2 eggs

2 tablespoons milk

2 tablespoons brandy

1 tablespoon Worcestershire sauce

1 clove garlic, chopped

2 teaspoons salt

$1/4$ teaspoon freshly ground black pepper

2 cups fresh bread crumbs

1 pound unseasoned ground raw pork

Preheat the oven to 350°F.

Place the turkey, onion, parsley, eggs, milk, brandy, Worcestershire sauce, garlic, salt, and pepper in a food processor and blend for 10 seconds, stopping once to scrape down the sides of the container. Add the bread crumbs and continue to puree until the mixture is smooth. Transfer this mixture to a bowl and combine it with the ground pork, mixing well. To make sure the flavors are balanced, sauté a spoonful in a skillet and taste (do not eat the raw mixture); adjust the seasonings.

Place the mixture in a 9 by 5-inch loaf pan. Cover the pan with foil, then place it in a larger pan partially filled with hot water (the water should reach at least a third of the way up the sides of the inner pan) and bake for about $1\,1/2$ hours, or until the juices run clear. (Note: The water helps keep the terrine nice and moist; the water will never come to a boil.) Remove the pan from the oven and then carefully lift the loaf pan from the hot water bath. If serving the terrine as a hot entrée, let it sit for 15 minutes to "firm up" before slicing. However, my recommended use is for outdoor fare, which means the terrine should be chilled first. This improves the flavor and firms up the texture for slicing into thin "deli-cuts."

FOR PICNIC SANDWICHES: This terrine is particularly wonderful with a bold-and-spicy whole-grained mustard, the crunch of a good garlic dill pickle, and some sliced tomatoes, all either tucked into a whole-wheat pocket bread or nestled between 2 slices of a really good sourdough.

Southwest Shredded
Beef Sandwiches

After a chilly day on the slopes or the cross-country ski trail, this is a particularly fulfilling treat! How good a recipe is it? A woman called me from the Eugene airport one day, desperately seeking a copy. She had lost hers and was about to embark on a ski weekend with the family. They were COUNTING on the Southwest Shredded Beef filling, and she knew she better not let them down or it would be mutiny on the trails.

This can be prepared ahead and refrigerated or frozen, so always make a double batch and you'll be prepared for those last-minute excursions—or for that desperate time when you can't find the recipe.

Yield: *12 servings*

1 (3 to 3¹/₂-pound) boneless chuck roast

1 (7-ounce) can diced green chiles

4 tablespoons ground cumin

2 tablespoons chili powder

Salt to taste, plus 1 teaspoon

Freshly ground black pepper to taste

1 tablespoon canola or safflower oil

2 cups chopped yellow onions

1 (10-ounce) can diced tomatoes and green chiles (I don't usually recommend brands, but RO-TEL is the one you want in this case)

2 (14¹/₂ ounce) cans stewed tomatoes

1 cup minced pickled jalapeño slices (available in Mexican food section of most markets)

¹/₄ cup chopped fresh cilantro

12 onion buns, split (and toasted, if desired)

Coarsely grated Cheddar cheese
Shredded lettuce

Preheat the oven to 325°F.

Place the roast on a sheet of heavy-duty aluminum foil (18 by 25 inches). Combine the diced green chiles, 2 tablespoons of the cumin, the chili powder, salt to taste, and pepper. Spread the mixture over the top of the roast and then wrap the foil around it, sealing well. Place in a baking pan and bake for 3½ to 4 hours, or until the meat is so tender it falls apart. Be careful when unwrapping the roast; the steam will burn!

When the meat is done, lift it from the pool of drippings in the foil and allow it to cool on a plate until it is easy to handle. Meanwhile, pour the meat drippings into a small container and skim off the fat. You will have about ½ cup of meat juice remaining, which should be reserved.

Shred the cooled roast with a fork or your fingers into small strips and fibers; set aside. A 3-pound roast will yield about 4 cups of shredded meat.

In a large pot, heat the oil and sauté the onions until soft, about 3 minutes. Add the reserved meat juices, the shredded meat, tomatoes with green chiles, tomatoes, jalapeño peppers, cilantro, the remaining 2 tablespoons of cumin, and 1 teaspoon of salt. The mixture will seem very soupy at this point. Simmer it gently, uncovered, over medium-high heat until thickened (but still rather saucy), about 30 minutes.

The filling can be prepared ahead of time and refrigerated or frozen. When ready to use it, thoroughly reheat the mixture by bringing it to a boil and simmering it for about 5 minutes on the stove, or microwaving it on High until very hot and bubbly. To assemble the sandwiches, partially split each bun horizontally, sprinkle on some of the shredded cheese, then top with a portion of the hot filling, another sprinkling of cheese, and some shredded lettuce.

If you plan to take this wonderful filling out into the wilderness for a picnic or on a cross-country ski trip, after you have reheated the mixture to a boil and let it simmer until it is good and hot, pack it immediately into two 1-quart wide-mouthed Thermos bottles.

PIZZA WITH CARAMELIZED ONIONS, OLIVES, AND HERBS

I thought I was being quite original and daring when I set out to create a masterful pizza made entirely from a glorious mound of caramelized onions and herbs. Then I stumbled upon Georgeanne Brennan's Pissaladière in her beautiful cookbook, Potager. It called for 15 onions. Of course, my pizza is not a pissaladière. To be so named, it would have to contain anchovies, because pissala means "a puree of tiny, salted and fried anchovies and sardines" that is, in Nice, traditionally mixed with the cooked onions before spreading them onto rolled-out bread dough. You will not, I guarantee, find a single anchovy lurking within the ingredients below.

YIELD: *6* ENTRÉE OR *12* SIDE-DISH SERVINGS

Pizza dough (purchase enough dough for a "large" pizza, unrolled,
        from your favorite pizzeria; most will sell it to you that way
        if you just ask)
7 tablespoons olive oil
2 tablespoons butter
10 yellow onions (about 3$^{1}/_{2}$ pounds), thinly sliced
10 cloves garlic, slivered
4 bay leaves
2 teaspoons light or dark brown sugar
1 teaspoon salt
1 teaspoon white pepper
2 tablespoons dry white wine
2 tablespoons balsamic vinegar
Cornmeal for the pan

$^1/_3$ cup freshly grated Parmesan cheese

3 tablespoons finely chopped fresh basil

3 tablespoons finely chopped fresh oregano leaves

1 $^1/_2$ cups niçoise olives, pitted and sliced

Refrigerate the dough while you proceed with the recipe.

In a large, heavy-bottomed skillet over medium heat, combine 6 tablespoons of the olive oil and the butter. Add the onions, garlic, and bay leaves, then sprinkle with the brown sugar, salt, and white pepper, tossing gently to thoroughly coat the onions with the seasoning. Cover, reduce the heat to low, and cook for about 20 minutes without stirring. Remove the lid, increase the temperature to medium-high, and continue cooking and stirring for 15 minutes. For the final phase, increase the temperature to high, and, stirring constantly, continue cooking until the onions are a rich golden brown. This will take about 10 more minutes (your total cooking time will be about 45 minutes). Stir in the wine and vinegar, and deglaze the pan by stirring well to loosen any cooked-on bits from the bottom of the pan; set aside.

Preheat the oven to 500°F.

On a lightly floured work surface, pat and roll the dough to fit a 16-inch round pizza pan or a 16 by 12-inch baking sheet. Sprinkle the pan with a thin layer of cornmeal, then press the dough into the pan, rolling the edges slightly to create a rim. Brush the remaining tablespoon of olive oil over the surface, then arrange the onions evenly over the dough. Sprinkle on the cheese and fresh herbs, then add the olives. Bake until the crust is a rich golden brown, 15 to 20 minutes. Cut into wedges or squares and serve.

FLANK STEAK WITH JAMAICAN JERK SAUCE

Although chicken and pork benefit from this spicy sauce, flank steak is always my first choice.

YIELD: *6 TO 8 SERVINGS*

    1 large yellow onion, coarsely chopped
    8 green onions, trimmed (using all of the white portion and about one
        third of the green), cut into 1-inch chunks
    10 cloves garlic, peeled
    1 (2-inch) piece fresh ginger, peeled
    1 fresh jalapeño chile pepper, seeded and minced
    2 tablespoons seeded and minced sweet green bell pepper
    2 teaspoons *each* ground allspice and dried thyme
    1 teaspoon *each* dried oregano, grated nutmeg, and ground cinnamon
    ½ teaspoon cayenne
    2 teaspoons salt
    1 teaspoon freshly ground black pepper
    Juice of 2 lemons
    ½ cup cider vinegar
    About 2 pounds flank steak

In the bowl of a food processor, combine all the ingredients except the steak. Mix on "pulse" until the onions are lightly pureed.

Arrange the flank steaks in a shallow dish or a heavy-duty plastic resealable bag. Spread the sauce on both sides of the meat, then refrigerate and marinate for 4 hours, turning several times. Bring to room temperature before cooking.

When ready to serve, remove the meat from the marinade and grill over hot coals or broil in the oven until medium to medium-rare in doneness, about 4 minutes on each side. Let the steak rest for about 4 minutes before serving. Cut across the grain, at an angle, for the most tender presentation.

Pizza Supreme Sandwich

Yield: 2 to 4 servings

 2 yellow onions, thinly sliced

 2 tablespoons olive oil

 1 loaf French bread, measuring approximately 15 inches long, 4 inches wide, and 3 inches high

 $^1/_4$ pound mozzarella cheese, thinly sliced

 $^3/_4$ pound sweet Italian sausage, crumbled and browned

 3 tablespoons sliced black olives (half of $2^1/_4$-ounce can)

 $^1/_2$ cup spaghetti sauce (any commercially canned variety will do)

 2 ounces pepperoni, thinly sliced

 About 5 fresh mushrooms, thinly sliced

 1 small green bell pepper, seeded and thinly sliced

 Freshly grated Parmesan cheese

 1 cup coarsely grated medium or sharp Cheddar cheese

 Sandwich garnishes: thinly sliced tomatoes, shredded lettuce, vinaigrette dressing

In a skillet, over medium heat, sauté the onions in the oil until softened and transparent, about 10 minutes; set aside.

With a serrated knife, cut the loaf of bread in half lengthwise, creating a slightly thicker bottom half. With your fingers, gently hollow out the bottom half, leaving a $^1/_2$-inch border around the edge, and about $^1/_2$-inch thickness on the bottom.

Place both halves cut-side-up on a baking sheet and broil until golden. Remove from the oven and spread half the mozzarella slices along the bottom of the hollowed-out portion. Next, layer on the sausage, olives, and sautéed onions, then drizzle on the spaghetti sauce. On top of the sauce, layer the pepperoni, mushrooms, bell pepper, Parmesan cheese, and Cheddar cheese. Place top half of bread over the cheese, and bake until the cheese melts, about 15 minutes, in a 375° oven. Halve and serve immediately, with the garnishes on the side.

SIDE DISHES AND ACCOMPANIMENTS

OVEN-ROASTED BALSAMIC ONIONS

YIELD: *8 SERVINGS*

4 large yellow onions
3 tablespoons olive oil
Salt and freshly ground black pepper to taste
$1/3$ cup balsamic vinegar

Preheat the oven to 350°F.

Halve the unpeeled onions lengthwise through the root and stem ends. To guarantee that the onions will sit upright in the baking dish, cut a thin slice from the rounded side of each half. Place the onions, cut side up, in a baking dish just large enough to hold them. Drizzle each onion with a bit of the olive oil, then season with salt and pepper. Roast the onions until tender and golden, about 50 minutes. Remove the onions to a warm serving platter and return them to the oven after it has been turned off. Add the balsamic vinegar to the baking dish and stir and scrape to loosen any cooked-on bits of flavorful onion. Pour the sauce into a small saucepan and simmer to reduce it to a thick and syrupy state, about 10 to 15 minutes. Drizzle the sauce over the onions and serve hot or at room temperature.

POTATOES DIJON
WITH CARAMELIZED ONIONS

YIELD: *4 TO 6 SERVINGS*

3 tablespoons butter

2 tablespoons olive oil

2 onions, thinly sliced into rings

$1/2$ cup dry white wine

$1/2$ cup heavy cream

2 tablespoons Dijon mustard

$1/2$ teaspoon *each* fennel seed, dried basil, dried thyme

3 large russet potatoes (unpeeled), thinly sliced (about 4 cups
   sliced)

Salt and freshly ground black pepper to taste

Paprika and fresh flat-leaf parsley, chopped, for garnish

In a medium-size heavy skillet over medium heat, melt 1 tablespoon of the butter with the olive oil. Add the onions and sauté gently until golden brown, about 15 minutes. Remove from the heat and set aside.

Meanwhile, in a medium saucepan, simmer the wine until reduced to $1/4$ cup, about 6 minutes. Whisk in the cream, mustard, fennel, basil, and thyme and continue cooking until the sauce has thickened slightly, about 4 minutes. Add the onions to the sauce and set aside.

Melt the remaining 2 tablespoons of butter in a large nonstick skillet over medium-high heat. Add the potatoes and cook, turning frequently, until the slices are tender and well-browned on both sides, about 10 minutes. Season with salt and pepper. To serve, arrange half the potatoes in a casserole dish, then spoon half the onion mixture over them. Add the remaining potatoes, then drizzle with the remaining onion sauce. Garnish with parsley and paprika and serve.

PENNSYLVANIA DUTCH
SWEET AND TANGY ONIONS

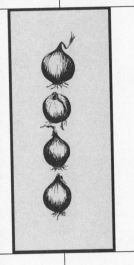

YIELD: *6 SERVINGS*

4 tablespoons ($^1/_2$ stick) butter, or more as needed

8 medium yellow onions, sliced into $^1/_4$-inch-thick rings

2 tablespoons sugar

2 tablespoons all-purpose flour

$^1/_2$ teaspoon salt

$^1/_4$ teaspoon freshly ground black pepper

$^1/_3$ cup cider vinegar

$^1/_3$ cup dry white wine

In large pot or Dutch oven over medium-low heat, melt 4 tablespoons of the butter. Add the onion rings and cook gently, uncovered, stirring occasionally, for about 45 minutes, or until the onions are a delicate golden and very tender. If necessary, add additional butter to keep the onions from sticking during the cooking. Stir in the sugar, flour, salt, and pepper, mixing well, then add the vinegar and wine, and continue cooking and stirring until thickened, about 3 to 4 minutes.

French Onions—
Sans Soup

As flavorful as French onion soup, without the bowl. This is a delectable accompaniment to roast beef or grilled steaks.

Yield: *8 servings*

6 medium yellow onions, sliced

8 tablespoons (1 stick) butter, plus 4 tablespoons ($^1/_2$ stick), melted

$^1/_4$ cup all-purpose flour

$^1/_2$ teaspoon salt

$^1/_4$ teaspoon white pepper

1 cup light cream

1 cup homemade or canned beef broth

$^1/_4$ cup dry white wine

$^3/_4$ pound Gruyère or Swiss cheese, coarsely grated

1 French bread baguette, sliced into $^1/_2$-inch rounds

$^1/_3$ cup freshly grated Parmesan cheese

Preheat the oven to 350°F. Lightly grease a 2-quart shallow baking dish.

In a large skillet over medium heat, warm 4 tablespoons of the butter and sauté the onions, stirring frequently, until they're soft and transparent, about 10 minutes. Transfer the onions to the baking dish. Set aside.

In a saucepan over medium heat, melt another 4 tablespoons of butter. Whisk in the flour and stir for 2 minutes. Whisk in the salt, pepper, light cream, and broth and continue stirring until thickened, about 2 minutes. Remove from the heat and whisk in the wine. Pour this sauce over the onions and sprinkle with the cheese. Brush one side of the bread slices with the melted butter and place them, buttered side up, over the sauce, covering the top completely. Bake for 20 minutes, then sprinkle lightly with the Parmesan cheese and continue baking until the bread is completely browned, 10 to 15 minutes.

Fall
into
Winter

OVEN-ROASTED ROOTS
AND BULBS OF WINTER

This is another wonderful accompaniment to roast beef or chicken.

YIELD: 6 SERVINGS

2 large yellow onions

1 large red onion

3 parsnips

3 large turnips

3 large rutabagas

$^1/_2$ large fennel bulb

$^1/_2$ celery root

3 tablespoons olive oil

1 teaspoon salt

$^1/_2$ teaspoon white pepper

1 teaspoon dried rosemary, crumbled

Preheat the oven to 475°F.

Trim and peel the onions, leaving the roots intact. Halve each onion lengthwise through the root end, then cut each half into 4 or 5 wedges, leaving a portion of the root with each piece. Peel and trim the parsnips, then cut lengthwise into $^1/_4$-inch slices. Peel and trim the turnips and rutabagas, then halve each one and cut each half into $^1/_4$-inch-thick slices. Trim the fennel bulb and celery root, then cut crosswise into $^1/_4$-inch-thick slices.

Place all of the prepared vegetables into a large roasting pan and drizzle them with the olive oil. Gently toss the vegetables to coat each one thoroughly with a bit of the oil, then spread them out evenly around the pan. Sprinkle with the salt and pepper, then roast for 15 minutes. At this point, sprinkle on the rosemary, gently stir the vegetables, turning as many as possible, then return the pan to the oven and roast for another 15 minutes, or until the vegetables are tender and golden, and have acquired a lovely crisp exterior.

Onions
Braised with Madeira

～ ～ ～

This is a terrific accompaniment to roast turkey, chicken, or pork. Also delicious along-side roasted polenta.

Yield: *8 to 10 servings*

- 2 tablespoons butter
- 2 tablespoons olive oil
- 6 yellow onions, sliced into 1-inch-thick rounds
- 1 teaspoon salt
- $^{1}/_{2}$ teaspoon white pepper
- $^{1}/_{3}$ cup Madeira

In a heavy skillet over medium-low heat, warm the butter and oil. Add the onions, cover the pan, and simmer gently for 10 minutes. Add the salt, pepper, and Madeira and continue cooking, uncovered, for another 10 minutes, until the onions are just beginning to turn golden.

POTATO, ONION, FENNEL GRATIN

YIELD: *10 SERVINGS*

2 tablespoons olive oil

2 medium fennel bulbs, trimmed (reserve a few of the feathery stalks
       for garnish) and finely chopped

2 large yellow onions, coarsely chopped

1 teaspoon fennel seed

4 cups homemade or canned chicken broth

$1/4$ cup all-purpose flour

$1/2$ cup heavy cream

Salt and white pepper to taste

$2^3/4$ pounds russet potatoes

$2^1/2$ cups coarsely grated Swiss cheese

$1/4$ cup coarsely grated Parmesan cheese

In a large, heavy skillet, warm the oil and sauté the fennel, onions, and fennel seed over medium-high heat for 5 minutes. Stir in $1/2$ cup of the chicken broth and continue cooking rapidly until the broth has evaporated and the vegetables begin to brown. This will take about 10 minutes. Deglaze the pan with $1/4$ cup more of the chicken broth, stirring and scraping to release any of the cooked-on bits of food; continue cooking for another 5 minutes or so for an even richer color, then deglaze the pan again with another $1/4$ cup of broth, and continue stirring until it has evaporated.

Finally, whisk the flour into the vegetables, then whisk in the cream and the remaining 3 cups of broth. Bring the liquid to a boil, reduce the heat to medium or medium-low, and continue stirring until the sauce has thickened slightly, about 5 minutes; season with salt and pepper and set aside.

Preheat the oven to 350°F. Lightly grease a 2½ to 3-quart casserole.

Peel the potatoes and cut them crosswise into very thin slices. Arrange about a quarter of the fennel-onion mixture in the bottom of the casserole. Cover with a quarter of the potatoes and a quarter of the Swiss cheese. If desired, season each layer lightly with salt and pepper to taste. Repeat the layers, ending with the potatoes; reserve the remaining cheese for later. (Note: The potatoes may be prepared to this point up to 24 hours ahead, covered and refrigerated.)

Bake, covered, for 30 minutes. Uncover, sprinkle with the reserved Swiss cheese and the Parmesan, and continue baking for another 45 minutes, or until the potatoes are very tender and the top is golden.

SOUTHWEST
SIZZLING ONIONS

Serve these alongside any Mexican or American Southwestern dish such as fajitas or tacos, or even a simple roast chicken. They're quite wonderful, particularly when you bring them to the table sizzling hot and cloaked in the heady aroma of fresh cilantro.

YIELD: *4 TO 6 SERVINGS*

3 medium yellow onions, peeled

2 tablespoons peanut oil

$1/4$ cup finely chopped fresh cilantro

Salt and freshly ground black pepper to taste

Splash of balsamic vinegar

Halve each onion lengthwise through the root end, then cut each half crosswise into $1/4$-inch-thick slices. Separate the slices into individual pieces.

Heat a large, heavy skillet over high heat until very hot. Add the oil and swirl to coat the bottom and sides of the skillet thoroughly. Before the oil begins to smoke, add the onions all at once. Let them sizzle for about 30 seconds without stirring to brown the bottom layer, then stir and continue stir-frying until the onions are thoroughly browned and beginning to become rather limp, about 5 minutes. Ideally, they should retain some of their firmness. At the very last moment, add the cilantro, salt and pepper, and the balsamic vinegar, then stir and toss quickly for another 30 seconds or so to deglaze the pan. Remove from the heat immediately, then transfer to a serving platter.

GREEN PEA PODS
WITH SPICY RED ONIONS

Emerald green pea pods join forces with gently pickled red onions to form a most noble side dish. I find it to be a jazzy accompaniment to lightly seasoned, grilled chicken breasts or flank steaks.

YIELD: *8 TO 10 SERVINGS*

2 quarts plus 3 cups water

³/₄ cup red wine vinegar

1 tablespoon whole yellow mustard seed

2 teaspoons cuminseed

1 teaspoon salt

2 to 3 large red onions, thinly sliced

¹/₃ cup olive oil

2 teaspoons sugar

1 pound Chinese pea pods, trimmed, with strings removed

In a large pot, combine the 3 cups of water with ¹/₃ cup of the vinegar, the mustard seed, cuminseed, and ¹/₂ teaspoon of the salt. Bring the mixture to a boil, then simmer for about 2 minutes. Add the onions, remove from the heat, and let the onions cool in the liquid. Drain the onions through a strainer, then toss the onion and seed mixture with the remaining 6 or 7 tablespoons of vinegar, the olive oil, remaining ¹/₂ teaspoon of salt, and the sugar. (Note: The onions may be prepared to this point up to 24 hours ahead and refrigerated.)

When ready to serve, rapidly boil the 2 quarts of water and blanch the pea pods until they turn bright green and are just barely tender, about 2 minutes; drain well, then run them under cold water to set the color and stop the cooking; drain again. Arrange the pea pods around the outer rim of a serving platter, spoon the onions into the center, and serve.

1 pound storage onions = about 4 cups chopped

1 basket of pearl onions (this is the typical way they are sold) = 20 to 40 onions, depending on their size

Fall into Winter

Risotto with a Melange of Peppers

~ ~ ~

A wonderful use for your final crop of backyard peppers and new crop of storage onions.

Yield: *6 generous servings*

2 tablespoons butter

2 tablespoons olive oil

1 cup arborio rice (or another short-grained rice, such as California
   Pearl)

1 medium yellow onion, halved, then sliced into $\frac{1}{4}$-inch-thick
   half-rings

$\frac{1}{2}$ teaspoon minced garlic

$\frac{1}{2}$ cup dry white wine

4 cups well-seasoned homemade or canned chicken broth

1 *each* large red, yellow, and green bell pepper, roasted, peeled, and
   seeded (see Note), thinly sliced, and cut into $\frac{1}{2}$-inch lengths
   (about 2 cups)

2 tablespoons finely minced fresh basil, or 2 teaspoons dried

$\frac{1}{2}$ cup freshly grated Parmesan cheese, plus additional for serving

Salt and freshly ground black pepper to taste

In a heavy-bottomed pan that holds at least 2 quarts, warm the butter and oil and gently sauté the rice, onion, and garlic over medium heat until the grains become translucent. Add the wine and continue cooking until it begins to cause the rice to swell, about 8 minutes. Now, continue cooking, adding about $\frac{1}{2}$ cup of broth at a time, and stirring at least every minute or so. As the hot broth is absorbed, add another $\frac{1}{2}$ cup or so, continuing to stir. After about 12 minutes into this process, add the peppers and basil.

Continue stirring in the broth, $^1/_2$ cup at a time, until the rice releases its outer layer and turns creamy and the grains are firm but not hard in the center. This will take another 20 minutes or so.

Just before serving, stir in the grated cheese; then adjust seasonings, adding salt and freshly ground pepper. Pass more grated Parmesan at the table.

Note: To peel the peppers, make several slits in each pepper to prevent them from bursting. Arrange them on a baking sheet and broil on all sides until thoroughly blistered, but not burned, about 6 minutes. Place them in a plastic bag, in the freezer, for about 10 minutes; the skins will be loosened by the steam, and will peel away easily.

STEVE'S FIRESIDE
SPANISH RISOTTO

I decided to name this one for my darling husband after his joshing observation the night I presented the newly developed recipe: "Say, we used to eat something like this when I worked on the fire line in the Forest Service one summer. It was called Spanish Rice, and it came in a can." Well . . . not ex-ACT-ly, my pet.

YIELD: *6 GENEROUS SERVINGS*

2 tablespoons olive oil

1 cup chopped yellow onions

1 cup arborio rice (or another short-grained rice, such as California Pearl)

1 (14$^1/_2$-ounce) can ready-cut (diced in juice) Italian-style tomatoes

4 cups well-seasoned homemade or canned chicken broth

6 small Anaheim chiles, roasted, peeled, seeded, and chopped ($^2/_3$ cup; see Note)

$^1/_2$ teaspoon salt, plus extra to taste

$^1/_2$ cup freshly grated Parmesan cheese, plus additional for serving

Freshly ground black pepper to taste

In a heavy-bottomed 2-quart pot over medium heat, warm the oil and sauté the onions for about 3 minutes. Add the rice and continue to cook gently, stirring constantly, until the grains become translucent. Add the tomatoes and cook until they are heated through.

Meanwhile, put the chicken broth in a separate pot and keep it at just below a simmer. Once the tomatoes have heated through, add about $^1/_2$ cup of the hot broth at a time, stirring at least every minute or so. As the broth is absorbed, add another $^1/_2$ cup or so, continuing to stir. After about 12 minutes into this process, add the chiles and the $^1/_2$ teaspoon salt.

Continue stirring in the broth, $^1/_2$ cup at a time, until the rice releases its outer layer and turns creamy, and the grains are firm but not hard in the center. This will take about 20 more minutes.

Just before serving, stir in the grated cheese, then adjust the seasonings, adding salt and freshly ground pepper. Pass more grated Parmesan at the table.

Note: To peel the peppers, using about 6 small Anaheim chiles (each one measuring about 4 to 5 inches in length), make several slits in each pepper to prevent them from bursting. Arrange them on a baking sheet and broil on all sides until thoroughly blistered, but not burned. Place them in a plastic bag, in the freezer, for about 10 minutes; the skins will be loosened by the steam, and will peel away easily.

Autumn Relish
of Roasted Corn, Onion,
and Peppers

Altogether, the richly sweet and zesty goodness of balsamic vinegar, the fiery undertones of jalapeño, and the taming influence of olive oil and roasted corn, onions, and peppers, adds up to a lovely, lively condiment. Perfect with grilled chicken.

Yield: about 2½ cups

1 cup freshly cooked corn kernels (use only local, in-season corn)

1 *each* red bell pepper and yellow onion, roasted and finely diced
(½ cup each; see Note)

¼ cup finely minced celery

¼ cup balsamic vinegar

3 tablespoons olive oil

2 tablespoons chopped fresh cilantro

½ jalapeño pepper, seeded and finely minced

Salt and freshly ground black pepper to taste

Combine all the ingredients except salt and pepper in a small bowl. Season with the salt and pepper. The relish may be served immediately, or prepared up to 24 hours ahead and refrigerated.

Note: To roast red pepper and onion, pierce the pepper in several places to prevent bursting, then rub it with olive oil and place on a baking sheet. Quarter a yellow onion lengthwise through the root end. Lay the quarters on the baking sheet alongside the pepper and brush with oil. Roast the vegetables in a 350°F. oven for about 30 minutes. Once roasted, the pepper may be skinned by placing it in a plastic bag and chilling in the freezer for about 10 minutes (this will loosen the skin). Remove from the freezer and slip off the peel.

Fried Onion-Ginger Chutney

The onions are tamed to a tender sweetness in this chutney because they're fried first. Combined with the sensations of hot, sweet, and sour—so typical of equatorial cuisines— it's bound to be exotic and delightful. It's especially great with braised or grilled pork chops or roast chicken.

YIELD: ABOUT 1 CUP

> 2 tablespoons extra-virgin olive oil
>
> 2 white onions, very thinly sliced
>
> 1 tablespoon minced garlic
>
> 2 tablespoons minced fresh ginger
>
> 2 whole star anise, crushed
>
> 1 tablespoon curry powder
>
> $^1/_2$ teaspoon white pepper
>
> $^1/_8$ teaspoon ground mace (you may substitute ground cinnamon)
>
> $^1/_4$ cup distilled white vinegar
>
> 2 tablespoons molasses
>
> Salt to taste

In a large frying pan, heat the olive oil over medium-high heat until hot but not smoking. Add the onions and fry quickly, stirring constantly, for about 5 minutes, or until they're a deep, dark brown. Add the garlic and ginger and continue cooking for 1 minute more, then stir in all the remaining ingredients and simmer, stirring fairly constantly, for an additional 5 minutes, or until the chutney is very thick. Remove from the heat, cool, and either serve immediately, or cover and refrigerate for up to 1 week.

HROUS (HOT PEPPER AND ONION PASTE)

This is an age-old favorite of southern Tunisian cooking. If you were to make the traditional preparation, you would sprinkle large quantities of onions with salt and turmeric, then allow the mixture to age and ferment in clay jars for several weeks until the onions became jaw-achingly tangy. Then you would stir in chile peppers and spices. This recipe is a bit of a short-cut, but a delicious condiment for flavoring tomato sauces, stews, soups, and—of course—couscous dishes.

Additionally, you could mix a little Hrous with olive oil and use it for bread-dipping at the table.

YIELD: *1 cup*

$^1/_2$ pound yellow onions, thickly sliced

3 to 4 tablespoons kosher or pickling salt

$^2/_3$ teaspoon ground turmeric

12 to 15 dried New Mexican chile peppers

1 $^1/_2$ teaspoons coriander seed

2 tablespoons caraway seed

$^1/_2$ teaspoon ground cinnamon

$^1/_3$ cup distilled white vinegar

4 to 5 tablespoons olive oil, more as needed

In a deep dish, combine the onions with the salt and turmeric. Let stand at room temperature for about 3 days, until the onions become very soft and juicy. Transfer the onions to a sieve lined with cheesecloth. Rinse well, then let them drain. Gather the ends of the cloth and squeeze the onions to extract all of their liquid.

Stem and seed the chiles. Cut them into strips and toast them over low heat in an ungreased frying pan, removing them from the pan as soon as they start to give off their aroma, about 5 minutes. Let cool.

In a blender, spice grinder, or a clean coffee grinder, in batches, grind the toasted chiles with the coriander, caraway, and cinnamon.

Combine the spice mixture with the drained onions, the vinegar, and the olive oil, and, wearing rubber gloves, knead to mix well. Pack into a 1 $\frac{1}{2}$-cup jar and top with more olive oil. Hrous will keep for 3 to 5 months in the refrigerator.

A Relish of
Sun-Dried Tomatoes,
Onion, and Basil

This is a great spread or dip for bagel chips, melba toast, or toasted baguette rounds.

Yield: about 2 cups

10 to 15 oil-packed sun-dried tomatoes, drained (reserve the oil) and
    finely chopped

1 cup finely chopped red onions

¼ cup finely chopped fresh basil

¼ cup balsamic vinegar

¼ cup reserved oil from the tomatoes, or virgin olive oil

2 tablespoons drained and rinsed capers

2 tablespoons chopped black olives

½ teaspoon salt

¼ teaspoon hot pepper sauce

In a small bowl, combine all the ingredients. Refrigerate for several hours at least (or up to several weeks) to bring the flavors together.

COCKTAIL ONIONS

These are like the ones you always got at your grandmother's house along with the black olives on Thanksgiving.

YIELD: ABOUT 3 PINTS

> 3 pounds pearl onions (each one measuring no larger than 1 inch,
> preferably much smaller)
> 1 cup plus 1 $^1/_2$ tablespoons pickling salt
> 7 cups distilled white vinegar, 5 percent acidity
> 2 cups water

Scald the onions in boiling water for about 2 minutes, then quickly dip them into cold water; peel the onions. Layer the onions in a large bowl alternately with the 1 cup of pickling salt. Refrigerate for 24 hours, stirring several times once the juices from the onions begin to form. (Note: This step is called short brining, and helps ensure a crisp pickle because it actually draws out moisture from within the vegetable and firms up the flesh in the process.)

Drain the onions, then rinse well and drain again. Combine the vinegar, the remaining 1 $^1/_2$ tablespoons of pickling salt, and the water in a nonaluminum saucepan; simmer for 5 minutes.

Meanwhile, wash 3 pint and 1 half-pint canning jars. Prepare the lids according to the manufacturer's directions. Pack the onions in the jars, leaving $^1/_2$-inch head space. Pour the hot vinegar solution over the onions to just cover the onions. Wipe each jar rim with a clean, damp cloth. Attach the lids. Process in a boiling water canner for 10 minutes (15 minutes at 1,001 to 6,000 feet; 20 minutes above 6,000 feet). Let the jars cool overnight without moving. Store in a cool, dark place.

TO BULB OR NOT
TO BULB

There are times
when a bulb
doesn't form,
even when it's
supposed to.
When this
happens, the
reason can
usually be
traced back to
the wrong set of
growing
conditions.
Either the
grower goofed
during
cultivation, or
the weather was
wrong, or the
soil wasn't right.

A ZESTY
PICKLED PEARL ONION

This pickled onion has a bit of zip, plus it's on the sweet side. So, if you're wanting some-thing beyond the traditional cocktail onion, this might be for you. If it seems too sweet, it's perfectly safe to cut down on the sugar.

YIELD: *ABOUT 3 PINTS*

> 3 pounds pearl onions (each one measuring no larger than 1 inch,
>   preferably much smaller)
> 1 cup plus 1 tablespoon pickling salt
> 7 cups distilled white vinegar, 5 percent acidity
> 3/4 cup sugar
> 2 cups water
> 3 tablespoons mustard seed
> 1 1/2 teaspoons pickling spice
> 3 cloves garlic, halved
> 3 small hot red peppers, or 1 1/2 teaspoons red pepper flakes
> 3 bay leaves

Scald the onions in boiling water for about 2 minutes, then quickly dip into cold water. To make peeling easier, trim away the root ends with a very sharp knife; peel the onions. Layer the onions in a large bowl, alternately with the 1 cup of pickling salt. Refrigerate for 24 hours, stirring several times once the juices from the onions begin to form. (Note: This step is called short brining, and helps en-sure a crisp pickle because it actually draws out moisture from within the vegetable and firms up the flesh in the process.)

Drain the onions, then rinse well and drain again. Combine the vinegar, the remaining 1 tablespoon of pickling salt, the sugar, and water in a nonaluminum saucepan; simmer for 5 minutes.

Wash 3 pint and 1 half-pint canning jars. Prepare the lids according to the manufacturer's directions. Pack the onions in the jars, leaving $1/2$-inch head space. To each jar add 1 tablespoon of mustard seed, $1/2$ teaspoon of pickling spice, 2 garlic halves, 1 red pepper (or $1/2$ teaspoon pepper flakes), and 1 bay leaf. Pour the hot liquid over the onions to just cover them. Wipe each jar rim with a clean, damp cloth. Attach the lids. Process in a boiling water canner for 10 minutes (15 minutes at 1,001 to 6,000 feet; 20 minutes above 6,000 feet). Let the jars cool overnight without moving. Store in a cool, dark place.

And sometimes it just happens.

However, there are times when growers will deliberately short-circuit an onion's bulbing behavior in order to grow a top-quality green onion.

Fall

into

Winter

SPROUTING
ONIONS

Onion bulbs are really living, breathing vegetables, which carry within them— even in their dried and cured state—the potential for new life. Once they've sent out a bright green shoot through the center, their quality is shot. Certainly, they're edible, but the tissue

LONDON PUB-STYLE
PICKLED ONIONS

The traditional pickled onion from the British Isles—the one found on the Plowman's lunch plate—uses a hearty malt vinegar, which provides a zesty flavor and amber tone. If you don't want any sweetness, it's okay to omit the sugar entirely, or cut it back dramatically; some cooks think the sugar provides a balance for the vinegar.

YIELD: *3 PINTS*

3 pounds pearl onions (each one measuring no larger than 1 inch, preferably much smaller)

1 cup plus 1 scant tablespoon pickling salt

7 cups malt vinegar, 5 percent acidity

$1/4$ cup sugar

2 cups water

3 tablespoons mustard seed

1 tablespoon whole black peppercorns

$1 1/2$ teaspoons whole allspice

3 small red chiles or $1 1/2$ teaspoons hot red pepper flakes

3 bay leaves

Scald the onions in boiling water for about 2 minutes, then quickly dip them into cold water. To make peeling easier, trim away the root ends with a very sharp knife; peel the onions. Layer the onions in a large bowl, alternately with the 1 cup of pickling salt. Refrigerate the onions for 24 hours, stirring several times once the juices from the onion begin to form. (Note: This step is called short brining, and helps ensure a crisp pickle because it actually draws out moisture from within the vegetable and firms up the flesh in the process.)

Fall
into
Winter

Drain the onions, then rinse well and drain again. Combine the vinegar, sugar, the remaining tablespoon of pickling salt, and the water in a nonaluminum saucepan; simmer for 5 minutes.

Wash 3 pint pickling jars. Prepare the lids according to the manufacturer's directions. Pack the onions in the jars, leaving $1/2$-inch head space. To each jar add 1 tablespoon of mustard seed, 1 teaspoon peppercorns, $1/2$ teaspoon whole allspice, 1 red pepper (or $1/2$ teaspoon pepper flakes), and 1 bay leaf. Pour the hot liquid over the onions to just cover them. Wipe each jar rim with a clean, damp cloth. Attach the lids. Process in a boiling water canner for 10 minutes (15 minutes at 1,001 to 6,000 feet; 20 minutes above 6,000 feet). Let the jars cool overnight without moving. Store in a cool, dark place.

surrounding that lovely new shoot is going to be soft in texture, with an off flavor. That's not to say, however, that at desperate moments I haven't carved around the bad part in order to make do with the good.

Fall

into

Winter

ONION VINEGAR

What a fabulous-tasting vinegar this is! Drizzle it over a platter of sliced fresh summer tomatoes and cucumbers, fresh mozzarella, and chopped basil. Perhaps sprinkle the whole affair with some roasted garlic to really dazzle your friends. Other vinegars can be used, such as a white wine vinegar, or even a fine-quality balsamic. If you do use the balsamic, cut back on the sugar by a tablespoon or so.

YIELD: *3 TO 4 PINTS*

> 6 large yellow onions, chopped
>
> 1/2 cup salt
>
> 3 cups distilled white vinegar
>
> 2 cups cider vinegar
>
> 2 tablespoons sugar

Sprinkle the onions with the salt and let stand at room temperature, covered, for 24 hours, stirring occasionally. Put the onions in a gallon crock. Bring the vinegars to a boil and stir in the sugar. Pour the vinegar over the onions and cover loosely. (The mixture will foam for a few days, so be sure to use a container that is large enough to prevent exploding, such as a food-grade plastic bucket with a lid.)

Steep for 2 weeks in a cool place, such as a garage or pantry. Then strain through a double thickness of cheesecloth into a bowl, pressing and squeezing through the cheesecloth to extract all the juice. Pour the vinegar into clean jars, and cork or cap. Store in a cool, dark place away from direct sunlight.

CELERY VINEGAR

Mild and wonderful with fresh lettuce.

YIELD: *3 TO 4 PINTS*

> 1 large bunch of fresh celery with leaves, chopped
> 1 large yellow onion, chopped
> 2 tablespoons celery seed
> 2 cups cider vinegar
> 3 cups distilled white vinegar
> 1 teaspoon salt
> 1 1/2 tablespoons sugar

Place the celery and onion in a gallon crock and add the celery seed. Bring the vinegars to a boil in a medium-size saucepan, add the salt and sugar, and stir until dissolved. Pour the vinegar over the chopped celery and cover. Let stand in a cool place, such as a garage or pantry, for at least 2 weeks. Strain through a double thickness of cheesecloth and let stand at room temperature, covered, overnight. Then pour the vinegar into clean containers (you may have a bit of sediment left on the bottom of the original container). Cork or cap, and store in a cool, dark place away from direct sunlight.

5

WINTER INTO SPRING

When the fruit trees stand bare in the cold, hard earth, and lovely summer tomatoes are a fanciful memory, winter has arrived. It's a season of intense contrasts, from vigorous outdoor activities such as cross-country skiing, to intimate conversations by a roaring fire. The body's inner clock is ticking away, keeping track of the shorter days and frosty nights.

Indeed, once our souls have been marked by that November chill, the only hope for soothing revival comes by way of the kitchen. Special toe-warming, satisfying preparations with a nurturing factor so high that if we were cats, we would be curled up and purring by the hearth.

There's soup, for one thing. Winter, after all, is Soup Season. And because homemade winter soups are as much nourishment for the soul as the body, they're worth the effort. Even if you don't do all those correct presoup things, such as stockpiling leftover bones and vegetable trimmings in the freezer, you can still throw together a powerful pot of soul soup.

In fact, a homemade pot of soup sheds brightness on the season's darker side like no other concoction. At its most basic level, a soup's preparation becomes a personal thing between the cook and the pot. It requires a good deal of time on the cook's part—standing over the pot reflecting on life and all its components, including, perhaps, all the winter vegetables that sing their sweetest song in the worst kind of weather.

Life's bound to look a little better after that.

Finally, the steaming pot makes it to the table, and everyone is served. Spoons dip, and a universal slurp is heard 'round the kitchen. It's a lip-scorching experience, outrageous in its spontaneous effect, awakening senses and lifting spirits. The weather turns from miserably cold to delightfully brisk, and, for a little while at least, the day's hard edges are soft and fuzzy.

Once again, Mother Nature has wisely presented us with an allium that embraces the season in which it thrives. Through the ages, leeks have been associated with cold-weather recipes: the simmering stews, hearty soups, and savory pies. Like other alliums, all it takes to tame the fiery flavor of leeks is a little bit of heat and time—two commodities that are in plentiful supply in most winter kitchens.

Leeks (Allium porrum)

At a time of year when most vegetables are but a twinkle in the farmer's eye, or nestled cozily in greenhouses waiting for the spring thaw, the leek is toughing out the winter in not-so-cozy fields.

Winter leeks were planted the previous May, and can be harvested by September. But if left in the field, they'll continue to grow into November. Once they've reached maturity, leeks will not get any bigger, and store nicely right where they are—in the ground. Growers continue to harvest the crop as needed, until the plants go to seed the following May.

Nippy weather is one thing, but one would think that surviving the freezing temperatures generally associated with winter might be beyond even the heartiest leek. However, these plucky bulbs are rarely affected by a big freeze. The upper leaves may be burned, but the plants won't die.

Common Varieties

Like all other alliums, leek varieties abound. In the raw state, their characteristics can range in flavor from heavy, rich, and bitter to light and slightly sweet. For cooking purposes, however, they can be used interchangeably since the flavors aren't quite as pronounced once heat has been applied. The following are some of the more readily available varieties grown in the United States.

Large American Flag—Also known as Broad London, this is the most common of the varieties, both commercially and in backyards. It's a hardy plant (which is saying a lot for a vegetable already considered stalwart by any standard), that can withstand colder climates better than most of the other varieties.

Blue Leaf—Similar to the Large American Flag, with leaves broader at the base and a deeper blue-green color.

Carentan—Also known as Winter leek, this variety is a very thick, shorter-stemmed strain with deep blue-green color and extremely erect leaves.

Blue Solaise—Considered an heirloom variety, the creamy white base of this particular leek blushes to a lovely violet when grown in colder climates.

Giant Musselburg—Known for its long, thick, white stem and drooping bright to medium-green leaves. This variety can grow from nine to fifteen inches in height, and swells to three inches in diameter at the base.

Selection and Preparation of Leeks

Harvesting leeks in winter is no easy task. The ground is cold and hard, and even the pros can't dig up more than three or four dozen an hour. Once the leeks are brought in from the field, every leek has to be cleaned thoroughly of dirt, with all traces of yellowed, frostbitten leaves removed.

Because all this work adds up to higher prices at the cash register, it's important to select the best leeks money can buy. Look for straight, cylindrical stalks with clean bases. Avoid leeks with dried-out leaves—a sure sign they aren't very fresh.

As the season heads into spring, be wary of leeks that are bulbous at the root end or that have a long, pencil-thin stalk shooting up out of the center of the otherwise flat leaves. Either situation is the result of harvesting after the plants have gotten too far along in their second spurt of growth. Such leeks will be woody, with less flavor.

At home, wash the leeks thoroughly and cut off the roots. Then slice each leek once from the green end almost to the base. Fan the two sections apart and pass the leek through running water to remove all the grit that has accumulated.

Winter into Spring

OSO Sweet Onion
(Allium cepa)

Jim Huston was lingering over a bowl of soup one beautiful spring afternoon in a Lancing, Michigan, restaurant. Sitting in the middle of this bowl of soup was a big ol' sweet Vidalia onion. The onion was richly flavored and light golden in color—the result of slow and deliberate cooking on the part of the chef.

Huston really liked that soup, and was impressed with this tasty use for the Vidalia. The son of an onion grower, himself an onion broker, Huston always appreciates a good onion that's been properly treated by a caring cook. And he's especially fond of the sweets.

"Why can't we have these all year long?" he lamented to his dining partner, John Battle, referring to the brief spring-into-summer appearances of such sweet onions as the Vidalia, Walla Walla, and Texas 1015. Battle, also a broker of onions, agreed that it would be a nice thing.

Unlike most polite lunchtime chatter, which rarely travels beyond the valet parking booth, Jim Huston's conversation led him to South America. He was determined to provide the United States with a super-sweet onion throughout the most unlikely of seasons, winter. To do so, the tenacious broker knew he had to go where the seasons were reversed from ours. Somewhere one could justifiably be sipping a piña colada at the exact same moment all of us northerners were experiencing snow-drifts up to our hubcaps. Someplace like South America.

So during the winter of 1986, Jim Huston crossed the equator and began his search for an undiscovered super-sweet onion. Eventually, he did find an onion with potential. Seeds were gathered from this variety of orb and Huston's researchers started tweaking around with it.

The results were highly encouraging, so Huston and his band of onion specialists tracked down the right place to grow their onion: in Chile, at the base of the Andes mountains, where the rich and fertile volcanic soil is so wonderful. Even though it took time, Huston put the onions through several test plantings. More important than passing time, he had to be sure that this sweet hybrid of an onion would consistently yield fabulous results.

By 1988, Huston's team felt that the OSO Sweet onion had attained the sort of super-sweet quality he had been looking for. And in 1989, they brought up their first one hundred tons to test the market. That shipment of sweet onion heaven moved about as smoothly through the marketplace as a hot fudge through ice cream. Huston was highly encouraged. In the years that followed, production improved and in each city where the OSO Sweet appeared, consumers ate it up.

But in 1992, Jim Huston retired. By now, the group of Chilean growers who had been producing the OSO Sweet for him knew what a remarkable product they had. They formed the South American Venture Incorporated (SAVIN), and urged Huston's associate (and lunch partner!), John Battle, to get on board so that a North American connection could be maintained.

Battle accepted the challenge, dedicating a large chunk of his company, Battle Produce, to carry on where Huston left off with the OSO Sweet. By the end of the 1994–95 season, more than six thousand tons of OSO Sweet onions had been consumed in the United States. And although that's just about one third of the average Walla Walla Sweet harvest, and a tenth of Vidalia's annual supply, John Battle considers it a giant step in the right direction: super-sweet onions all year long.

OSO Sweet Onion Facts

The OSO Sweet is harvested in Chile in early December. By the end of the month, it has found its way to North American markets, where lucky cooks can add it to their winter shopping lists through March. The OSO Sweet onion has a sweet, mild aroma, with no fumes when cut. The texture is crisp and juicy like an apple, with a subtle onion/fruity flavor. According to scientific tests conducted by Michigan State University, the OSO Sweet contains nearly 50 percent more sugar than the other sweet onion varieties.

OSO Sweet Onion Celebration

At the end of the 1994–95 season, to celebrate the OSO Sweet's success, a luncheon was held for a select few fans. John Battle had the last few remaining cases of onions shipped to New York City's restaurant Daniel. Owner/Chef Daniel Boulud had agreed to design a special luncheon for about fifty magazine, newspaper, and television food professionals from around the country. As you can see from the menu that Chef Boulud created, the OSO Sweet was showcased in a variety of delectable ways.

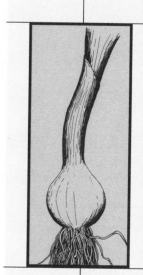

Luncheon Menu

—

Canapés
Crispy Toast of Tomato and OSO Sweet Onions with Cilantro

—

OSO Sweet Onion Tartlette with Duck Confit
and Aged Pyrenee Cheese

—

Chilled Vichyssoise of OSO Sweet Onions with Caviar

—

Roasted Bass with OSO Sweet Onion Compote, Morels,
Fava Beans, and a Caramelized OSO Sweet Onion Jus

—

Braised OSO Sweet Onions Stuffed with Squab,
Sweetbreads, Porcini, and a Black Truffle Sauce

—

Douceurs et Fantasie

—

APPETIZERS

ARTICHOKE, LEEK, AND HAM QUICHE

This is the kind of appetizer that tends to bring people together in a compact circle around the platter. Yes, it's that good.

YIELD: *8 SERVINGS*

2 (6-ounce) jars marinated artichoke hearts

3 cloves garlic, minced or pressed

1 cup finely chopped leeks (white and pale green portions only, 1
     large leek)

$^1/_2$ cup finely minced good-quality ham (such as Black Forest)

1 cup coarsely grated Swiss cheese

$^1/_2$ cup coarsely grated Parmesan cheese

1 $^1/_4$ cups ricotta cheese

$^1/_2$ cup sour cream

4 eggs

$^1/_2$ teaspoon salt

$^1/_4$ teaspoon white pepper

$^1/_4$ teaspoon dried thyme

1 11-inch quiche crust, prepared in a quiche or tart pan with a
     removable bottom, partially baked (page 207)

Preheat the oven to 375°F.

Drain the artichoke hearts, reserving the marinade. Chop the artichoke hearts into ¼-inch dice and set aside. Pour about half the reserved marinade into a skillet and heat over medium-high heat. Add the garlic and leeks and sauté until the leeks are tender and the marinade has reduced and thickened, about 5 minutes. Add the chopped artichoke hearts, stir to combine well, then remove from the heat and set aside to cool.

In a medium-size bowl, combine the ham, cheeses, sour cream, eggs, salt, pepper, and thyme. Stir in the artichoke mixture, then pour into the prepared quiche crust and bake for about 45 minutes, or until the filling is set and a knife inserted in the center comes out clean. (Note: The filling will still "jiggle" slightly.) Remove the quiche from the oven and serve either warm or at room temperature.

CHINESE POTSTICKERS

There's no getting around it, making potstickers from scratch is a time-consuming undertaking. Which is why winter is a good time to make them. This is when we tend to spend more time in the kitchen anyway, since the chilly days and nights keep us indoors. Recipes for filling potstickers are numerous; most dumpling aficionados have a pet concoction they've fine-tuned over the years. Typically, most potstickers contain a ground or chopped meat, as well as some vegetables and seasonings (fresh ginger, bean sprouts, and shredded cabbage are the standard ones). I happen to love the flavor and texture leeks bring to a potsticker filling.

And if you have any doubts, there are about 350 passengers on the Royal Viking Sun who can back me up. A few years ago, on the final leg of a cruise from San Francisco to Hong Kong, I was demonstrating the preparation of this, my favorite Chinese dumpling, to fellow passengers the day before docking in Shanghai. The Chef de Cuisine, Manfred Jaud, had never before seen the simple little device one can use to create these meat-filled Chinese dumplings. He has always assigned the task of filling and crimping— a time-consuming proposition—to a sous chef. So when I showed him how this procedure could be streamlined with the use of a dandy little hinged plastic potsticker press (available in most gourmet cookware and specialty-food shops for about $5), he was charmed. In fact, my parting gift to Chef Jaud before leaving the cruise in Hong Kong was a potsticker press. He said it was to be one piece of equipment that would remain locked in his desk drawer—"for all the time, for safekeeping, unless, of course, I am using it."

Like Chef Jaud, you would be surprised how simple it is to make these elegant little half-moon morsels traditionally called guotie (pronounced gwau-tyeh) with the help of a potsticker press. Once you have several dozen potstickers filled and sealed, the cooking begins. Unlike most Chinese dumplings, potstickers are fried on their flat bottoms before steaming. This gives them a slightly crunchy character and robust flavor. Once the bottoms are a nice golden hue, chicken broth is added and the pot is covered. The dumplings are steamed until the broth has been absorbed, the wrappers are translucent, and the potstickers are plump and tender.

One word of advice: To prevent potstickers from actually sticking to the bottom of the pan, it's best to use either a nonstick or a heavy-bottomed pan that cooks evenly and does not scorch.

YIELD: *30 TO 35 POTSTICKERS*

1 (10-ounce) package frozen chopped spinach, thawed and
squeezed dry

1 pound ground raw pork

1 cup minced leeks (white portion only)

$^1/_2$ cup minced green onion (white and green portions)

3 tablespoons minced fresh cilantro

2 tablespoons soy sauce

2 tablespoons dry sherry

1 tablespoon peeled and grated fresh ginger

2 teaspoons sesame oil

4 large cloves garlic, minced or pressed

1 package (containing at least 35, 3- to 3$^1/_2$-inch in diameter)
potsticker wrappers

1 egg white, lightly beaten

$^1/_2$ cup vegetable oil, such as peanut oil

2 cups canned or homemade chicken broth

Hot pepper oil (see Note)

Sesame-Soy Dipping Sauce (recipe follows)

In a bowl, combine the spinach, pork, leeks, green onion, cilantro, soy sauce, sherry, ginger, sesame oil, and garlic; mix well.

To assemble the potstickers, lay a wrapper on the potsticker press. Spoon 2 teaspoons of filling into the center of the wrapper. Brush the edges of the wrapper with lightly beaten egg white and press the 2 halves of the press together firmly. If you do not have a press, then after filling and brushing with egg white bring the edges together around the filling and, with your fingers, firmly crimp and press the edges to form a seal. Gently remove the folded and crimped dumpling and lay it

(*continued*)

on a flat surface, crimped edges up, to form a flat bottom. Repeat with the remainder of the filling and wrappers. (Note: The potstickers may be prepared to this point, covered lightly, and frozen, then sealed in airtight packaging and stored in the freezer for up to 6 months. When ready to serve, just proceed with the recipe; no thawing is necessary.)

To cook the potstickers, heat 2 tablespoons of the oil in a 12-inch heavy skillet over medium-high heat. Add as many potstickers as you can get in the pan without crowding, and cook until they're golden brown on the bottom, about 3 minutes. Add ½ cup of the broth and cover the pan immediately (as soon as the broth comes in contact with the oil there will be a major amount of splattering and sizzling, so be careful). Reduce the heat to medium-low and cook the dumplings until most of the liquid has been absorbed and the potstickers are nicely plumped and a deep golden brown on the bottom, about 5 to 7 minutes.

Remove from the heat and keep them warm in a 200°F. oven while you cook the remaining potstickers in the same manner. To serve, provide your guests with individual small dishes containing the sauces.

Note: This zesty-flavored oil is available in most Oriental food sections of well-stocked supermarkets. To make your own hot pepper oil, sauté 2 teaspoons dried chili flakes in ½ cup peanut oil for 3 minutes; remove from the heat and let the mixture stand until it is cool. Although not a traditional variation, I like to stir in 1 tablespoon chili-garlic sauce (also available in most Oriental food sections).

SESAME-SOY DIPPING SAUCE

Yield: about ⅔ cup

½ cup soy sauce

2 tablespoons Chinese black vinegar, or 1 tablespoon *each* white
    vinegar and Worcestershire sauce

1 tablespoon minced garlic

1 teaspoon minced fresh ginger root

1 teaspoon sesame oil

In a small container, combine all the ingredients.

Sweetheart Tart

A perfect nibble for February 14—when leeks are primo and love is in the air.

YIELD: *6 SERVINGS*

2 tablespoons olive oil

2 large leeks (white and pale green portions), thinly sliced
  (2½ cups)

½ cup finely chopped fine-quality ham (such as Black Forest)

2 tablespoons dry sherry

1½ cups coarsely grated Monterey Jack cheese

1 (9-inch) quiche crust, fully baked (page 207)

4 eggs

¾ cup half and half

½ teaspoon salt

¼ teaspoon white pepper

Preheat the oven to 350°F.

In a medium-size frying pan, heat the oil and sauté the leeks until soft. Add the ham and dry sherry and sauté for another few minutes to combine; set aside.

Sprinkle the cheese on the bottom of the cooked and cooled pie shell, then add the leek mixture. In a bowl, whisk together the eggs, half and half, salt, and white pepper and pour over the leeks. Place the tart on a baking sheet and bake until the center of the pie barely wiggles when gently bumped, about 40 minutes.

Mushroom
and Leek Pastries

Yield: 32 pieces

2 tablespoons olive oil

1 pound fresh mushrooms, finely minced

$^1/_2$ cup finely chopped leek (white and pale green portions only, 1 medium leek)

3 cloves garlic, minced

$^1/_3$ cup sherry

$^1/_2$ teaspoon salt

$^1/_2$ teaspoon white pepper

2 eggs

$^1/_2$ cup light cream or half-and-half

$1^1/_2$ cups fresh fine bread crumbs (a good-quality sourdough is preferable)

1 cup freshly grated Parmesan cheese

1 tablespoon minced fresh basil, or 1 teaspoon dried

2 sheets (each measuring 10 by 10 inches) puff pastry, thawed if frozen (pastry sheets are available in the frozen food section of most supermarkets)

In a large skillet or pot, heat the olive oil and sauté the mushrooms, leek, and garlic until the juice from the mushrooms has cooked away, about 5 minutes. Add the sherry, salt, and pepper, and continue cooking until most of the sherry has evaporated and the mixture has thickened and dried, about 5 minutes; remove from the heat and set aside to cool. When the mixture has cooled, stir in the eggs, cream, bread crumbs, Parmesan cheese, and basil. (The filling can be made to this point and refrigerated for 1 or 2 days before proceeding.)

Preheat the oven to 375°F. and grease several muffin or cupcake tins.

Roll each puff pastry sheet on a lightly floured surface to measure 12 by 12 inches. Cut the sheets into 3 by 3-inch squares. Lay the squares in the tins, pressing the center down slightly but not forcing the pastry completely onto the bottom. Drop a rounded spoonful of mushroom mixture in the center of each square. (The pastries can be prepared to this point, covered lightly with plastic wrap, and refrigerated for several hours.)

When ready to serve, place the muffin tins in the preheated oven and bake for 20 to 25 minutes, or until the edges of the pastry are nicely browned and the filling is hot. Remove the pastries from the tins using a fork, and serve while hot.

FABULOUS
LEEK SOUPS

At a time of year when a lot of what you see in the produce market is a pale re-flection of sunnier seasons, leeks are a welcome addition. This is when they're at their peak, which makes them an essential ingredient on a soup lover's shopping list. And on these frosty winter days, a big bowl of steaming-hot soup is the per-fect antifreeze for proper maintenance of body and soul.

Unfortunately, in a world gone convenience-conscious, people seem to have forgotten that soup doesn't come so much from a can as from the right side of your brain. You know, the creative, free-spirited side. The side that brings us inspired stir-fry dinners, jazzed-up salad dressings, and dynamite homemade barbecue sauce.

We all have a right side, it's just that some are more developed than others. Which explains the leek soup recipes that follow. Consider them as nothing more than road maps, guiding you along to a culinary destination. Whether you select the direct route or opt for the scenic tour is strictly up to you—and what you hear up there in the right side of your brain.

Leek Soup Au Gratin

Here's a steamy soup or simple entrée to help you enjoy the leek bounty. The soup is patterned after the classic French onion soup au gratin, but can be assembled in short order—to warm you deliciously on long winter nights.

Yield: 6 servings

6 tablespoons butter

4 cups thinly sliced leek rings (white and pale green portions only)

1 quart homemade or canned beef broth

2 to 3 tablespoons dry sherry, or 1 to 2 tablespoons brandy

$\frac{1}{4}$ teaspoon white pepper

$\frac{1}{4}$ teaspoon salt

6 Toasted French Bread Croutons (see below)

2 cups *each* coarsely grated Monterey Jack and Swiss cheese

In a large pot, melt the butter and sauté the leeks over medium heat until softened, about 5 minutes. Add the broth, sherry, pepper, and salt, and simmer for another 10 minutes to blend the flavors. Adjust the seasonings and ladle the soup into 6 ovenproof soup bowls. Add the French bread croutons, sprinkle each bowl with $\frac{1}{3}$ cup of the Monterey jack cheese, and then top with $\frac{1}{3}$ cup of the Swiss. Place the bowls under the broiler until the cheeses melt and turn slightly golden, about 30 seconds. Serve immediately.

TOASTED FRENCH BREAD CROUTONS: Preheat the oven to 325°F. Place 6 slices of French bread cut $\frac{1}{2}$ to $\frac{3}{4}$ inch thick on a baking sheet. Bake for about 20 minutes, until the bread is thoroughly dried out and lightly golden. About halfway through the process, spread both sides of each slice with a small amount of butter. These can be prepared several hours ahead.

LEEK AND POTATO SOUP
WITH SWISS CHEESE

YIELD: *6 SERVINGS*

2 tablespoons butter

4 cups chopped leeks (white and pale green portions only, about 2
    pounds)

1 medium yellow onion, chopped

4 medium russet potatoes, peeled and chopped

4 cups homemade or canned chicken broth

1 1/2 cups light cream

Salt and white pepper to taste

1 1/2 to 2 cups grated Swiss cheese

In a large pot, melt the butter and sauté the leeks and onion for 3 minutes. Add the
potatoes and broth, cover and simmer for 15 minutes, or until the potatoes are tender. In batches, place the mixture in a blender or food processor and blend until
smooth. Return the soup to the pot, stir in the cream, and bring almost to a boil.
Ladle into soup bowls and top each serving with a portion of the grated Swiss
cheese.

Bombay Leek Bisque

Yield: 8 to 10 servings

6 medium white potatoes, peeled and diced to measure (8 cups)

2 cups chopped leeks (white and pale green portions only, about 1
  pound)

2 cloves garlic, minced

6 cups homemade or canned chicken broth

$^1/_4$ cup chopped fresh cilantro

1 tablespoon curry powder

$^1/_2$ teaspoon *each* salt and white pepper

4 tablespoons ($^1/_2$ stick) butter or margarine

1 to $1^1/_2$ quarts light cream

Combine the potatoes, leeks, garlic, chicken broth, cilantro, curry powder, salt, and pepper in a large pot. Cook, tightly covered, over medium heat for about 30 minutes, or until the potatoes are soft. In small batches, puree the potato mixture in a blender. Return the soup to the pot, and stir in the butter and a quart of the cream. If the mixture seems too thick, add additional cream as needed. Adjust the seasonings, reheat, and serve.

CREAMY CORN
AND LEEK SOUP

YIELD: 8 SERVINGS

1 tablespoon olive oil

2 medium leeks (white and light green portions), thinly sliced
(3 cups)

$^1/_2$ cup chopped yellow onion

3 cups milk

3 cups half and half

2 cups homemade or canned chicken broth

1 teaspoon salt

$^1/_2$ teaspoon freshly ground black pepper

3 cups frozen corn (when in season, substitute kernels from the cobs
of 4 ears of sweet corn)

1 ($16^1/_2$-ounce) can creamed corn

In a large pot over medium heat, warm the oil and sauté the leeks and onion for about 3 minutes. Add the milk, half and half, chicken broth, salt, and pepper and bring the mixture to a boil. Reduce the heat and simmer until the leeks and onions are very tender, about 15 minutes. Add the corn, cover, and continue cooking for about 10 minutes. Adjust the seasonings and serve.

CLAM AND LEEK CHOWDER

YIELD: 6 SERVINGS

4 slices bacon, diced

1 to 2 tablespoons reserved bacon grease

2 cups chopped leeks (white and pale green portions only, 1 pound)

1 cup finely chopped celery

4 medium potatoes, peeled and diced

3 (6-ounce) cans chopped clams, drained, juice reserved

1 quart light cream

Salt and white pepper to taste

$^{1}/_{8}$ teaspoon dried sage

1 $^{1}/_{2}$ tablespoons flour

1 $^{1}/_{2}$ tablespoons butter or margarine, softened

Chopped fresh flat-leaf parsley for garnish

Sauté the bacon until crisp in the bottom of a soup pot. Drain all but 1 or 2 tablespoons of fat from the pot. Add the leeks and sauté until just barely tender, about 10 minutes; add the celery and continue to sauté for a moment more. Add the potatoes and the drained clam juice (do not add the clams yet or they will be tough), and enough water to just barely cover the potatoes. Simmer the mixture, uncovered, until the potatoes are tender, 20 to 30 minutes, adding more water as necessary to keep the vegetables covered.

When the potatoes are tender, stir in the cream, and season with the salt, pepper, and sage; bring the mixture to a simmer. Meanwhile, in a small cup, blend together the flour and softened butter to form a roux. Stir this into the soup and continue stirring until the soup thickens slightly. Add the clams and simmer gently just until clams are heated through, about 1 minute. (Note: This broth is not very thick—if you want it thicker, add more flour.) Garnish with the chopped parsley and serve.

POTATO, PARSNIP,
AND LEEK CHOWDER

A traditional New England recipe with a few modifications.

YIELD: *6 SERVINGS*

4 slices bacon

1 pound parsnips

1 pound (about 3 medium) russet potatoes

1 tablespoon reserved bacon fat

1 cup chopped leeks (white and pale green portions)

3 cups homemade or canned chicken broth

1 teaspoon salt

2 cups light cream

About $\frac{1}{4}$ teaspoon white pepper

2 tablespoons butter (optional)

Blanch the bacon in boiling water for 5 minutes; drain and dice. Peel the parsnips and potatoes and dice into $\frac{1}{2}$-inch pieces. Place the diced potatoes in cold water to keep them from discoloring. Brown the bacon bits in a 3-quart saucepan. When crisp, remove from the pan and set aside. Remove all but 1 tablespoon of bacon fat from the pan, then sauté the leeks in the remaining bacon fat until softened and lightly browned, about 15 minutes. Meanwhile, bring the broth to a boil. When the leeks are cooked, add the parsnips and potatoes to the pan and pour in just enough of the boiling broth to cover the vegetables. Add the salt, bring the mixture to a boil, reduce the heat, cover, and simmer for 15 minutes, or until the vegetables are tender. Add the light cream and heat through (do not allow cream to boil). Add the pepper and more salt if desired; stir in the butter (if desired) just before serving and garnish with the crumbled pieces of bacon.

Apple Vichyssoise

Apples give a new twist to an old favorite.

Yield: *4 servings*

- 1 teaspoon butter or margarine
- 2 large leeks, washed and thinly sliced (white and pale green portions)
- 1 small yellow onion, chopped
- 3 baking potatoes, peeled and chopped
- 2 cups homemade or canned chicken broth
- 1 cup unsweetened applesauce
- Pinch of ground cinnamon
- $\frac{1}{4}$ cup heavy cream or low-fat yogurt
- Thinly sliced apple and chopped fresh flat-leaf parsley for garnish

Melt the butter over medium heat in a medium pot. Add the leeks and onion and cook until soft, about 10 minutes. Add the potatoes and cook over medium heat for 3 minutes. Add the broth and applesauce and simmer uncovered for 25 minutes, or until the potatoes are soft.

Puree the mixture in batches in a food processor or blender until very smooth. Stir in the cinnamon and refrigerate until cold. Just before serving, stir in the cream or yogurt. Divide the soup among 4 bowls and garnish with the sliced apple and chopped parsley.

CURRIED LEEK SOUP

YIELD: 6 SERVINGS

About 1 $^1/_2$ pounds leeks (white and pale green portions), cut into
      1-inch chunks (6 cups)

3 cups homemade or canned chicken broth

1 cup peeled, cored, and diced apples

1 cup diced yellow onions

1 cup diced potato (a red, white, or yellow Fin variety would be
      best)

1 large tomato, peeled, seeded, and diced (about $^3/_4$ cup)

$^1/_2$ cup diced carrot

1 teaspoon dried basil

$^1/_2$ teaspoon salt, or more to taste

$^1/_2$ teaspoon curry powder

$^1/_4$ teaspoon freshly ground black pepper, or more to taste

Combine all of the ingredients in a large pot. Bring the mixture to a boil over medium heat and simmer, covered, for 20 minutes, or until the potatoes and leeks are tender. Remove the soup from the heat and cool slightly, then blend the mixture in several batches in a blender or food processor until very smooth. To serve, reheat gently until heated through.

HERB-POACHED LEEKS
WITH PEPPERCORN VINAIGRETTE

YIELD: 4 TO 6 SERVINGS

6 large leeks, trimmed and halved lengthwise

2 cups homemade or canned chicken broth

$^1/_2$ cup dry white wine

3 carrots, coarsely chopped

3 celery stalks, coarsely chopped

1 medium yellow onion, coarsely chopped

6 sprigs fresh thyme

$^1/_2$ cup coarsely chopped fresh flat-leaf parsley

About 2 tablespoons whole black peppercorns

PEPPERCORN VINAIGRETTE:

2 tablespoons fresh lemon juice

2 tablespoons white wine vinegar

1 teaspoon Worcestershire sauce

1 teaspoon Dijon mustard

$^1/_2$ teaspoon coarsely ground peppercorns (a mixture of black, white, and green is a nice choice, though all black is fine)

$^1/_4$ teaspoon salt

$^2/_3$ cup salad oil ($^1/_3$ cup olive oil and $^1/_3$ cup canola oil is a nice blend)

(continued)

Place the leeks in a large, heavy skillet along with the chicken broth, wine, carrots, celery, onion, thyme, parsley, and peppercorns. Bring the broth to a boil over medium-high heat, then reduce the heat and simmer, covered, for 15 minutes, or until the leeks are tender. Remove the skillet from the heat and lift the leeks from the flavored broth with tongs or a wide, slotted spatula (refrigerate or freeze the broth for another day's batch of homemade soup). Try to keep the leeks as whole as possible.

To make the vinaigrette, in a small bowl, whisk together the lemon juice, vinegar, Worcestershire sauce, Dijon mustard, peppercorns, and salt. Whisk in the oil, then adjust the seasonings.

To serve, arrange the hot or slightly cooled leeks on a lovely platter, and at the moment before serving, drizzle them with the Peppercorn Vinaigrette.

Leek Salad with Ham and Cranberries

This recipe is from Oregon's premier fishing lodge, the Steamboat Inn. The cranberries definitely give it a holiday sort of feeling, so this might be just the Thanksgiving side dish you've been looking for.

Yield: *4 servings*

12 small leeks

6 cups homemade or canned chicken broth

$1/2$ cup fresh or frozen whole cranberries

1 tablespoon minced fresh flat-leaf parsley

$1/4$ cup olive oil

2 tablespoons vegetable oil

2 tablespoons lemon juice

1 teaspoon Dijon mustard

2 cloves garlic, minced

$1/2$ to 1 teaspoon salt

Freshly ground black pepper to taste

1 cup minced good-quality ham (such as Black Forest)

Wash and trim the leeks, using all the white portion and 4 inches of the green; set aside. In a saucepan, bring the chicken broth to a boil and add the cranberries. Cook the berries just until they begin to pop, about 5 minutes. Remove with a slotted spoon and set aside.

Add the leeks to the broth. Reduce the heat and simmer for 10 minutes, un-

(continued)

til the leeks are softened. Remove from the broth and cool. Save the broth for another use—it will have a wonderful flavor.

In a small bowl, combine the parsley, the oils, lemon juice, mustard, garlic, salt, and pepper. Mix well. Combine the ham and cranberries and add 2 tablespoons of the dressing, tossing gently to mix. Arrange 3 leeks on each of 4 salad plates and drizzle them with a small amount of the remaining dressing. Top with a portion of the ham/cranberry mixture.

Sun-Dried Tomatoes
and Swiss Sandwich

A delicious sandwich to keep in mind this winter for that first cross-country ski outing.

Yield: 4 sandwiches

$^1/_2$ cup drained sun-dried tomatoes

$^1/_2$ cup chopped pickled Greek peperoncini

1 (2$^1/_4$-ounce) can sliced black olives, drained

$^1/_3$ cup Fresh Spinach and Leek Presto Sauce (page 310)

$^1/_4$ cup mayonnaise, or more to taste

4 French rolls, split

Thinly sliced Swiss cheese

In a bowl, combine the sun-dried tomatoes, peperoncini, olives, Presto sauce, and the mayonnaise. Spread one side of each roll with a portion of the filling, a few slices of Swiss cheese, and a little more mayonnaise on the inside of the upper half of the rolls, if desired. Serve at once or wrap each sandwich with plastic wrap and refrigerate until ready to serve.

SUPER BOWL SUNDAY SUBS

These marinated vegetable salad submarine sandwiches, featuring the OSO Sweet onion, are a delightful way to tailgate in your own living room during this annual winter television event.

YIELD: *8 SERVINGS*

2 red bell peppers

2 OSO Sweet onions (or any sweet onion variety, such as Vidalia or
    Walla Walla)

$3/_4$ pound fresh mushrooms

1 small zucchini

1 small yellow squash

$2/_3$ cup sliced black pitted olives

$3/_4$ cup olive oil

3 tablespoons white wine vinegar

2 large cloves garlic, minced

$1^1/_2$ teaspoons Italian herb seasoning

$1^1/_2$ teaspoons salt

8 (9-inch) submarine sandwich rolls

Lettuce

12 slices provolone cheese

$1^1/_2$ pounds sliced deli meats (the combination is up to you)

Wash the peppers and prick them in several places with a fork. Place them on a baking sheet and roast under the broiler, turning occasionally, until the skin is blistered on all sides, about 6 minutes. Remove from the oven and place in a plastic bag in the freezer for 10 minutes to cool quickly (the steam helps loosen the skins).

Meanwhile, peel and slice the OSO Sweet onions into rings; cut the large rings in half. Wipe, trim, and thinly slice the mushrooms. Thinly slice the zucchini and yellow squash, then cut the slices into quarters; measure 1 cup of each.

Once the peppers have cooled, peel away the skin, then cut off the stem end and remove the seeds and membranes. Thinly slice the peppers and cut the slices crosswise into halves. Place the vegetables and sliced olives in a large shallow pan. In a small bowl, whisk together the oil, vinegar, garlic, and seasonings. Pour the mixture over the vegetables, gently toss to coat, then refrigerate for several hours, tossing occasionally so the vegetables will remain coated with the marinade.

At serving time, heat the oven to 350°F. Slice the rolls in half lengthwise, leaving one side still attached. Place the rolls on a baking sheet and toast for 2 to 3 minutes or until lightly browned. Remove from the oven. Line the bottom of each roll with some lettuce. Cut the cheese slices in half. On each roll, overlap 4 half-slices of cheese, then arrange the deli meats on top. Top with 1 cup of the marinated vegetable mixture. Cut subs in half if desired. Serve at once.

Leek Frittata

— — —

Yield: 6 servings

> ¹/₄ cup olive oil
>
> 2 large leeks (each measuring about 1¹/₂ inches at the root end),
>> cleaned, white and pale green portions, thinly sliced into
>> rings
>
> 8 eggs
>
> 2 tablespoons sour cream
>
> ¹/₃ cup freshly grated Parmesan cheese, plus additional for serving
>
> 2 tablespoons snipped fresh chives, plus chopped fresh chives for
>> garnish
>
> ¹/₂ teaspoon salt
>
> ¹/₄ teaspoon white pepper

In a 10-inch skillet or omelette pan (preferably one with a nonstick surface), warm 2 tablespoons of the olive oil over medium-high heat. Add the leeks and sauté, stirring occasionally, until the leeks are tender, 7 or 8 minutes.

Meanwhile, break the eggs into a bowl and whisk lightly. Whisk in the sour cream, Parmesan cheese, snipped chives, salt, and pepper. Once the leeks have cooled, transfer them to the egg mixture with a slotted spoon and stir well to combine.

Preheat the broiler.

Add the remaining 2 tablespoons of oil to the skillet and warm it over medium heat. Gently pour in the egg and leek mixture, reduce the heat to low, and cook slowly without stirring for about 8 minutes, or until the eggs are set and only the top remains uncooked. Remove the pan from the burner and place it under the broiler for 1 to 3 minutes, until the frittata top is lightly browned and the eggs are completely set.

To serve, loosen the underside of the frittata with a large spatula and slide it onto a serving platter. Sprinkle with additional Parmesan cheese, a sprinkling of chives, and serve. At the table, cut each diner a generous wedge.

LEEK AND
BLACK OLIVE TARTS

These are easy to make if you use frozen puff pastry.

YIELD: FOUR 4-INCH TARTS

6 tablespoons olive oil

8 cups very thinly sliced leeks (white and pale green portions, about
2 pounds)

1 clove garlic, minced

8 ounces fresh or defrosted frozen puff pastry

8 black niçoise olives, pitted and cut into quarters

Heat the olive oil in a skillet over medium-high heat. Add the leeks and garlic and cook until they are softened, about 10 minutes, stirring often to prevent burning; set aside.

On a floured surface, roll out the puff pastry to a thickness of $^1/_4$ inch. Cut out four $4^1/_2$-inch circles and place them on a parchment-lined or greased baking sheet. Place in the freezer until ready to use.

Preheat the oven to 400°F. Remove the puff pastry from the freezer. Place a 4-inch tartlet tin in the center of each circle of dough. Place another baking sheet on top of the tins. Then place a heavy pan on top of the second baking sheet (to weigh down the tartlet tins as the puff pastry puffs up around the tins, creating a large "cup," which you will later fill with the cooked leeks). Bake the puff pastry in the preheated oven for 15 minutes, or until golden brown. Remove them from the oven, let cool slightly (about 5 minutes), then gently pry the tarts loose from the tins.

Divide the leeks among the 4 tarts, spreading them to cover the bottom. Top with the quartered olives and serve immediately.

LEEKS WITH PEPPERS AND CHEESE IN CUSTARD

This makes a wonderful lunch or light supper. It chills beautifully, so it's also at home on a picnic.

YIELD: *4 SERVINGS*

4 large leeks, trimmed of dark green tops, washed

2 tablespoons butter

2 shallots, minced

1 jalapeño pepper, seeded and minced

$^1/_2$ red bell pepper, seeded and chopped

$^1/_2$ cup diced cooked ham

2 tablespoons Madeira or dry sherry

1 cup heavy cream

2 eggs

$^1/_4$ teaspoon salt

$^1/_8$ teaspoon white pepper

$^1/_2$ cup grated Jarlsberg or well-aged Swiss cheese

$^1/_4$ cup freshly grated Parmesan cheese

$^1/_8$ teaspoon freshly grated nutmeg

Preheat the oven to 350°F. Lightly grease a 2-inch-deep, $1^1/_4$-quart baking dish.

Cook the leeks in a pot in boiling salted water until tender, about 10 minutes. Drain; cut in half lengthwise, and reserve.

Melt the butter in a medium-size skillet over medium heat. Add the shallots, peppers, and ham and sauté for 3 minutes. Stir in the Madeira and cook, stirring constantly, until all the liquid has evaporated, about 2 minutes. Remove from the heat.

Layer the leeks in the bottom of the baking dish, and spoon the ham mixture between the leeks.

Whisk together the cream and eggs in a bowl until smooth. Stir in the salt and pepper, the Jarlsberg, 2 tablespoons of the Parmesan, and the nutmeg. Gently pour this mixture over the leeks. Sprinkle the remaining 2 tablespoons of the Parmesan over the top. Bake until puffed and golden, about 30 minutes. Cut through the leeks using a very sharp knife, and serve squares or rectangles directly from the baking dish.

ENTRÉES

BOUILLABAISSE

A true bouillabaisse of Marseille is made with at least eight different kinds of fish. I've opted for five kinds. Do make sure they're very fresh. You'll be delighted with the results.

YIELD: *8 SERVINGS*

> 2 dozen fresh clams, well scrubbed (use only clams that are
> tightly closed)
>
> $^1/_4$ cup cornmeal
>
> 1 tablespoon plus 1 teaspoon salt
>
> 4 slices bacon, cut into 1-inch pieces
>
> 2 carrots, peeled and sliced into $^1/_4$-inch-thick rounds
>
> 1 green bell pepper, cored, seeded, and diced
>
> 1 onion, diced
>
> 3 cups chopped leeks (white and pale green portions only, about
> 3 large leeks)
>
> 5 new potatoes (about 1 pound), quartered (consider a yellow-
> fleshed variety, such as Yukon Gold)
>
> 2 (14$^1/_2$-ounce) cans plum tomatoes, coarsely chopped
>
> 1 cup homemade or canned chicken broth
>
> 1 cup dry red wine
>
> 1 bay leaf
>
> $^1/_2$ teaspoon dried thyme
>
> $^1/_4$ teaspoon white pepper, or to taste

(continued)

All the countries of Great Britain have a national emblem from the plant world. England chose the rose; Ireland has the shamrock; for Scotland, it's the thistle; and for Wales, it's the leek. The connection between leeks and Wales harkens back to an ancient victory over the Saxons, when Welsh soldiers gained the upper hand by tucking leeks into their hats to distinguish themselves from their enemies.

Winter into **S**pring

Pinch of sugar

2 dozen jumbo raw shrimp, shelled and deveined

2 pounds raw scallops

1 1/2 pounds boneless red snapper, cut into chunks

1/2 pound fresh cooked crab meat

Chopped fresh basil leaves for garnish

8 Garlic-Basil Croutons (recipe follows; optional)

1 1/2 cups Rouille (recipe follows)

To clean out the clams, place them in a large pot and cover them with cold water. Sprinkle with the cornmeal and 1 tablespoon of the salt. Let stand for 1 hour. Rinse, and drain.

Sauté the bacon in a large kettle or Dutch oven until crisp, about 5 minutes. Drain off all but 3 tablespoons of the bacon grease, then add the carrots, green pepper, onion, leeks, and potatoes. Cover and cook, stirring occasionally, for 10 minutes. Stir in the tomatoes, broth, wine, bay leaf, the remaining 1 teaspoon of salt, the thyme, white pepper, and sugar. Simmer, uncovered, for 10 minutes.

Add the shrimp, clams, scallops, snapper, and crab meat to the kettle. Cover, and cook until the clams open and the fish is cooked through, about 10 to 12 minutes.

To serve, place an assortment of fish in large individual bowls; then ladle the vegetables and soup over the fish. Sprinkle each serving with the basil garnish, then top with several croutons and a dollop of rouille, passing more at the table.

GARLIC-BASIL CROUTONS

YIELD: *6 CUPS*

4 tablespoons (1/2 stick) butter

3 cloves garlic, minced

1 tablespoon chopped fresh basil

1 (12-inch-long) loaf of French bread, cut into 1-inch chunks (about
      6 cups)

Salt and freshly ground black pepper to taste

Preheat the oven to 350°F.

Combine the butter, garlic, and basil in a pot over medium heat. When the butter melts, drizzle the bread with the butter-herb mixture. Sprinkle with salt and pepper, then spread the cubes on a baking sheet and bake for 15 minutes, until the cubes are golden.

ROUILLE

YIELD: ABOUT 1½ CUPS

1 red bell pepper
1 small hot red chile pepper, cored and carefully seeded
4 cloves garlic
1 medium potato, peeled and cooked
½ teaspoon salt
Freshly ground black pepper to taste
¾ cup olive oil
A few drops of fresh lemon juice

Prick the bell pepper with a sharp knife, then put under the broiler, turning it frequently as the surface bubbles and turns dark. Place the roasted pepper in a plastic bag and freeze for about 10 minutes so the steam can loosen the skin. Remove from the freezer, then peel and remove the seeds and membranes. Place the roasted pepper in a food processor, add the chile pepper, garlic, potato, salt, and freshly ground black pepper. Puree until smooth. While the machine is running, slowly drizzle in the olive oil. Process until the mixture is thick and smooth. Transfer the rouille to a bowl and add the lemon juice.

SEAFOOD AND SAUSAGE GUMBO

❧ ❧ ❧

You'll spare no expense with this "down-home" gumbo: crab, lobster, shrimp, and scallops round out the seafood platter. But the combo is dynamite. You could leave the okra out, but then you couldn't call it gumbo. I like to serve this over a moist medium-grain white rice.

YIELD: *8 SERVINGS*

12 ounces kielbasa or Cajun sausage, cut into 1-inch slices

¼ cup olive oil

12 ounces okra, stems removed

3 large leeks (white and pale green portions only), coarsely chopped

1 red bell pepper, seeded and coarsely chopped

1 green bell pepper, seeded and coarsely chopped

6 cloves garlic, finely minced

6 cups homemade or canned chicken broth

2 (14½ ounce) cans plum tomatoes, slightly crushed, undrained

2 teaspoons ground cumin

½ teaspoon cayenne

½ teaspoon salt

¼ teaspoon hot pepper sauce

½ teaspoon white pepper

1 bay leaf

1 pound medium or large raw shrimp, peeled and deveined

12 ounces raw scallops, rinsed and drained

12 ounces cooked lobster meat

8 ounces cooked crab meat

2 tablespoons chopped fresh flat-leaf parsley

In a large, heavy pot or Dutch oven, sauté the sausage over medium heat until brown, about 10 minutes. Remove it from the pot with a slotted spoon and set aside.

Add the oil to the pot, along with the okra, the leeks, bell peppers, and garlic. Stir, and cook for about 10 minutes or until the leeks are softened. Add the chicken broth, tomatoes, cumin, cayenne, salt, white pepper, and bay leaf. Simmer, uncovered, for 30 minutes. Add the shrimp and scallops to the gumbo and simmer for another 5 minutes. Remove the bay leaf, if you can find it, then add the lobster, crabmeat, and parsley, adjust the seasonings, and heat through for 2 to 3 minutes. Serve immediately.

LAMB STEW WITH
WINTER-INTO-SPRING VEGETABLES

It used to be a French tradition to include turnips in every lamb stew. But by the turn of the century, potatoes began taking their place. Today, a lamb stew is frequently made with a mixture of both. This recipe incorporates the last of the winter leeks with many of the first-of-spring vegetables.

YIELD: 6 SERVINGS

2 tablespoons vegetable oil

3 pounds boneless lamb shoulder, trimmed of excess fat, cut into
1 1/2-inch cubes

1 tablespoon butter

4 medium leeks (white and pale green portions), coarsely chopped
(about 3 cups)

3 cloves garlic, finely chopped

2 tablespoons all-purpose flour

1 tablespoon tomato paste

3 medium tomatoes, peeled, seeded, and diced (during winter
months, substitute 2 [16-ounce] cans whole, peeled tomatoes,
drained)

Several sprigs fresh thyme, or 1/2 teaspoon dried

1 bay leaf

Salt and freshly ground black pepper to taste

VEGETABLE MONTAGE:

18 pearl onions

1 1/2 pounds small red or white new potatoes

1 1/4 pounds carrots

1 1/4 pounds turnips

2 tablespoons butter

Salt to taste

1 cup fresh or frozen peas

Heat the oil in a deep, heavy-bottomed frying pan over high heat. Working in batches if necessary, add the meat and brown on all sides; remove the meat from the pan. Add the butter, leeks, and garlic to the pan, sprinkle with the flour, and cook, stirring frequently, for 1 to 2 minutes, until the leeks are lightly browned. Return the lamb to the pan and add enough hot water to barely cover. Add the tomato paste, tomatoes, thyme, bay leaf, and salt and pepper. Bring to a boil, reduce the heat, and simmer until the lamb is tender when pierced with a sharp knife, 1 to 1½ hours. Skim any fat from the surface of the stew. (The stew may be prepared to this point up to 48 hours ahead, covered tightly, and refrigerated.)

To make the vegetable montage, peel the onions; cut the unpeeled potatoes, carrots, and turnips into 1-inch chunks. Simmer the potatoes, carrots, turnips, and onions in a saucepan with the butter, salt, and just enough water to barely cover the vegetables, until they are tender and most of the water has evaporated, about 30 minutes. During the final 5 minutes of cooking, add the fresh peas (if fresh are unavailable, add the frozen green peas at the end of the cooking phase).

When ready to serve, skim the fat, reheat the stew, then gently fold in the Vegetable Montage and cook for 10 or 15 minutes longer. Adjust the seasonings and serve the stew in a deep platter.

Winter Stew
of Beef and Leeks
in Chives-Laced Popovers

YIELD: *6 SERVINGS*

2 tablespoons olive oil

2 pounds stewing beef (such as boneless chuck), cut into 2-inch
 cubes

3 large leeks (white and pale green portions), halved lengthwise and
 chopped (3 cups)

2 tablespoons all-purpose flour

1/4 cup balsamic vinegar

2 cups water

1 cup homemade or canned beef broth

1 cup dry red wine

2 bay leaves

Salt and freshly ground black pepper to taste

Popovers (recipe follows)

In a heavy-bottomed, flameproof casserole or Dutch oven, warm the oil and sauté the beef over medium-high heat until browned, 8 to 10 minutes. Add the leeks and sauté for another 3 to 4 minutes, stirring often. Sprinkle the leeks and beef with the flour and cook for another 2 minutes to brown the flour lightly. Whisk in the balsamic vinegar and deglaze the pan, scraping up all the crusty-brown bits on the bottom. Add the water, broth, wine, and bay leaves, reduce the heat, cover, and simmer until the meat is very tender, about 2 hours. You may need to add additional wine and broth during the cooking process to keep a nice sauce.

To serve, arrange 2 popovers on each of 6 dinner plates. Split open the popovers and spoon the stew into them.

POPOVERS

YIELD: 12 POPOVERS

> 1 cup all-purpose flour
>
> 1 cup milk
>
> 1/2 cup half and half
>
> 4 eggs
>
> 1 tablespoon butter, melted
>
> 1 tablespoon snipped fresh chives
>
> 1/2 teaspoon salt
>
> 1/2 teaspoon sugar

Preheat the oven to 475°F. Brush each compartment of a 12-cup muffin tin with oil or melted butter.

About 1 hour before the stew is ready, in a bowl, whisk together all the ingredients. Once well combined, continue mixing for 2 to 3 minutes (you may use an electric mixer or blender, if desired).

Heat the muffin tin in the oven for 2 minutes. Remove the tin from the oven and quickly fill each muffin cup about half to three quarters full with the batter. Bake for 15 minutes, then reduce the heat to 350° and bake until the popovers are a rich golden brown and nicely puffed, about 20 minutes more. Do not open the oven door during baking, if at all possible.

Hearty Beef and Leek Stew

— — —

This is a classic offering, to be sure: a delicious medley of winter vegetables and beef.
Don't forget the buttered noodles on the side.

Yield: 6 servings

1/4 cup olive oil

2 pounds boneless beef chuck, cut into 1-inch cubes

Freshly ground black pepper to taste

5 leeks (about 1 1/2 inches in diameter; white portion and 2 inches of
       green), well rinsed and coarsely chopped

4 carrots, peeled and cut into 3-inch lengths

4 parsnips, peeled and cut into 3-inch lengths

1/4 pound mushrooms, halved

1 1/2 cups homemade or canned beef broth

1 1/2 cups good-quality red wine (an Oregon Pinot, or California
       Beaujolais, or Burgundy, for example)

2 tablespoons red currant jelly

2 teaspoons dried thyme leaves, crumbled

1 teaspoon dried rosemary leaves, crumbled

6 cups halved new potatoes (red, white, or Yukon Gold)

8 cloves garlic, minced

2 (16-ounce) cans plum tomatoes, drained

1/4 cup chopped fresh flat-leaf parsley

Preheat the oven to 350°F.

    Heat the olive oil in a large skillet.

    Thoroughly brown the beef in small batches in the skillet over medium-high
heat, about 6 minutes per batch. Transfer the beef to a heavy flameproof casserole

and sprinkle generously with black pepper. Place the leeks, carrots, parsnips, and mushrooms in the same skillet. Sauté over medium heat to brown them slightly, 8 to 10 minutes. Remove the vegetables from the skillet and set them aside.

Add the broth and wine to the skillet, bring to a boil, and deglaze the pan by scraping up any brown bits from the bottom. Stir in the red currant jelly, thyme, and rosemary. Cook for 1 minute, then pour over the meat in the casserole. Add the potatoes and garlic to the casserole, and bring the mixture to a boil. Cover, transfer to the oven, and bake for 45 minutes.

Remove the casserole from the oven and add the reserved vegetables. Stir in the tomatoes and the parsley, adjust the seasonings, and return the casserole to the oven. Bake, uncovered, until the beef is very tender, about 45 minutes more. Serve.

Salmon with OSO Sweet Onion Ringlets

Michel Richard, owner/chef of Citrus restaurant in Los Angeles, developed this wonderful melange of onions and salmon. He used it in his own cookbook, "Home Cooking with a French Accent," and was kind enough to let me use it here as well. Merci! Michel.

YIELD: *4 SERVINGS*

ONION CRUST:

  $^3/_4$ pound OSO Sweet onions

  1 cup all-purpose flour

  1 quart peanut oil

ONION SAUCE:

  2 tablespoons unsalted butter

  $^3/_4$ pound OSO Sweet onions, halved and thinly sliced (3 cups)

  $^1/_4$ cup Champagne vinegar or other white wine vinegar

  1 quart homemade or canned unsalted chicken stock

  $^1/_4$ cup heavy cream (optional)

  Salt and freshly ground black pepper to taste

  4 ($^3/_4$-inch-thick) boneless and skinless salmon fillets, 6 to 8 ounces
     each

  Flour and beaten egg for coating fish

To make the onion crust, slice the onions into $^1/_8$-inch-thick rings and separate. Toss the rings with the flour. Heat the oil in a pot to 325°F. Shake off the excess flour from the rings and fry a quarter of them just until light golden brown, about 5 to 8 minutes. They will be refried later for garnish. Set this batch aside in the warm oven on paper towels. Fry the remaining onions in 2 or 3 batches until very dark gold and crunchy, about 15 minutes. Drain well on paper towels, then coarsely chop the browned onion rings for coating the salmon.

To make the sauce, melt the butter in a large, heavy saucepan. Add the onions, cover, and cook over medium-low heat, stirring occasionally until translucent, about 10 minutes. Increase the heat to medium-high and stir the onions until golden brown, about 3 minutes. Pour in the vinegar and boil until reduced to a thick glaze, about 1 to 2 minutes. Add the chicken stock and simmer, stirring occasionally until the mixture is reduced to $1\frac{1}{2}$ cups, about 40 minutes. Puree the mixture in a blender until very smooth. Return the sauce to the rinsed saucepan, add the cream, if using, and the salt and pepper; set aside while you prepare the fish.

Preheat the oven to 350°F. and oil a large, heavy baking sheet.

Season the salmon fillets with salt and pepper. Dip the rounded side of each fillet in flour, then in the beaten egg, and then the Onion Crust, pressing it into the surface. Place the fish on the baking sheet, onion side up, and bake for 20 minutes, or until the salmon is opaque and flakes when gently poked with a fork.

To assemble the dish, gently rewarm the onion sauce in the saucepan over medium-low heat. Refry the onion rings reserved from the crust until they're golden brown, about 3 minutes. Ladle a portion of the sauce into the center of each of 4 plates. Top with a salmon fillet and sprinkle with the reserved onion rings.

Scallop and Leek Sauté
with Capers and Anisette

~ ~ ~

Yield: 4 servings

3 tablespoons butter, plus extra for pasta

3 cups sliced mushrooms (about $^1/_4$ pound)

2 cups sliced celery

$1^1/_2$ cups sliced leeks (white and pale green portions)

$^3/_4$ teaspoon chopped fresh dillweed

$^3/_4$ teaspoon salt

$^1/_4$ teaspoon white pepper

2 tablespoons anisette (licorice-flavored liqueur) (see Note)

2 tablespoons rinsed and drained capers

$^3/_4$ pound raw bay scallops, rinsed and drained (this removes any "fishiness" from fresh or frozen scallops)

$1^2/_3$ cups light cream

1 pound uncooked fettuccine (preferably spinach or herb-flavored)

About 2 tablespoons softened butter

Melt the butter in a large skillet and sauté mushrooms, celery, and leeks until the leeks are soft and the mushrooms have released their liquid, about 7 minutes. Add the dill, salt, white pepper, anisette, and capers and continue cooking until the liquid is almost evaporated, about 1 minute. Add the scallops and continue cooking until the scallops become opaque, about 3 minutes. Add the cream and cook until the cream reduces by about half and the mixture thickens, about 5 minutes; adjust the flavorings.

Meanwhile, cook the pasta in a large pot of boiling water until tender, according to package directions. Drain, then toss with butter to coat. On each of 4 dinner plates, place a serving of pasta, then top with a portion of the scallop mixture. Serve immediately.

Note: Anisette is an essential ingredient in this recipe. The faint licorice flavor is a delicious complement to scallops. However, if you happen to have Pernod in your liquor cabinet, this could also be used (begin with 3 tablespoons, adding more to taste). Fresh fennel leaves, finely chopped, may also work, but the flavor would be slightly different.

LEEK AND CHEESE RAVIOLI

YIELD: 6 TO 8 SERVINGS

$^1/_4$ pound bulk pork sausage

2 cups chopped leeks (white and pale green portions,
  2 medium-to-large leeks)

$^1/_8$ teaspoon white pepper

1 cup coarsely grated Monterey Jack cheese

96 egg-roll wrappers

Egg paste (whisk together 1 egg with 1 tablespoon flour)

3 tablespoons vegetable oil

6 to 9 tablespoons hot water

1$^1/_2$ cups plain yogurt

1 teaspoon dried mint leaves

Brown the pork sausage in a medium-size skillet over medium-high heat, breaking up the meat into small pieces as it cooks, about 5 minutes. Drain the fat, then add the leeks and white pepper and continue cooking until the leeks are tender, about 4 minutes. Remove from the heat and cool thoroughly, then stir in the cheese.

Cover the egg roll wrappers with a damp cloth to keep them from drying out as you work. Place a heaping teaspoon of the filling in the center of one wrapper, then brush all around the filling (out to the edge) with the egg paste. Adjust a second wrapper on top of the filling and press down around the filling with your fingers to remove air pockets as you seal the ravioli (always start pressing nearest the mound and pressing outward). To completely seal the ravioli and trim them at the same time, cut the edges with a ravioli cutter, removing about $^1/_8$ inch of dough around all the sides. (If you don't have a ravioli cutter, trim the edges and then press shut with the tines of a fork.)

The ravioli can be prepared a day ahead, covered with a floured towel, and refrigerated. Or make them up to 1 month ahead, freeze on a baking sheet, then wrap in plastic when solid. Do not thaw before cooking.

If you are going to prepare an entire batch, it's best to have 2 or 3 frying pans going at once to eliminate washing and drying the pans several times during the process. Heat a thin layer of oil in each skillet over medium-high heat. Arrange as many ravioli as you can in each pan without overlapping. Sauté just until the bottoms are a rich golden brown, about 3 minutes. Gently pour in about 3 tablespoons of hot water per pan (add the water near the side of the pan), cover each pan, turn down the heat to medium, and cook for about 2 more minutes. Lift the ravioli from the pan and place them on paper toweling to absorb the oil. Then store them in a 200°F. oven until all the remaining ravioli are cooked.

Serve with a dipping sauce of the yogurt mixed with the mint leaves.

Pork Chops with Apple, Rosemary, and Leek Dressing

YIELD: *4 SERVINGS*

2 leeks (white portion only)

$^1/_4$ cup vegetable oil

1 medium russet potato, grated, with skin

1 sprig fresh rosemary, leaves removed and finely chopped,
    or $^1/_2$ teaspoon dried

1 tart apple, peeled, cored, and diced

About $^1/_2$ cup homemade or canned chicken broth

2 slices firm whole-grain bread, crumbled

Salt and freshly ground black pepper to taste

4 loin pork chops

Split the leeks lengthwise, wash thoroughly, then chop. In a large skillet, over medium-high heat, warm 2 tablespoons of the oil and sauté the leeks until soft, about 6 minutes. Add the potato, rosemary, and apple, cover the pan, and continue cooking for about 3 minutes. Add the chicken broth to moisten the mixture, and continue cooking until the potatoes are tender, about 20 minutes (you may need to add a bit more broth toward the end of the cooking process). Add the bread and salt and pepper. Turn the heat to low and keep the dressing warm while you prepare the pork.

In a separate skillet over medium-high heat, heat the remaining 2 tablespoons of oil making sure the oil is hot before you add the chops. Brown the pork chops for 6 to 8 minutes on each side. (Alternately, you could grill the chops, browning both sides well.) Serve each chop with a spoonful of the dressing.

BRAISED LEEKS WITH
TURNIPS AND CARROTS

A delicious combination. It stands on its own as a side dish, or can be tossed with pasta. The vegetables absorb the flavor of the broth as they cook. And then, once the liquid has been reduced, a dab of butter brings this dish to a golden conclusion.

YIELD: *4 SERVINGS*

> 4 small turnips
>
> 2 medium carrots
>
> 2 to 3 large leeks (white and pale green portions only)
>
> $^1/_2$ cup homemade or canned chicken broth
>
> 1 tablespoon butter
>
> 1 tablespoon finely chopped fresh flat-leaf parsley
>
> 1 teaspoon dried basil
>
> Salt and ground white pepper to taste

Peel the turnips and carrots. Slice the turnips into $^1/_4$-inch-thick rounds, then slice the rounds into strips of uniform thickness. Slice the carrots $^1/_4$ inch thick on the diagonal, then slice them again into narrow strips of uniform thickness. Slice the root end from each leek, then cut the leeks into $^1/_2$-inch rounds.

Place the vegetables in a large skillet with the broth. Bring the mixture to a boil over medium-high heat, lower the heat, and boil until the broth has reduced to about 2 tablespoons, about 5 minutes. Reduce the temperature to medium, add the butter and sauté until the vegetables are tender and delicately browned, about 10 minutes. Toward the end of the cooking, add the parsley and basil, and season with salt and pepper.

Fresh Spinach
and Leek Presto Sauce

This is a delectable, speedy, make-ahead sauce I created one winter when the supply of fresh basil was poor. Use it in place of the traditional pesto—as a topping for pasta, stirred into a batch of steamed vegetables, or spread on French baguettes with cheese and grilled. Refrigerated, it maintains good color and flavor for at least a week. It could probably go longer, but I haven't managed to keep a batch alone long enough to be sure.

Yield: 1¼ cups

$^1/_2$ cup olive oil

2 cups chopped leeks (white and pale green portions only, 2 large
    leeks)

3 cloves garlic, minced

3 cups fresh spinach leaves, thoroughly washed and firmly packed to
    measure

2 teaspoons dried basil

$^1/_2$ teaspoon salt

$^1/_4$ cup freshly grated Parmesan cheese

In a skillet, heat $^1/_4$ cup of the oil and sauté the leeks and garlic until the leeks are very soft, about 7 minutes; remove from the heat and cool slightly. Spoon the leek and oil mixture into a blender or food processor. Add the spinach, basil, and salt. Process until the mixture is finely chopped. With the motor running, pour the remaining $^1/_4$ cup of olive oil in a slow but steady stream through the feeder hole. Blend to a coarse puree, then stop the motor, add the cheese, and process for just a moment more.

BROCCOLI AND LEEKS WITH ROASTED PEPPERS, OLIVES, AND FETA CHEESE

This is a colorful dish to serve during the holidays. And the flavors are truly marvelous.

YIELD: 4 SERVINGS

1/2 large bunch of broccoli

2 large leeks (white and pale green portions only)

1 tablespoon olive oil

2 cloves garlic, minced

5 kalamata olives, pitted, coarsely chopped

1 medium red or yellow bell pepper, roasted (page 205), peeled, and
    diced

1 tablespoon finely chopped fresh flat-leaf parsley

2 teaspoons finely chopped fresh marjoram, or 1/2 teaspoon dried

1/2 cup feta cheese, crumbled

Salt and freshly ground black pepper to taste

1 to 2 tablespoons fresh lemon juice

Lemon wedges for garnish (optional)

Cut the broccoli into medium-large florets. Set aside the stalks for another purpose (see Braised Leeks with Turnips and Carrots, page 309), or peel them, cut into rounds, and include a few of them. In a saucepan or steamer, steam or blanch the broccoli until it has cooked as much as you like, 3 to 5 minutes for tender-crisp.

Trim away the root ends of the leeks and cut the leeks into 1/4-inch-thick rounds. In a large, nonstick skillet over medium heat, warm the oil and sauté the leeks with the garlic for about 7 minutes, or until the leeks are tender. Add the steamed broccoli, olives, pepper, parsley, and marjoram, and sauté over medium-high heat until the vegetables are warmed through. Scatter the cheese over the top, season lightly with salt and pepper, and drizzle the fresh lemon juice over all. Garnish with wedges of lemon and serve this dish as a warm side dish or salad.

CARROT AND LEEK TART

This is another unique vegetable offering from Oregon's popular fly-fishing resort, the Steamboat Inn. It's a simple, do-ahead recipe that's one of Co-Owner Sharon Van Loan's most requested hits. With Sharon's blessing, I've added the leeks, which add a subtle yet rich onion flavor.

YIELD: *8 SERVINGS*

> 1 $^1/_4$ pounds carrots, peeled and cut into $^1/_4$-inch slices
>
> 1 teaspoon sugar
>
> 2 tablespoons butter
>
> 2 cups chopped leeks (white and pale green portions,
>> about 2 medium-to-large leeks)
>
> 1 teaspoon fresh lemon juice
>
> $^1/_4$ teaspoon chopped fresh dillweed
>
> $^1/_4$ teaspoon salt
>
> 2 dashes cayenne
>
> 1 10- or 11-inch quiche crust, fully baked (page 207)
>
> 1 tablespoon chopped fresh chives or minced flat-leaf parsley for
>> garnish

Preheat the oven to 400°F.

Place the sliced carrots and the sugar in a pot of boiling salted water. Cook for 10 to 12 minutes, until the carrots are tender but crisp. Drain, then set aside 8 slices each of small-, medium-, and large-diameter slices.

In a small skillet over medium-high heat, melt the butter and sauté the leeks until the leeks are tender, 4 to 6 minutes. Remove from the heat and let the mixture cool slightly.

Transfer the carrots and leeks (along with the butter they were sautéed in), to the work bowl of a food processor and process to a coarse puree. Add the lemon juice, dillweed, salt, and cayenne. Give the filling another short burst with the blades, then transfer the mixture to the fully baked tart shell and spread it in an even layer over the bottom of the shell.

Bake for about 10 minutes, until the tart is heated through. Cut the tart into 8 wedges. Sprinkle with the chives or parsley, transfer to individual serving plates, and serve immediately.

Leeks have been cultivated for about four thousand years. In fact, leeks were considered more popular than garlic because they were less potent, and in medieval Europe, were considered legal tender.

Winter into Spring

Oven-Roasted
OSO Sweet Onions with
Herbs and Balsamic Vinegar

⌐   ⌐   ⌐

Equally at home in the company of meat, poultry, or fish, this delectible treatment is one of the most direct celebrations of this super-sweet onion.

Yield: *4 servings*

2 (8-ounce) OSO Sweet onions, peeled, cut into 8 wedges each

$^1/_3$ cup balsamic vinegar

$^1/_3$ cup extra-virgin olive oil

5 cloves garlic, minced

8 sprigs fresh flat-leaf parsley

1 tablespoon chopped fresh basil

2 teaspoons chopped fresh oregano

2 teaspoons chopped fresh rosemary

$^1/_2$ teaspoon salt

$^1/_2$ teaspoon freshly cracked black pepper

Preheat the oven to 450°F.

Place the onion wedges in a single layer in a shallow, lightly greased baking dish. Drizzle evenly with the vinegar and olive oil. Sprinkle with the garlic and herbs. Season with the salt and pepper. Roast for 15 to 20 minutes, until the onions are beautifully caramelized and tender. Remove from the oven and serve immediately or at room temperature.

OSO Sweet Onions with Fresh Spinach and Leek Presto Sauce

— — —

Another marvelous approach to stuffed onions that makes a magnificent side dish with roast pork and chicken.

YIELD: *4 SERVINGS*

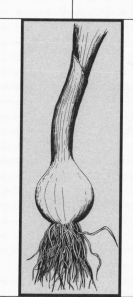

1 recipe of Fresh Spinach and Leek Presto Sauce (page 310)
4 OSO Sweet onions or other sweet onion
Olive oil
$^{1}/_{2}$ cup homemade or canned chicken stock
$^{1}/_{4}$ cup bread crumbs, tossed in about 1 tablespoon melted butter

Preheat the oven to 300°F. Prepare Fresh Spinach and Leek Presto Sauce and set aside.

Peel the onions and slice off the tops. Brush a heavy skillet with olive oil, heat well, and quickly sear the onions, cut side down. Transfer the onions, cut side up, to a baking dish. Deglaze the skillet with the chicken stock and add to the onions. Bake until almost tender, about 45 minutes (Note: The dish may be prepared up to 24 hours ahead to this point, covered, and refrigerated.) Scoop out the middle of the onions, saving them for another purpose, and fill with the spinach mixture. Sprinkle with the bread crumbs and bake in a 375° oven until heated through, about 25 minutes.

Spinach and Leek Sauté
with Yellow Fin Potatoes

A quick and tasty side dish that can be ready in about 10 minutes if the potatoes have been boiled ahead of time.

Yield: *4 to 6 servings*

2 pounds yellow fin potatoes, peeled and boiled (if yellow-fleshed
   potatoes are unavailable, any new potato can be substituted)

$^1/_2$ pound spinach, stemmed and washed

2 tablespoons peanut or other light vegetable oil

2 cups chopped leeks (white and pale green portions, about 2
   medium-to-large leeks)

1 or 2 cloves garlic, minced

1 (1-inch) piece fresh ginger, peeled and thinly sliced

1 teaspoon mustard seed

1 teaspoon ground cumin

Red pepper flakes to taste (optional)

1 teaspoon ground turmeric

$^1/_2$ teaspoon chili powder

1 teaspoon salt, or to taste

Cut the potatoes into cubes to measure about 4 cups; set aside. Coarsely chop the spinach and set it aside. Heat the oil in a large saucepan, add the leeks, garlic, and fresh ginger and sauté briefly, about 30 seconds. Add the mustard seed, cumin, red pepper flakes, turmeric, and chili powder. Stir well and cook over medium heat until the leeks are softened, about 10 minutes. Gently stir in the potatoes to coat them with the seasonings, then add the spinach in handfuls. Add the salt, stir again carefully (to keep the potatoes intact) but thoroughly, cover, and cook for 3 minutes or so, until the spinach has cooked down a bit. Serve at once.

ANGEL HAIR PASTA
WITH LEEKS

YIELD: 4 SERVINGS

2 pounds leeks

3 tablespoons olive oil

$^1/_2$ teaspoon curry powder

Pinch of red pepper flakes

$^1/_2$ cup dry white wine

12 ounces uncooked angel hair pasta

$^1/_4$ cup half and half

$^1/_2$ cup freshly grated Parmesan cheese, plus additional for serving

Clean the leeks, then slice the white and pale green portions into thin rings or half-rings (depending on whether or not you had to cut the leeks thorough during cleaning to remove any deep grit).

In a large frying pan over medium-low heat, warm the oil and gently sauté the leeks, curry powder, and red pepper flakes for 15 minutes. Add the wine and simmer for another 5 minutes. Adjust the seasonings, then set aside.

Cook the pasta in a large pot of salted boiling water until al dente, about 3 minutes, drain well, rinse, then drain again. Add the cooked and drained pasta to the frying pan with the leeks. Stir in the half and half and the Parmesan cheese. Toss the ingredients to mix well, cook briefly over low heat, then serve, passing additional Parmesan at the table.

WINTER PASTA PRIMO

— — —

A delicious blend of vegetables, herbs, and pasta.

YIELD: *6 SERVINGS*

2 cups broccoli florets

2 cups julienned carrots

2 cups julienned turnips

2 cups cauliflower florets

$1/_4$ cup olive oil

3 cloves garlic, finely minced

2 cups sliced leeks (white and pale green portions, about 2 medium-
to-large leeks)

$1/_2$ cup fresh chopped herb combination (basil, chervil, and parsley is
a nice mixture)

1 pound uncooked fresh pasta (such as linguine)

$1/_2$ cup freshly grated Parmesan cheese, plus additional for serving

Salt and freshly ground black pepper to taste

$1/_2$ cup lightly toasted pine nuts (see Note)

Blanch the broccoli, carrots, turnips, and cauliflower separately in a large pot of
boiling water. You can do this by lowering each batch into the water in a strainer
and lifting each batch out as soon as the vegetables are tender but still holding their
shape (broccoli will only take about 1 minute; carrots and turnips, about 3 minutes; cauliflower, about 2 minutes). Drain each batch in a colander and rinse under cold running water to halt the cooking process; set aside.

In a large pan, heat the olive oil over medium heat. Add the garlic and leeks
and sauté until the leeks are tender, about 10 minutes. Add the herbs and blanched

vegetables, and sauté just until heated through, about 1 minute. Transfer about half the mixture to a bowl, cover to keep warm, and set aside.

Bring a large pot of salted water to a boil. Drop in the pasta and cook, stirring frequently, until tender but still firm to the bite (al dente). Drain, then transfer to the pan with the other half of the vegetable mixture. Add the cheese, salt, and pepper and toss to mix well. To serve, spoon the pasta onto 6 individual serving plates then top with the remaining vegetables and sprinkle with the pine nuts. Serve immediately, offering additional cheese at the table.

Note: To toast pine nuts, place on a baking sheet and toast in a 350° oven until lightly golden, about 7 minutes.

LEEK AND SHERRY TIMBALES

If you don't happen to have bona fide timbale molds on hand, any 5- or 6-ounce oven-proof, tall-sided dishes will do.

YIELD: *8 SERVINGS*

> 6 tablespoons butter, plus additional for molds
>
> 4 cups chopped leeks (white and pale green portions, about 4
>   medium-to-large leeks)
>
> 2 ribs celery, chopped
>
> ¼ cup sherry
>
> 1¼ cups light cream
>
> 4 eggs
>
> 1 teaspoon salt
>
> ¼ teaspoon white pepper
>
> 1 cup grated Monterey Jack cheese

In a skillet, melt the butter and sauté the leeks and celery over medium heat until softened, about 3 minutes. Add the sherry and simmer for another 3 minutes to reduce the liquid slightly. Remove from the heat and cool slightly.

Meanwhile, in a bowl, combine the cream, eggs, salt, and white pepper. Stir in the cooled leek mixture and the cheese.

Butter 8 (5- or 6-ounce capacity) molds well, then fit a round of parchment or wax paper in the bottom of each mold; butter the paper. Fill the molds with the leek mixture. (At this point, the timbales can be refrigerated for several hours before cooking.) When ready to cook, preheat the oven to 350°F. and place the molds in a pan. Pour enough boiling water around them to come halfway up the sides of the molds. Bake for about 40 minutes. The timbales are done when a knife inserted in the center comes out clean. Let the timbales rest for at least 5 minutes before unmolding. To unmold, run a thin knife around the inner edge of each mold and invert onto a serving plate.

OSO Sweet Onion
and Potato Gratin

~ ~ ~

A rich and comforting dish that cries out for good old meatloaf!

Yield: *8 servings*

8 tablespoons (1 stick) butter

4 tablespoons all-purpose flour

2½ cups heavy cream

2½ pounds Yukon Gold potatoes, peeled and thinly sliced

2½ cups OSO Sweet onion rings

2 cups thinly sliced mushrooms

Salt and freshly ground black pepper to taste

⅓ cup chopped fresh flat-leaf parsley

⅓ cup Parmesan cheese, freshly grated

1½ cups coarsely grated Monterey Jack cheese

Preheat the oven to 350°F. Lightly grease a deep baking dish.

Melt the butter in a medium-size heavy-bottomed saucepan over medium-low heat. Whisk in the flour and stir until smooth. Whisk in the cream and continue stirring until the mixture begins to thicken, about 3 minutes; set aside.

Place half of the potatoes in the baking dish and top with half the onion rings and half the mushrooms. Season lightly with salt and pepper and sprinkle with half the parsley. Top with half the Parmesan and half the Monterey Jack cheese. Cover with half the reserved sauce. Repeat the process with the potatoes, onions, mushrooms, seasoning, parsley, and sauce, finishing with the remaining cheeses. Cover and bake for 2 to 2½ hours, removing the lid for the final 30 minutes to brown the top.

For more ways to cook with OSO Sweet Onion, head back to the sweet onion recipes in Chapter 2.

~

LEEKS WITH BARLEY
AND WILD RICE PILAF

YIELD: 6 SERVINGS

1 cup uncooked wild rice

4 tablespoons ($^1/_2$ stick) butter

$^1/_4$ to $^1/_2$ pound pancetta, thinly sliced, then minced (see Note)

2 leeks, washed and thinly sliced (white and pale green portions, about 2 cups)

1 bunch of red chard, if available (use regular, if not), chopped

4 ribs celery, coarsely chopped

1 cup uncooked barley

1 bay leaf

$^1/_2$ cup sherry

7 cups homemade or canned chicken broth

Salt and freshly ground black pepper to taste

Minced fresh or dried thyme to taste

Rinse the wild rice in a strainer under cold running water several times. Heat the butter in a large saucepan and sauté the pancetta, leeks, chard, and celery over low heat for 15 to 20 minutes. Stir in the wild rice and barley and cook for several minutes, stirring, until the barley turns slightly golden. Add the bay leaf, sherry, broth, salt, pepper, and thyme; bring to a boil, then cover, reduce the heat to low, and cook for about 40 minutes, or until the rice and barley are tender. If there is any unabsorbed liquid, simply boil until it is gone. (Note: The dish can be prepared up to 2 days in advance, covered, and refrigerated. Reheat in a microwave at High power for about 15 minutes or in a preheated 350° oven, covered, for 20 to 30 minutes, adding more liquid if necessary.)

Note: Pancetta is Italian bacon; if unavailable consider using a good quality ham.

Leeks Braised in Butter
and Sherry Au Gratin

This simple side dish is a wonderful accompaniment to steak or roast chicken.

Yield: *4 to 6 servings*

6 tablespoons butter

4 cups chopped leeks (white and pale green portions only, about 4
   large leeks)

2 tablespoons dry sherry

$^1/_4$ teaspoon salt

$^1/_4$ teaspoon white pepper

$^1/_3$ cup heavy cream

$^1/_4$ cup coarsely grated Monterey Jack cheese

$^1/_4$ cup freshly grated Parmesan cheese

Melt the butter in a heavy, ovenproof skillet over medium-high heat. Add the leeks
and sauté until softened, about 3 minutes. Add the sherry, salt, and white pepper
and continue to cook until the leeks are tender, about 5 minutes. Stir in the cream
and cook for a couple of minutes longer to reduce the liquid slightly; remove from
the heat. Sprinkle with the Monterey Jack cheese and then the Parmesan. Place the
pan under the broiler and broil just until the cheese melts and begins to turn golden
around the edges, about 3 minutes. Serve immediately.

Potato and Leek Puree with Fresh Basil

Vegetable purees are very popular these days, and one of my favorite combinations is this one. The leeks give the mild, creamy potatoes a strong boost of onion flavor and a lovely green color.

Yield: 6 servings

1¹/₂ pounds russet potatoes (about 5 medium), peeled and cut into chunks

2 tablespoons olive oil

2 cups chopped leeks (white and pale green portions, about 2 medium-to-large leeks)

¹/₄ cup fresh basil leaves

About ¹/₄ to ¹/₃ cup butter, melted

About ¹/₃ to ¹/₂ cup cream or milk, heated

Salt and freshly ground black pepper to taste

Place the potatoes in a large saucepan with enough water to cover them by about ¹/₂ inch. Bring the water to a boil over high heat, reduce the heat to low, cover, and simmer until the potatoes are soft, about 20 minutes.

Meanwhile, in a skillet, warm the olive oil and sauté the leeks over medium-high heat until soft, about 7 minutes. Let the leeks cool slightly, then puree them in a blender or food processor along with the basil leaves; set aside.

When the potatoes are tender, drain well, then mash them into a puree, adding butter and cream to taste. Gently fold in the leek puree, adjust the seasonings with salt and pepper, and serve.

TO PREPARE AHEAD: Spoon the prepared puree into a lightly oiled baking dish. Refrigerate up to several hours. When ready to serve, dot with butter and reheat in a 350°F. oven until hot, about 35 minutes.

Roasted Balsamic
Potatoes with Leeks

With the heady scent of rosemary floating above these gloriously roasted potatoes and leeks, chicken is the natural companion, roasted or grilled.

Yield: *6 servings*

> 3 large leeks (1 to 1 $^1/_2$ inches in diameter at the base)
>
> 3 tablespoons olive oil
>
> 2 pounds red, yellow fin, or Yukon Gold potatoes, cut into 1-inch
>> chunks, unpeeled
>
> $^1/_3$ cup balsamic vinegar
>
> About $^1/_2$ teaspoon salt
>
> $^1/_4$ teaspoon white pepper
>
> 2 teaspoons chopped fresh rosemary; or a scant $^3/_4$ teaspoon dried,
>> crumbled

Preheat the oven to 400°F.

Prepare the leeks by first cutting off the dark green portion. Halve each leek lengthwise through the root end, leaving the root end intact on each half. Wash thoroughly to remove any dirt inside the leaves, then drain well, and pat dry with paper towels.

Pour the olive oil into a large, shallow baking dish (measuring about 10 by 15 inches). Add the potatoes and leeks and toss to coat with the oil. Cover the pan with foil, sealing it well, and roast for 20 minutes. Remove the foil, and increase the temperature to 450°. Drizzle on the balsamic vinegar, salt, and pepper, then toss the vegetables again to coat them evenly. Continue roasting, tossing the vegetables occasionally, until they are golden brown, 30 to 40 minutes more. Just before serving, sprinkle with the rosemary and gently toss again.

INDEX

Index

Index